NEW YORK UNIVERSITY SERIES IN
EDUCATION AND SOCIALIZATION IN AMERICAN HISTORY

The Publication of this work has been aided by a grant
from the Andrew W. Mellon Foundation

Front row sitting (reading from left to right): Samuel Stillman Greene, Louis Agassiz, Barnas Sears, William Russell, George Barrell Emerson. Back row standing (reading from left to right): Arnold Guyot, Dana Pond Colburn, Herman Krusi, Jr.

The Classless Profession: American Schoolmen in the Nineteenth Century

by

Paul H. Mattingly

New York: NEW YORK UNIVERSITY PRESS 1975

Contents

Contents

Acknowledgements

The clichés of an academic preface cannot be fully appreciated until one has faced the task of cramming an acknowledgment of scholarly indebtedness into a few short phrases. The debts are real and intimidating. Unfortunately, without them scholarship has no backing. The most important debts are to people, especially to my wife, Jane. She always remembered, when I forgot, that this study was only a study. David Harnett has been a constant critic of all the drafts to endlessly good effect. While I was at the University of Wisconsin where this research began, several historians—-Merle Borrowman, Merle Curti and William R. Taylor—offered reactions and stimuli from their very different perspectives. Even more important, my friends and fellow graduate students in Madison created an intellectual atmosphere which in retrospect I know was unique. Its impact has changed my thinking in ways which I hope this study partly shows. At New York University several colleagues, particularly Stephanie Edgerton and Allan Horlick, have continued in several ways these earlier lines of inquiry and have insisted on possibilities of interpretation which I would not have considered without them.

Several institutions have contributed financial support in different ways at different times. The University of Wisconsin, especially the departments of History and Educational Policy Studies, offered strategic help at the crucial beginning stages. New York University and its office of Research Services assisted with research funding and, in many ways even more importantly, released time. The National Research Council's Committee on Basic Research in Education, chaired by James S. Coleman, selected this study for funding by the National Institute of Education. Under these auspices I completed the book in its present form.

Without such assistance the study would, of course, not have reached its present stage. The reader will have to judge the merits of that nurture. Here I merely want to make a subjective distinction. The formal institutions, the universities and the offices, provided the most obvious and catalytic backing for this history. However, the roots of support began before their kindly intervention and, I hope, will continue afterward to some benefit. This longer backing, unlike the institutional kind, is not only pivotal but indispensable. I hope the dedication puts this emphasis right.

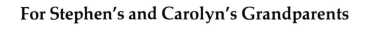

For Stephen's and Carolyn's Grandparents

Introduction

This book is not a chronology of the professional schoolman in nineteenth-century America. Instead, it is an interpretation of certain historical questions which continue to bear upon educators in the twentieth century. The study assumes a critical stance in order to refine and understand the meaning of the schoolman's past experience. This particular orientation necessarily builds upon the work of previous historians but with some important differences. At its best, interpretive history should become particularly conscious of its joint responsibility to both past and present; it should attempt a greater sensitivity to the interrelationships among historical events, to the multiplicity of actors and causes of past change, to the dynamics between ideas and group experiences. At the same time this sense of historicity cannot be unmindful of the hereditary lines between past problems and current dilemmas. If it achieves new dimensions of understanding, it will be because it has made different disciplines serve each other. At its best the interdisciplinary viewpoint will make historical analysis germane and illuminating to an informed reading public as well as a scholarly audience.

The heart of this study deals with the basic conditions of the lives of teachers, before and after professionalization became an institutional process. What kinds of persons initiated the professional improvement of schoolkeepers; what classes of people were attracted to the work; what differences did their own experiences make, particularly the differences of their own origins and education upon their social aspirations and career achievements; how did different historical conditions produce different educational and social values; and how were those values transformed in their turn by successive generations of teachers? The focus then concerns the collective mentality of America's teaching corps, their shifting belief systems as well as the changing routines of their lives.

The title of this book, *The Classless Profession*, should suggest several things about its thesis. First, nineteenth-century schoolmen were not all that firmly fixed in the social structure of American society. Second, they achieved a special process of professionalization which strove to be above or outside considerations of social status and political maneuvering. Third, they sought to characterize themselves as classless, though their actual achievement was not as enlightened and democratic as their self-image suggested. Fourth, in the effort to welcome young talent to teaching, regardless of social origins, they screened certain types of young men into and certain types out of schoolkeeping.

In summary, the argument of the book runs like this: in the early nineteenth century anxious citizens, usually ministers but also a sprinkling of

lawyers and doctors, decided that the key to a truly American and democratic
public school resided in the teachers of public classrooms. These other
professionals, the Friends of Education as they were called then, tried to
impart to schoolmen standards modeled upon the new goals and institutions
in their own professions. At the end of the 1830s as the benevolent effort of
these Friends spawned widespread public interest in their cause, the nation's
economic crisis altered their involvement in the work of education. Economic
constrictions also removed their hope of duplicating for young teachers a
professional experience similar to their own. The Friends of Education did,
however, attract sufficient numbers of young men into teaching, young men
who created in concert with educational leaders like Horace Mann and Henry
Barnard an institutional network for professionalizing teachers. Initially this
network was a loose system of voluntary associations, the most effective of
which were the teachers' institutes. For most of the century the focal point of
this system was the American Institute of Instruction (1830–1918), the earliest national association for professional schoolmen. The historical experience of this national association illuminated the significant changes and
personalities throughout the teaching profession until the end of the nineteenth century.

Ultimately the schoolmen's professional ideology, condensed into the key
notion of character, suffered a reinterpretation as it was transmitted near
midcentury from the first generation of professional teachers (1830–1860) to
the second (1860–1890). Although many social and political factors impinged
on this transformation, the significant features of this shift can be found in
the dynamic interchange between the teachers' own ideology and its supportive institutions. For both generations character possessed quasi-spiritual
properties; it was always a bit more profound and sublime than its explicit
manifestations in deed or word. Both generations felt character could be best
fostered where actions were voluntary, that is, neither coercive nor selfish.
This general interpretation meant that specific educational institutions which
claimed to inculcate character designed different ways to do it. In part this
institutional variety made the nature of character serve seemingly different
ends, and, especially in teacher-training institutions, discussions about
character resisted a single definition of the term. The voluntary implications
of character made the idea adaptable to different plans and individual purposes. It was a characteristic which flourished during the ante-bellum period,
America's Golden Age of Oratory and Evangelism.

The basic meaning of the term "character" remained generally unchanged
throughout the century; it referred to a moral potential within each person
and was somewhat susceptible to improvement and refinement given the
proper influences. Functionally its meaning changed because of the different
class origins of the two generations of schoolmen.[1] The first generation,
benevolent and authoritative, did not pass on to its successors its confidence

in the power of pedagogy. In a sense their own moral rhetoric and social-class fears obscured the importance of both morality and social class as facts of professional teaching. As a consequence, moral and social-class considerations were more often taken for granted than comprehended by the second generation, which thought they had realized the mandate of character entrusted to them by their mentors. Where earlier character had referred to specific attitudes of intellectual discipline and self-possession, the later version of character developed a tacit equation with testable experiences and practical behavior. The second generation's emphasis upon skill training, teaching methods and the production of good teachers did not imply a rejection of earlier interpretations of character. Rather, the practical grasp of work and production, more pressing to their less privileged social origins, took for granted a moral foundation which they seldom examined critically. Still, both generations recognized social conflict and political partisanship as the clearest enemies of character. The first generation, however, differed on the point in that they knew the apolitical meaning originated from a political choice. The second generation and its successors made a habit of their apolitical thinking and treated the habit as a moral principle. .

If the politics of education, the legal and formal process of educational policy-making, seem to be peripheral in this study, it is because I wished to deal with such developments on several levels of meaning. My first duty, I felt, was to understand *their* point of view and that viewpoint was not openly political. They did not examine social and educational problems in terms of the conflicting interests and working allegiances of social groupings; they certainly did not think of professionalization that way. They never sought to legislate guidelines. Like their orientation, my study may have overqualified the more official and familiar political realities of their time. Still even now, I prefer my choice and its limitations. It has made me attend to the problems of analytic interpretation and the dynamics of change rather than those of factual presentation. So often historians have examined the official forums of power to get to the heart of social reality. Too often they end, however expertly, by summarizing the official accounts of official actions. But these official policies are only fragments of the matter of politics. More emphatically, the politics of education can be best understood in a historical context which treats policy changes on their several levels of meaning. Before the full impact of the teaching profession in American can be assessed, one must understand the structure and shifting realignments within the schoolman's ranks over time. Here I have tried to reconstruct the collective, generational ideologies and patterns within which individuals and institutions functioned. Once established, that context enables one to grasp the politics of education realistically.[2]

Within the actual political and generational interrelationships two methodological features merit notice. First, the official and unofficial rationales of pertinent groups and individuals have highlighted the role of ideas. Ideas have become here historical facts and institutional phenomena themselves and not exclusively, as pragmatic historians have it, as evidence with lesser authority than hard facts. Second, individual participants in historical change have become more rather than less important because of this interweaving of ideas and institutions. In the context of broader intellectual and structural patterns the role of choice, which so intrigued the thinking men of the nineteenth century, has often been totally obscured in social and institutional history. Changes appeared to follow from impersonal causes. Here, instead, the fates of individuals determine how voluntary and involuntary certain shifts have been. To the extent that individual careers followed or departed from established traditions, one can assess rather precisely the relative significance of men, ideas and institutions.

In a sense the structure of the study itself has taken on a nineteenth-century mode of presentation. Each chapter is intended to stand by itself while reworking or viewing from different perspectives the same phenomenon, the transformation of the professional schoolman. Though this transformation is the thematic topic, each chapter puts different weight on a single individual, an institutional milieu or a historical moment. Each may seem to return again and again to the same point in time and come forward to relatively the same point as others. The desired effect would be an unobtrusive reminder to the reader that many of the experiments and strategies occurred simultaneously, though they are discussed separately. In addition, the historical transformation itself dictated this structure, for the professional goal of character became historically significant precisely because its own dynamics were susceptible to different interpretations. Yet, in spite of these variations the goal of character provided the necessary adhesive for rendering diverse groups of schoolmen functionally harmonious. The order of the chapters will, I hope, aid an understanding of the ideological force of character.[3] To offset any possible confusion let me describe my own understanding of each chapter and its fit into the argument as a whole.

Chapter I depicts the experience of a teacher before distinct institutions and rationales existed for professional teachers. Through a single individual's (William A. Alcott's) experience, one can pace professional success in the early nineteenth century. In the context of his career one can see when and how crucial roles and strategies became either advantageous or outmoded in the eyes of schoolmen then. At the very least the travails of the rural teacher here were those a first generation of school reformers like the Reverend Samuel May sought to change.

Chapter II examines the first efforts, the failures and partial successes, to remedy teaching's ills and upgrade the teacher's status. In the 1820s the Reverend Thomas Gallaudet offered an early description of a teacher-training school, one which had to be substantially changed once the first teacher's seminary at Andover, Massachusetts actually got under way in the 1830s. The principal of that early experimental school, the Reverend Samuel R. Hall, initiated some dramatic modifications of the ideal school to meet realities which Gallaudet could never have foreseen. The first actual experiment underscored the educator's dependence upon a ministerial style and evangelical power.[4] There are here no comparative analyses to explain interesting yet secondary questions, such as why were ministers more attracted to schooling than other professionals. Instead of broadening the study that way, the inquiry tried to refine the comparisons internally. In particular, the prominent questions became, How did their academic ideals, borrowed from other professions, square with the realities of the public schoolroom? and in turn, How did their altered institutional and educational arrangements affect the rural youth who were most attracted to the work? The essential point of this chapter demonstrates the kind of ministerial person and pedagogy dominating the professional style of the first-generation schoolman. In addition, there is an explanation of the general impermanence of professional institutions, resulting in a reliance upon "temporary" agencies for the range of professional work from recruitment to training. Gradually the acceptance of these voluntary organizations—institutes, lyceums, literary societies, lecture circuits, etc.—came to govern the nature of professional norms and aspirations.

Chapter III interprets the social and intellectual dynamics of these norms concentrated as they were in moral character, the first clear prerequisite for the professional teacher. The focus of this chapter is restricted to the uses of character in thought and behavior and probes several of the significant ambiguities, which followed from the idea. The force of character seldom seemed to have implied political power in the schoolman's eyes, though none doubted its benevolent and constructive social impact. Since the ideology of character existed before the professional institutions for teachers, the implications of character were made explicit before any discussion of the actual professional schools and associations which housed the notion successfully. In my mind it was important to know how character as a public school and professional ideal sidestepped considerations of special preferment for some groups over others. This analysis has explored the place of Horace Mann in the professional lore of the time, singling out particularly his dramatic career shift into education as a context for understanding the meaning of character. I have concluded that the historical importance of this idea was not its promise of moral harmony but its effective service in detaching educational issues from political reality. Professional problems thereby became personal and moral rather than political problems. Hence the actual political consequences of professional work in teaching were substantially muted, then and since.

Chapter IV describes the coalescence of these three historical factors: the awareness of distinctly professional problems, the lessons of early efforts in professional training, the emergence of a professional ideology. In this context I discuss the most effective teacher-training institution before the Civil War, the teachers' institute, and not its founding only but its design and redesign in the hands of two generations of schoolmen. The protagonists here are Henry Barnard, the first secretary of the Connecticut and Rhode Island Boards of Education and eventually the first U.S. Commissioner of Education, and David N. Camp, Barnard's protégé and in several of his many offices his successor. A theme of ongoing importance develops here and in subsequent sections, namely the interplay between a first generation which guided itself by upper-class notions of education and the second generation which subscribed to the values of a lower middle class. Both classes experienced unexpected changes as the work of teaching came under the direction of representative schoolmen, teachers who after the Civil War worked in public and normal schools where they had learned, teaching students of the same social class as themselves. Only when the distinctions between and within several generations are taken together, I have assumed, does the notion of a generation make sense in a historical analysis.

Chapters V, VI and VII attempt to refine in various ways the institutional consequences of this upper-to-lower-middle-class transition within the ranks of professional schoolmen. Chapter V examines the eroding power of the national assembly of teachers, the American Institute of Instruction, and stresses the sociological shifts within the profession. Chapter VI discusses the importance of the professional conception of voluntary association as well as the bureaucratizing tendencies of this conception at midcentury. Chapter VII traces the rise of the normal school as a generic institution and as the center of the teaching profession in the late nineteenth century. This last analysis fixes upon Bridgewater (Massachusetts) Normal School, which in the eyes of nineteenth-century schoolmen and in actual fact was one of the most prominent and oldest schools of the genre.

Finally, Chapter VIII analyzes the passing of the normal school's power and the rise of a new center for professional policy-making, the superintendency. Within this shift a third generation of teachers began to emerge and to create a clear hierarchy of social class within the profession. At that point both the second generation and the American Institute of Instruction, which epitomized the intellectual contribution of nineteenth-century schoolmen, actually waned. Even if other events had not sealed the fate of the Institute in 1918, the aspirations and orientations of the third generation would likely have sought other organizational forms than the Institute and the state normal schools anyway. Still, the passing of the American Institute of Instruction marked "complete" the work of two generations of American teachers and defined those educational alternatives which could not be tolerated by a generation of educators we have come to call Progressive.

Perhaps a word should be said about this study vis-à-vis the most recent historical work on Progressive schoolmen and their bureaucratic devices.[5] While far more consciously interpretive than most twentieth-century scholarship on American education, this new historical literature supports partially or fully the following propositions. First, Progressive schoolmen and their sympathizers concealed devious orientations to manipulate the school and control those social classes and ethnic groups which could not escape its clutches. Their bureaucracy became the logical consequence of this arrogant stance and, particularly in cities, remained essentially unchanged from the midnineteenth century forward. Once in motion, the educational bureaucracy implemented a rigid form of public instruction and preserved a class-stratification which is the antithesis of American democracy.

By contrast, this study began with the assumption that historical change produces different kinds of bureaucracy and that the task of historical analysis is the illumination of distinctions between and among significant institutional forms. In that context, the historical record has suggested the very real possibility that the nineteenth-century system of voluntary associations could well deserve the descriptions of rigidity and arrogant efficiency which many historians now reserve for the bureaucracy of twentieth-century schooling. In any case, unlike much of the current literature on educational bureaucracy, the theory of bureaucracy emerges here from those actually implemented by nineteenth-century schoolmen. The variously urban and nonurban geographical bases of this professional work as well as its peculiar evangelical and benevolent cast of thought have received particular stress. It is of first importance, I think, to see how nineteenth-century schoolmen could view their work as sensitive to the realities of democracy and intellect. Most especially, whatever verdict one finally reaches, an analysis of bureaucracy in the hands of nineteenth-century schoolmen must account for the voluntary and democratic goals they thought bureaucracy would serve. Explicitly and consistently they rejected regimentation and uniformity of thought and behavior as products of the American public school. If his choices were unconscionably arrogant, devious and exploitative—and at times they undoubtedly were—and if his interests varied with his public promises, the nineteenth-century schoolman cannot be understood as a significant social type by sacrificing historical complexity. Even where I found the schoolmen's work wanting, I have tried to respect certain historical realities which have been lately ignored. "Secularization" and "bureaucratization" not only did not preclude but, rather, sustained new forms of evangelism and religious fervor; "professionalization" and "urbanization" continued to be influenced by serious and legitimate nonurban pressures; schoolmen's demands for classlessness implied at least some kind of new choices for all social classes in the systematization of public instruction.

The key presence throughout this history has been the national association, the American Institute of Instruction. Its rise and fall between 1830 and 1918 provided the strategic boundaries of the study. The Institute has guided me to key individuals, issues and institutions. The interconnection between these historical factors shaped the institute, and by reconstructing rather than chronicling them they have also determined the course of this study. The Institute began by trying to attract all serious schoolmen into their councils in order to have teachers teach and reteach each other. They called it mutual instruction. Without doubt the association created channels of communication between teachers of different social classes, channels which the twentieth century thus far has not been able to match. In that sense the profession might have seemed classless and democratic but at the same time, one of the core themes here, it achieved this rapport (it was never equality, nor was it intended to be) at the price of an analytic mode of thought and at the sacrifice of certain professional options. The successful and unsuccessful preferences of professional schoolmen, inside and outside the Institute, contributed to the shape of their work and this study. Ironically, once their choices became unavoidable (and obviously political), their rhetoric became more strident and didactic. They advanced their classlessness, to take an example that has fascinated me, more and more as the century progressed, as their ranks became progressively and undeniably more stratified.

Some of the bolder changes within the Institute and the profession can be sketched with the following statistical summary (see Table 1, p. xix). The quantities represent the rates and numbers of schoolmen as they joined the American Institute of Instruction. This distribution indicates the institutional position certain schoolmen held at the moment they joined their fellow professionals at the Institute's annual meetings. In spite of other factors which gave disproportionate authority at times to particular groups, these figures offer a basis for understanding the intra-professional relationships conditioning the development of the schoolman's profession. The grammar school levels pace those of the academy men until public schoolkeeping achieved greater scope and order after 1850. Until the 1870s grammar schoolmen participated avidly and increased by double over the number of the private academy men. During the last three decades of the century both groups maintained their standing at half their midcentury force, yet together they could not match the enrollment of the incoming superintendents who came to dominate the last years of the Institute. The Friends of Education, the early sponsors of professionalization, became an insignificant force after the 1830s. Similarly, except for a few singular individuals and bursts of interest in the 1840s and 1880s, professors at the college and university levels had little directly to do with the improvement of professional teachers. Unlike the influence of the normal school teachers whose numbers rose at midcentury, then fell, the high school teachers steadily increased their numbers and standing until at century's end they matched the grammar school force. Thus

Table 1

Professional Groupings within the American Institute of Instruction, 1830–1908 [6]

Professional or School Affiliation	1830s	1840s	1850s	1860s	1870s	1880s	1890s	1900s	Totals	
Superintendent	5	5	13	26	25	23	32	47	176	18%
% in group [a]	3%	3%	7%	15%	14%	13%	18%	26%		
% by decade [b]	4%	4%	13%	18%	14%	28%	23%	33%		
Grammar School	30	13	29	43	57	13	27	28	240	25%
% in group	13%	5%	12%	18%	24%	6%	11%	12%		
% by decade	26%	26%	29%	30%	31%	16%	20%	20%		
High School	7	5	19	18	25	16	28	27	145	15%
% in group	5%	3%	13%	12%	18%	11%	19%	19%		
% by decade	6%	10%	20%	12%	13%	19%	20%	19%		
Academy	30	11	15	19	27	8	13	13	136	14%
% in group	22%	8%	11%	14%	20%	6%	10%	10%		
% by decade	26%	22%	15%	13%	14%	10%	10%	9%		
College/University	12	8	9	10	22	13	19	11	104	11%
% in group	12%	8%	9%	10%	21%	12%	18%	11%		
% by decade	11%	16%	9%	8%	12%	16%	14%	8%		
Normal School	4	4	14	19	22	8	14	12	97	10%
% in group	4%	4%	14%	20%	23%	8%	14%	12%		
% by decade	4%	8%	14%	13%	12%	10%	10%	9%		
Friends of Education	26	4	2	10	4	2	5	3	56	6%
% in group	46%	7%	4%	18%	7%	4%	9%	5%		
% by decade	23%	8%	2%	7%	2%	2%	4%	2%		
Numerical Total	114	50	101	145	182	83	138	141	954	
% of Total A.I.I. Membership	16%	20%	27%	31%	15%	31%	23%	32%	22%	

[a] "% in group" refers to the fraction of the total in a given position. For example, in the 1900s 26% of all the superintendents who ever joined the American Institute of Instruction joined in those years.

[b] "% by decade" refers to the fraction of the total in a given decade. For example, in the 1900s 33% of all who joined in those years were superintendents.

by contrast with the relative professional harmony schoolmen had actually achieved by midcentury, the end of the century revealed a new professional stratification: superintendents at the top of the hierarchy, public (grammar and high school) schoolmen in the center and on the lower levels the most privileged and specialized groupings of collegiate, academy and normal school teachers.

The dominant characteristic of the American Institute of Instruction as a professional association—the characteristic which ensured its demise in the twentieth century—was its unspecialized and nonexclusive, that is, its classless pretensions. It proposed to give all ideas a hearing and to receive representatives of all types of schools from all regions of the country. Expectedly, the maintenance of a working harmony and cooperation became its dominant problem. When men of different social classes instructed their fellows in professional pedagogies, division became an ever-present danger. Once begun, who knew where disagreements would end? Out of this ongoing difficulty developed the functional preferences for certain educational and social values. The all-pervasive feature of these values stemmed from the evangelical origins of teaching as a professional work. The preoccupation with educating men of moral character led American schoolmen curiously toward a social service which itself shunned dramatic social issues or political controversies. Moral men taught each other by example and other indirect strategies. Not only did this line of thought and behavior draw sustenance from American political and religious traditions, it also served the immediate needs of a new profession with a highly diverse membership. Clear specification of practical political programs to advance education would not only have divided the new profession (and the American Institute of Instruction) internally. It would also, schoolmen assumed, have precluded the impartial financial support of a multigrouped and multiclassed society. Instead, professional schoolmen chose to call their profession classless and publicly ignored the actual stratifications within their ranks and institutions.

The history of this profession and these institutions advanced a peculiar and novel set of notions about education. Its evangelical roots caused in no small way the schoolman's aversion to ideology and social theory (on grounds of rigidity and divisiveness). As a consequence, schoolmen have labored awkwardly, then and since, to ensure certain social and political effects without political programs or social coercions outside the classroom. Instead, they have traditionally kept their official attention within the confines of the classroom—simulating social changes—or else devoting themselves to the mechanics of the students' minds in the study of psychology. These rather exclusive and specialized efforts have had important professional and social ramifications, but, true to their assumptions, schoolmen rarely correlated these outward realities with their work in the classroom. Instead of moving to the necessary political analysis of their society and its ideologies, instead of generating their own theories of social and educational structures, schoolmen have done their utmost to rationalize their pragmatic stance. In an effort to understand why they preferred the nineteenth-century rhetoric of character and its pragmatic consequences, I offer this historical analysis.

Tables

CHAPTER I

Sponsors and Ambitious Yeomen

The Friends of Education

In the history of American patriotic oratory and rhetoric, one of the more enduring themes has been the notion of education as the harbinger of personal and national achievement. The pursuit of social advancement through education was rooted in the very earliest decades of the Republic when it was realized, at least by some, that the young nation's viability rested on the educational aspirations of its people. The January 1827 issue of the *North American Review* contained a review of James G. Carter's *Essays upon Popular Education*, in which the anonymous author observed:

> No schemer nor empiric will bring forward the great destiny which is before us, but it will be slowly and gradually wrought out, by principles already in operation. It will be wrought out by the consenting inquiries, and purposes, and endeavors of the whole people; but the grand lever, which is to raise up the mighty mass of this community, is *education*. We forget not the power of a free press, so often denominated the palladium of our liberties, we forget not our excellent form of government, we forget not the institutions of religion, but all these are to take their character from the intelligence of the people. The empire of these States must rise or fall with the mind. The *schools* hold, in embryo, the future communities of this land. The *schools* are the pillars of the republic.[1]

The reviewer was equally convinced that the contemporary system of common schools fell far short of even beginning to fulfill these expectations. "In the first place," he remarked, "better schools are wanted. We mean, that the Free Schools, or what are usually called, the Common, and in the country, District Schools, need to be made better, and more efficient organs of instruction and influence." [2] The concern for the apparent disinterest of the citizenry in educational improvement might have been somewhat mitigated had the reviewer been aware of a meeting held the previous October in Brooklyn, Connecticut, a hilly farming town in the northeastern corner of the state.

In the spring of 1826, the Reverend Samuel J. May of Brooklyn called a convention for the consideration of the condition and improvement of common schools. By way of advertisement a circular of information with a number of questions was distributed to interested parties. More than a hundred delegates attended, representing more than twenty towns in five counties. Either in person or by letter many of Connecticut's most distinguished educators participated: Professors Denison Olmstead and James L. Kingsley of Yale College, Reverend Thomas H. Gallaudet of Hartford and William Russell of Farmington, who was then editor of the first, and at the time only, educational journal in the English language. All members of the convention bore witness to a general indifference to the schools by Connecticut communities. After the meeting itself, a report was drafted and published in order to familiarize the public with the crisis in their schools. This document, May recounted later, "surprised and mortified the better part of the people of the State, and led to the commencement of essential improvements." [3] Recollecting the events years afterward Samuel May and Henry Barnard, the educational encyclopedist and first United States Commissioner of Education, agreed that the Brooklyn convention had been the first held for any such educational purpose in the United States.[4]

The real novelty of this convention, however, was the preoccupation it reflected about educational affairs. In the early 1820s such concern was not widespread among the public as a whole so much as among a particular group of enlightened citizens. Yet after 1826, and owing directly to the impetus of conventions like May's, interest in educational reform became more public and was maintained through community participation in lyceums, a novel experiment in educational improvement. For the moment, however, serious discussion of educational matters was left to an easily discernible yet loosely defined group of citizens, categorized in the parlance of the period as "the Friends of Education."

For the most part, the Friends of Education were not officially involved in the direct instruction of students. Usually they had had some school-teaching experience and had recognized, either during or after their classroom work, that education was a far more significant activity than popular opinion had allowed. Frequently, they were themselves trained in one of the three established professions—the ministry, the law or medicine. As distinguished citizens, moreover, they often maintained at least an official supervisory capacity over the process of education in their communities, since common practice suggested the appointment of leading citizens as School Visitors. May's own influence on the educational affairs of Brooklyn came more from his position as a well-known citizen than from any specific educational duties attended on his office as minister of the First Congregational Church. During the late 1820s, the Friends of Education used their positions of influence to command the attention of large gatherings of citizens to discuss the condition of common schools. The Brooklyn convention was the first of these ventures,[5] and among the most successful. Before the establishment of preparatory institutions for teachers, the promotional activities of the Friends of Education and the organizations which they founded provided the strategic instruments for rallying public support for educational reform.

Samuel May reflected a common pattern for the Friends of Education when he attempted to solidify the gains of his 1826 convention. He devised a conventionlike organization for his town, one which brought together local citizens and exposed them to the instruction and example of qualified teachers as well as to the candid reactions of their fellow townsmen. The lyceum, as the organization came to be called in imitation of Aristotle's school, attempted to do for a community what the style of a skilled instructor did for a schoolroom of young students. The special characteristic of this town meeting of the mind was the mutual instruction of citizens. Without an enlightened concern on the part of each immediate community, the Friends of Education believed, no broad regional change in education or society was possible.

Initially, the Friends of Education restricted their criticisms of the common schools to their own communities, only to realize quickly that they were not confronting mere local or statewide problems, but general and regional, social ones. In 1826 May, for example, lodged his first criticism against Connecticut's peculiar dilemma: the state had more money for education than any other in the United States yet spent less on its teachers and educational facilities than many states with lesser revenue. Connecticut had received $1,200,000 from the sale of the state's claims to the Western Reserve in 1795. The interest from this money was set aside to provide the bulk of annual support for Connecticut's public schools. By the mid-1820s the fund had grown sufficiently large that local communities seldom felt obliged to tax themselves in order to supplement their portion of the fund. Since civic priorities may be gauged by the distribution of public funds and since citizens of Connecticut seldom evidenced a willingness to tax themselves, so the Friends of Education argued, Connecticut's poorer school system was directly caused by the state's unusually ample endowment from the Western Reserve.

Over and above critiques of specific educational practices, such as the Connecticut school fund, and popular attitudes toward education, conventions of the type May called sought to polemicize New England's educational plight. These conventions, intended in great measure for the awakening of community interest in scholastic matters, tended to rely more on rhetorical exhortations than on suggestions for particular programs. The dedication of these Friends of Education was unquestionable, but they often employed their dedication in an inchoate fashion, a practice which disguised their lack of concrete proposals. In addition, their own experience in schoolkeeping, usually restricted to private schools conducted for privileged youth, limited their ability to formulate the specific issues and techniques that would be necessary to institute a forward-looking system of universal education, adaptable to the varied educational needs in New England.

May's background indicates the difficulties which the Friends of Education as prominent citizens faced in appreciating the needs of common school teachers. The eminent merchant family from which he came provided May with more than the advantages of Boston's best private schools and study at Harvard College; it ensured him the necessary financial resources to progress without interruption in his studies from elementary school straight through his professional training. As a consequence, May's career distinguished him from many less fortunate, not only because of this continual progress of study but also because of the young age at which he was able to enter college (sixteen) and the ministry (twenty-five). Though it is not likely that he required supplementary funds for his schooling—the usual motive for devoting one's college vacation to schoolkeeping—May engaged to teach a district school in Concord, Massachusetts for the fall of 1816, his third year at Harvard. For the next six winters he varied his studies by giving portions of the school year to schoolkeeping, usually in private schools at Hingham and Nahant, Massachusetts.

Once ordained and called to Brooklyn, May was required by the press of his ministerial duties to abandon the practice of school teaching, though custom almost automatically assured his appointment to the school committee. "Everywhere in our country, as well as in Europe," he later recalled, "it was taken for granted that protestant ministers must appreciate the importance of the right culture of the young, and always be ready to promote their education." [6] His own affluent background and almost exclusive experience in private education gave May little preparation for the deplorable condition of Connecticut's public schools. His subsequent reaction to the "intolerably tedious" work, which he engaged in for these schools in his adopted state, suggests how sanguine had been his previous understanding of the actual nature and practice of instruction in common schools.[7]

On October 22, 1826 Samuel May addressed the Brooklyn Lyceum on "Errors in Common Education." In retrospect, the most striking impression of this address is the extreme vagueness it conveyed of May's concept of education. In spite of several bold contrasts in his lecture, May's discussion did not evolve a clear and compelling set of proposals for administering changes in Connecticut common schools. The essay, in short, was the typical product of an intelligent, educated man concerned about the quality of the educational system, but unable to conceive of a precise context in which reform should occur. As such it was an expression of the varied sentiments, motivations and attitudes prevalent among the Friends of Education. His clearest effort to define education revealed the seriousness with which May and men like him began to view education.

> Education, in its broadest sense, may be understood to mean the complete and harmonious development of all the intellectual and moral powers of our nature—the subjection of ourselves to the supreme control of right principles, and the acquisition of all knowledge that may be necessary, in order to our filling well the sphere of duty, in which God has placed us. Thus defined, it is the *great purpose* of this present state of our being.[8]

The ambiguities of the address become somewhat clearer when the characteristics of his audience are recalled. Schooling, May realized, should aim at equipping citizens to meet the social dislocations which poor agricultural towns like Brooklyn were beginning to experience during the first quarter of the nineteenth century. As New England became increasingly industrialized and densely populated, more and more people found that during their lives they would have to adapt themselves to unfamiliar careers, different from those of their parents. Primary and secondary education for the mass of the populace should imbue people with the idea that learning was a continuous process. "Increased demands" and "new responsibilities," May noted, "render it necessary to seek highest acquisitions of knowledge and to ponder anew the correctness of our moral principles, in their operation upon new classes of duty. And thus the process of education goes on, or should go on, toward perfection." [9] Perfection, however, was not a quality to be obtained merely by formal schooling during one's youth, "It [learning] is the work, which ought to be continual progress, until, in the providence of God, we are deprived of our faculties." [10] May labored to bring the community to the realization that greater acquaintance with and acquisition of education was the only hope for greater social and personal enrichment.

Actually, for all its amorphous qualities, this address was an implicit challenge to those who considered education a matter of rote restricted to the classroom. "I am not disposed," May emphasized, "to find so much fault with the branches, which, it is pretended, are taught to children, as with the *manner* in which instruction is generally given—a manner unfriendly, I am confident, yes, utterly incompatible with the attainment of a thorough, practical knowledge of either of these sciences, and tending scarcely at all to that unfolding of mind and heart, in which, as has been already said, real education consists." [11] May objected to instruction which began by presenting "general rules, abstract principles, tedious definitions" to the learner. Principles of learning, he believed, could not properly be established in the classroom by reliance upon prescription or fiat, since outside the classroom a child learned by inference "by reasoning from particulars to generals." [12] Rote and routine, moreover, were objectionable as methods of instruction, because they interfered with the development of a young mind. Pupils' minds, May assumed, contained natural facilities for understanding which could be developed by the process of instruction. In exercising only the faculty of memory, the contemporary methods of instruction, May concluded, resulted in paralysis rather than in learning.

May considered an instructor's style as important as his familiarity with various subjects, his disposition toward teaching as essential as his actual knowledge. The art of instruction, May explained, depended upon a teacher's ability to draw out of students' insights, inferences and inductions from facts which the student was known to possess. A qualified teacher stimulated his pupils to follow out independently trains of thought that he had suggested. Indeed May went further and claimed that once the skillful teacher had won the voluntary attention of his charges "any subject of knowledge may become . . . instrumental to the expansion of most of the mental faculties." [13] May's essay placed an extraordinary confidence in the teacher's style, a confidence that the teacher's own personal manner would ensure the proper train of thought for each of his students. Precisely how the teacher with his own principles and values would keep from interfering with the natural development of individual students was unclear. In part, May's confidence in the teacher's style was a function of his assumption that the community itself would act as a check upon educational practices and innovations.

In fact, communities did not provide the necessary check to the teacher's individual style in the late 1820s and early 1830s. Undertakings like the Brooklyn Lyceum increased concern for education less among the citizens than among the teachers themselves. As a consequence of the growing educational literature and the work of the Friends of Education, by the end of the 1820s many educational experiments had begun. While this experimentation indicated a degree of constructive adventurousness in a serious work, the variety of innovations in educational methods and techniques began to point up the basic weakness of the stress men like May placed upon the style of a teacher. Without the scrutiny of each community the manner of a particular teacher went unexamined, and the teacher was left to his own initiative and devices to determine the proper mode of imparting knowledge. Within a relatively short period of time, men like May began to add to their concern for communal enlightenment about education a regard for the evaluation of instruction and teachers.

At first, when confronted by methods of instruction whose limitations surprised and shocked them, the Friends of Education seldom turned to the special training of teachers as an immediate and efficient means of improving common school education. Indeed few Friends of Education, especially those who were ministers, questioned that the educator, once called by heaven to the work, could not suitably instruct himself in the skill of teaching. May's efforts in educational reform exalted the community's role precisely because education was in their eyes a social and not exclusively a pedagogical process. The Friends of Education undoubtedly took this view, in part, because their accustomed influence upon communal affairs, educational or otherwise, was seldom direct or authoritative. They assumed, as did May, that the indirect force of personal style would be somehow sufficient to meet any educational need, given appropriate awareness on the part of each citizen. Ultimately the very teachers who attended the lyceum began to demonstrate to the Friends of Education the errors of this assumption. May's anxious benevolence in behalf of a new pedagogy quickly enlarged into a wholesale questioning of the social and institutional order which had favored May and other Friends of Education.

Professional Quickening

The service of early exhortations to educational improvement was not entirely beneficial. By the early 1830s articles began to disparage those who interpreted the appeal for an "enlightened" style in education as a license to practice all kinds of innovative techniques and experimental methods upon children.[14] Insufficient attention, it was felt, was being given to the proper theory of education as a means of tempering practice and rendering it judicious. Teaching had always assumed some measure of discipline, a measure which, of course, the Friends of Education easily recalled when they remembered their own days of school teaching. Very quickly the Friends of Education began to do more than call for enlarged standards of education and improved qualifications of teachers. Focusing their educational concerns on the central role played by the teacher himself, these men called not simply for general educational improvement but for teachers to provide educational leadership. Through the 1830s the Friends of Education drew upon the experience of their own professions and training as a precedent for recommendations to teachers. Their increasing calls for professional standards reflected how disorderly and undisciplined "improvement" was becoming;[15] they also indicated how readily educational control began to pass from their hands.

During the 1820s and 1830s there were very few facilities for the special preparation of teachers. Several private efforts were made to establish seminaries, but these were all short-lived. Even had they been successful, such efforts were too restricted to meet the broad, immediate needs for qualified teachers. In 1832 one Connecticut teacher estimated the teaching personnel of that state alone to be in excess of four thousand, while the first and best-known experimental seminary for preparing teachers during this same period graduated less than one hundred students in its entire twelve-year history.[16] Even if many young men had been properly disposed toward teaching as a profession, the expense for attending such an institution remained prohibitive throughout the early nineteenth century so long as these efforts were privately financed.

Appeals were constantly made for institutions of special preparation in the reports of school committees, School Visitors and Friends of Education. More and more during the 1830s the state government was urged to participate with money and other support in such an enterprise. However, the first state-supported normal school was not founded until 1838 in Massachusetts, and Connecticut did not follow suit until 1849. Before 1838, for young men who might have entertained teaching as a serious occupation as well as for the Friends of Education, professional training of teachers remained conceptually and institutionally a vague and informal phenomenon.

Between the third and fifth decades of the nineteenth century—between the period when preparation of teachers was initially discussed and the establishment of actual, specialized facilities for this purpose—strategies for improving teachers' qualifications underwent a transformation which, though less dramatic, was as profound as the development which followed the founding of state-supported normal schools. The informal and somewhat haphazard character of the lyceum and the indirect influence exercised by the Friends of Education did not lend themselves to dramatic reforms such as were begun after 1838.[17] Nevertheless, these organizations and individuals provided the only context within which many young men could realize their aspirations for becoming professional teachers before 1838, when the first school dedicated to the special preparation of teachers was established. In large measure, the young men for whom teaching gradually emerged as a professional possibility did much themselves to change the public view of education both with their independent experiments and with their participation in lyceum activities. The development of more specialized institutions and professional techniques for teachers accelerated in the 1830s because many young men without professional prospects began to transfer their energies into the improvement of an occupation which had hitherto not been considered a full-time activity.

May and his associates tended to extrapolate from their own experiences as students and masters in private schools and academies when fashioning their image of a public school teacher. The majority of common school teachers in the early nineteenth century, however, had experienced few such social advantages either in background or in training. Only by intense self-motivation, ambition and effort, so the Friends of Education insisted, could the common school teacher transcend his milieu and approach an analogy with other professions. One whom they thought successful was William A. Alcott. Almost the exact contemporary of May, Alcott's early life left him ten years May's junior in professional opportunity and stature by the time both were thirty. Alcott's family were farmers in moderate circumstances, working the poor farming country of western Connecticut. These ties confined his education to district schools for three or four months in the summer and four months in the winter. After his eighth year Alcott studied in the schools during the winter term, supplementing this rudimentary instruction with his mother's tutoring and, for a year, with a school kept by the parish minister.

Alcott's aspiration was to become a printer, but his service was required on the family farm for a portion of each year. The only nonagricultural pursuit open to him was schoolkeeping, which could be carried on close to home. In 1816 at the age of eighteen, equipped only with his unsystematic education, Alcott began work as a schoolmaster. Only after teaching six years did it occur to him that schoolkeeping might be a permanent occupation. It took an additional four years—ten altogether—before Alcott realized that his own teaching style might be improved by knowledge of theories and methods of instruction.[18]

The strategies for "improvement" which Alcott employed on his own before 1826 suggest quite specifically the problem the Friends of Education encountered in promoting teaching as a profession. The circumstances under which Alcott undertook his first school appointment in Wolcott, Connecticut, did not prompt serious considerations of teaching as anything more than a temporary or accidental occupation. His own community had little cause to reflect upon methods of improving their teachers, for at that time, Alcott explained, the art of "governing" a school was regarded as a "peculiar gift of heaven." Indeed the suggestion that instructional ability could be developed "would have been deemed a strange innovation—not to say a dangerous heresy." [19]

Generally, teachers in rural communities like Wolcott came immediately from the ranks of the school's student body. Near the end of his study in the district schools, Alcott had been employed frequently as a monitor and, outside the classroom, as a tutor. Usually schools employed monitors and tutors when the size of the student body became too great for one man and help was needed to keep order. The oldest students of a class were invited to assume the responsibility of monitor on the basis of past deportment and physical size. His early success as a disciplinarian, Alcott remarked later, was "noised abroad," and he developed a reputation for "good learning." In actual fact and by his own admission his only talent was in spelling, indicating the truth of his own remark "that if this good learning" had "been duly analyzed, . . . I was [but] a good monkey or parrot." [20] His selection as a schoolmaster was not questioned, since approval was given by a one-man committee composed first of his father and then his uncle. Alcott scarcely needed to append the remark that two weeks before entering the schoolhouse, he had not sought the position nor had ever given school teaching consideration as a serious occupation.

In the third year of teaching, Alcott began to realize the value of having his talents "noised abroad." "I was invited [in 1819] to take charge of a school, at a considerable distance from my former sphere of labor. What report with her thousand tongues, had testified of me, I never knew; I only learned that they wanted a 'smart master', and therefore came for me. . . . They wanted one who had the 'gift' of governing." [21] Not only did reputation serve to enlarge Alcott's sphere of activity and the number of alternatives open to him, but an engagement on the basis of general reputation gave him a particular kind of security. During the following year, for example, Alcott was able to divide his duties as schoolmaster with those of a civil officer in his native town some distance away, all without fear of adverse criticism by either community. Travel between the two towns and the two offices sometimes required canceling his school:

> I have sometimes wondered how it came to pass that the people of the district did not complain. But "the king," you know, "can do no wrong, and he who gets his name up, may lie in bed all day." I had acquired . . . a high reputation in that neighborhood as a schoolteacher; and therefore it was, perhaps, that a few irregularities did not easily injure me.[22]

Until he decided to commit his energies completely to schoolkeeping, Alcott viewed his reputation in the same way the community did, as a tribute and an evaluation of his inherent skill.

A serious commitment to teaching as a more permanent career came in Alcott's sixth year of schoolkeeping. Afterward, his estimate of the value of reputation took on a different character. Even in retrospect, his description of this commitment to teaching retained a tone of painful compulsion:

I was now twenty-four years of age; and no occupation was determined on for life. It was ideal to think of spending my time as I had done, divided among so many various employments. I wished to devote myself, for life, to keeping school; but what encouragement had I to do so? Few districts employed male teachers except in winter; and in those which did, I was entirely unacquainted.[23]

However hesitant and cautious it may have been, Alcott's commitment marked a shift in his attitude toward the usefulness of reputation. He began to speak of "securing his district," of selecting the town he should serve rather than having the town select him. He also hoped to capitalize on his notoriety as a schoolmaster to require any town to appoint him for some period of tenure longer than the one term which was then customary. Reputation to Alcott became less a natural consequence of inherent skills and more a manipulable instrument for achieving his own ambitions.

During six years of striving to achieve respect and confidence as a teacher, Alcott determined to inaugurate some dramatic new reforms in his school. He had concluded that any success an individual teacher could hope to achieve toward improving the school system was a function of the public awareness of the bold and estimable character of his work. The innovations, Alcott reasoned, would surely have a beneficial effect on the students and, he hoped, they would serve also to enhance his own reputation, a circumstance which would in turn enable him to initiate further changes. He began with technical improvements: backs for benches, storytelling at the beginning of the day to ensure punctuality, ventilation of schoolhouses during recess, slates to occupy nonreciters.

The changes were popular, but they hardly affected the fundamental alterations in educational policies and practices which Alcott envisioned. After six years, his schoolhouse practices had become so well known that he felt able to trade on his wide reputation and suggest a bolder innovation aimed not at the students but at the system of school teaching itself. He focused on altering the employment procedures of teachers. Alcott volunteered to have his salary substantially reduced in exchange for a year-long contract. His terms were nine dollars a month, to which the school committee agreed on the condition that Alcott shorten the school year to eleven months. Such negotiations with the school committee carried on by a single teacher, for his own welfare as well as that of the school, demonstrated both to the citizens and to other teachers that an individual schoolmaster could effect substantial changes:

The circumstance [of Alcott sacrificing a portion of his own salary] excited some surprise throughout the town. What could it mean for a strong, healthy man, in his twenty-fifth year, to engage for a year, in a large school, at a hundred dollars, they could not conceive. There must, they thought, be some other object intended or aimed at, or some deep-laid scheme to be effected.[24]

His extraordinary sacrifice of salary, Alcott believed, would itself argue "the difference ... between the efforts of a teacher who feels that he is concerned in an employment which is to be his permanent employment—one in which and by which he is to gain his daily bread, and what is of more consequence, his reputation—and those of one who is only desirous of teaching a term or two as a preparation for something else, merely to busy himself until he can get a place which is more profitable." [25] At the very least, Alcott was convinced, the town would have to recognize the seriousness of his purpose as a schoolmaster and the extraordinary talents and sacrifice which should be expected from the local schoolmaster.

Alcott's experiment was only partially successful. When he applied for a continuation of the same arrangement the next year, the school committee would agree to a six-month contract, although they raised his salary to thirteen dollars a month. The community at large seemed to be perfectly satisfied with his manner of instruction—though, as Alcott noted, few visited the school to see his teaching firsthand. Yet according to the custom of financial support, especially in Connecticut, citizens objected to spending beyond the State Fund allotment; to do so would necessitate taxing themselves. "In short," Alcott asserted, "a reform was begun, externally. Had I known at this time a little better how to carry the spirit of reform into the internal concern of the school, much more might have been accomplished. A good work was begun; but it was not completed." [26] Alcott's extraordinary exertion during the next few years resulted in injury to his health and necessitated a break in his teaching career. After suitable rest Alcott began study for the medical profession, and after six months, he received a license to practice surgery and medicine. After three years in this profession he returned to teaching. In his *Confessions* written some years later Alcott made a most interesting comment in his motivations during this period, "I had only resorted to another profession as a discipline to my mind, and that I might have, as the common saying is, 'two strings to my bow,'—that is, that I might have, as a last resort, and in case of necessity, the benefits of a profession which though respectable I knew I could never love." [27]

When Alcott reentered the classroom, he found that his stature in the community was as much a function of his medical training as of the years he had already spent in schoolkeeping, educational planning and experimentation. It was an asset and yet a disappointment that the public should consider his medical license a higher achievement than his years in the common schools. "I had the prepossessions of the people in my favor. . . . They had all heard of my former reputation, ... and were therefore prepared to hope much—perhaps too much—from my exertions." [28] His fellow townsmen considered schoolkeeping a much inferior pursuit to that of medical practice and some were, therefore, prone to regard Alcott with a degree of suspicion. For the most part, however, medical studies enhanced his reputation, even to the point of arousing excessive expectations in regard to his teaching work.

Alcott's resumption of school teaching began initially with a sense of experimentation, much like his previous effort. Nevertheless, his newest educational enterprise in 1825 reflected how much Alcott had altered his own attitudes toward educational improvement in the years spent away from teaching. "Here I had resolved," he stated, "on a grand experiment in school keeping, although I meant to begin cautiously. It was not my intention to attack or even to slight old usages. My object was to change the spirit of the school, rather than to innovate largely upon its forms." [29] His second experiment was predicated upon gradual rather than dramatic innovations. Instead of a reliance solely upon technical devices to manifest his effectiveness in instruction, Alcott made his second experiment contingent upon an unselfish commitment to education. While still proud of his previous record of skilled instruction and of the authority it gave him in educational matters, Alcott began to consider teaching not only a permanent occupation but an actual profession. The transformation from an occupation to a profession was recorded in his manual for professional teachers, *Confessions of a Schoolmaster.* In the work he described a ten-year process of conversion to the benevolent and selfless work of instruction. The form and content of the *Confessions* demonstrated the purity of motive which Alcott believed defined the true professional. After 1825 Alcott began to stress the formation of individual character as much as the efficiency of pedagogical skill among the essential qualifications of a professional teacher. In a short period of time he reoriented his immediate concern for professional improvement from schemes for enhancing his own reputation and toward more direct forms of enlightening the public about education.

By 1826 Alcott could clarify from his own experience the essential problem that confronted any young man who aspired to become a professional teacher. On the one hand, his teaching style, Alcott assumed, should be informed almost completely by the intensity of his commitment to instruction. The best teacher labored without reservation and preferred work "in and out of season," to cite the phrase Henry Barnard employed later to characterize Alcott's own efforts. To intensify and hence improve his manner of instruction, the teacher had to give his full attention to the school and the pupils in his charge. On the other hand, the success of his teaching style was traditionally evaluated by the local community through its school committee and public approbation, rather than by experienced teachers who understood his professional difficulties. At the same time, the teacher who developed improvements had little to do with the process of judging them. In the 1820s teachers like Alcott conceived of the district community as wholly untutored in educational matters, and yet as possessing total power in admitting or dismissing teachers and thus in supervising both the form and content of instruction.

The entire question of the traditionally intricate relation between teacher and community occupied a great deal of Alcott's attention after 1825. Confronted with the lack of any widely recognized educational standards outside the community to which a teacher might appeal, the only hope for freeing the school from total subjugation to public whim lay in educating the public to advances in teaching method and practice. This was bound to be a difficult task, and was one which Alcott was hesitant to impose upon the local teacher, already so burdened with duties in the classroom. Originally Alcott had assumed that the entire matter could be overcome by a teacher's attempting to cultivate public faith and confidence in himself, that is, by his acquiring a substantial reputation. If the local schoolmaster was trusted, Alcott reasoned, then the community would be willing to allow him a free hand in the schoolhouse. After 1825, however, Alcott came to feel that this was rarely a successful strategy, both because the school committees still retained the power of the purse and because most teachers simply could not gain sufficient reputation on their own to be free agents.

The solution to teacher-community conflicts, if there was to be one, would have to be conceived in less personalized terms. If there was no appeal to generally accepted norms of schoolkeeping, then the community would always retain the final word in educational debates. This being the case, Alcott realized, the community would simply have to become enlightened about the nature of the teaching enterprise and the specific conduct of its own school. The public through its school committees had always insisted upon the right to be fully informed about the conduct of the schools, a position which Alcott accepted enthusiastically. In fact, he insisted that the argument be pushed one step further, and that the public recognize an equally strong obligation to inform itself about education. After ten years in common schools, Alcott felt he was able to distinguish clearly between those duties of the teacher and those of the community to education. The question then became a technical one: how best to achieve this increased public knowledge. Preoccupied with this question and ever anxious to learn of recent developments in education, Alcott responded enthusiastically to the Reverend Samuel May's notice of the Brooklyn convention.

Apart from cultivating a personal reputation, there were two practices or customs already in existence by which a teacher might attempt to involve and inform the community on educational issues: parental visitations and school exhibitions. Concerned teachers and their sympathizers observed during this period that the one means by which improvement could be efficiently advanced was the visitation. It was realized that an accurate assessment of a teacher's practices could be made only by having been present in the schoolhouse during actual instruction. If visitations were conducted systematically and periodically, a teacher's personal reputation would not have to carry his government of the classroom. Unlike reputation, the visitation provided a more sure and direct means for the teacher to clarify his methods and aims to parents and interested citizens. Alcott prided himself upon his receptivity to parental visits and was fond of challenging adverse criticism by noting how little firsthand knowledge was employed either in supporting or questioning his manner of teaching.[30]

Visitations, however, presumed communal concern, and in presuming the very characteristic they hoped to cultivate, visitations remained effective more as an idea than as a practice. Communities tended to abrogate their responsibility for direct and broad supervision and support by delegating School Visitors. These visitors were poorly paid, if at all, and most frequently they themselves considered the office a mark of the community's respect for themselves rather than a serious responsibility to the community. As visits by parents and citizens grew more and more infrequent during the 1830s the initiative for involving the community in education passed back to the teacher. By 1840 the whole concept of visitation had been reversed. It then meant the practice of the local schoolmaster calling on parents to inform them of his work.[31]

Before the end of the 1820s the only other means for enlightening the public about improved educational procedures was the school exhibition. At the end of a school term several schools of the district assembled at the request of the school committee. Teachers put their pupils through recitations and exercises most of which they had prepared especially for the event. These were frequently large gatherings, sometimes held outdoors, and the occasion gradually became a popular social affair, a seasonal festival for the locality. Schoolmasters, however, began to object to the exhibition, since School Visitors viewed exhibitions as substitutes for their vistations. Teachers without interest and ability clearly had reason to object, for their success or lack of it was publicly displayed in such gatherings. But criticism was also voiced by able teachers, especially as they began to think of their work as a distinct and worthy profession. They objected to becoming performers for public entertainment.[32] The exhibition, as they saw it, was a staged and contrived representation of schooling and could hardly serve either to improve classroom procedures or for public enlightenment of them. In the teacher's view the exhibition, since it confused mere entertainment and serious instruction, was combining two distinct functions. Gradually commencement exercises assumed the more social aspect of the exhibition's activities, while the lyceum took on the more serious and professional responsibility of public instruction. The new attention to the lyceum's potential was a direct result of the alliance between the Friends of Education and rural youth whose origins could not support their ambitions.[33]

Lyceums and Restless Professionals

By 1826 Alcott had come to realize from experiences in his own community the limitations and weaknesses of the various strategies he had employed to advance himself as a teacher and to enrich the common school system in his district. Neither the high esteem in which he was held throughout the community nor the school exhibitions and visitations in which he participated had served to stimulate interest sufficient to accomplish the educational renovations Alcott's emerging professional awareness demanded. In his correspondence with the Reverend Samuel May, Alcott learned that the Brooklyn convention had met with such a surprisingly favorable reaction that May had determined that it should evolve into a more permanent organization. May had become acquainted with the lyceum movement, then just beginning under the inspiration of Josiah Holbrook, and he seized upon it as a means of carrying on the discussions begun at the convention.

The lyceum as an institution for public instruction had been a British tradition since the late eighteenth century. What connection there was, however, between a British lyceum and its American counterpart was tenuous at best. The essential—and in the context of May's intention—the crucial difference between the two lay in the permanent and formal quality of the British lyceum (in England the term always designated a building housing a library, meeting rooms, etc.) and the casual quality of the American variety. One lyceum lecturer emphasized to his audience this informal character:

> I hold it to be a positive benefit of the lyceum that individuals voluntarily associate for the purposes of mutual improvement—that all distinctions, except those of individual merit are unknown—that the object is to communicate instruction to each individual—and that the individual is compelled in a measure to task his powers, to test his proficiency, to ascertain and supply his defects, to compare himself with others, and by such comparison to learn to do justice to their pretentions and to realize his own claims, advantages, and obligations.[34]

Lyceum membership of the type May conceived would be unrestrictive, open to the entire community and strictly voluntary. In fact, the lyceum tried to ensure by its organization that every citizen would have an opportunity for full observation and self-expression on all topics, whatever the individual's background, education or occupation.

The lyceum aimed at a broad range of public instruction and was not focused primarily upon questions of immediate concern to teachers. Nonetheless, the lyceum did serve the teacher's efforts to improve education, and during the 1830s the expansion of lyceums throughout New England was extraordinary.[35] In part, this expansion was possible owing to the organization's adaptability to forms as varied as public addresses, conversation or upon occasion presentations of model school classes. The lyceum's chief service to the teacher was the incorporation of the best aspects of visitations and exhibitions. Like the visitation, the lyceum gave citizens a personal knowledge of an individual teacher, his skills and his plans; and like the exhibition it provided not only the demonstration of different teaching styles but the opportunity of discussing them. The very informality of the lyceum precluded, so its proponents believed, the evils of false display and selfish design which the exhibition was thought to encourage.[36] The lyceum was neither a wholly serious activity like the visitation nor a mere entertainment like the exhibition. It was, one lyceum exponent claimed, a "rational entertainment." [37] But, above all else, May's lyceum and its counterparts enabled the teacher to participate directly with the community in the evolution of educational and professional standards.

In championing the lyceum concept the Reverend Samuel May had stressed its service in advancing local community interest and knowledge both of teaching and of teachers.[38] There was, however, latent within the lyceum another service, one which Alcott wished to exploit. Although his own years in common schools had given him a firm appreciation of the value of serving a community sophisticated in educational matters, he was even more interested in employing lyceums for the professional benefit of teachers. Alcott's youth had made him acutely aware of the need for establishing and enhancing education as a recognized profession among those whose only career it was. One of the most serious impediments to such recognition had been the lack of a sense of communality among teachers themselves. "How much the young need wisdom," he exclaimed in his *Confessions of a Schoolmaster*, "especially at an age when they are exposed to danger! How valuable at this period, are faithful friends! Would that I could have had but one! Even one continued remonstrant would probably have saved me from many errors and much sorrow." [39] If teachers working throughout a state or county could assemble at a lyceum to discuss their problems and compare methods, they would, he felt, come away with at least a feeling of professional kinship. This awareness was every bit as important a contribution of a lyceum as increased public interest. The tendency to view the lyceum from the teacher's viewpoint rather than that of the public distinguished May and Alcott despite their broad kindred sense of educational commitment. May was after all primarily a minister, while Alcott was a teacher only. In this context May tended to stress the importance of communal support for and interest in public education; Alcott was more concerned with the professional improvement of common school teachers.

If a lyceum's purpose was to improve the public regard for the importance of education as well as to improve teacher efficiency through mutual instruction, its very success continued unforeseen consequences. In those communities where the operation of the lyceum demonstrated the value of patient search for efficient teachers, citizens became more willing to augment their portion from the state appropriations to attract such teachers. Indeed the competition for well-reputed teachers and for the establishment of model school institutions became for many New England towns the sign not only of social welfare but of benevolence and moral health. Innumerable articles in the educational literature asserted that the condition of the schoolhouse indicated precisely the character of the town.[40]

Concomitantly the teacher who participated in mutual instruction within a lyceum learned not only techniques of improved teaching but also of professional opportunities elsewhere. To the extent that a more competitive community and more ambitious teachers resulted from the proliferation of lyceums—the only organizations for educational improvement in this period—the effect of a successful lyceum was to draw efficient teachers from one local community to another and thereby to ensure in the occupation of teaching a heightened mobility. To many teachers like Alcott this mobility, although it freed the teacher from dependence upon one locale, prevented teaching from attaining the permanency and stability which characterized the highest forms of the established professions.

A combination of these factors operated in the professional careers of both William Alcott and his more famous cousin and fellow teacher, Amos Bronson Alcott. The Brooklyn Lyceum provided both Alcotts with advantages which their teaching styles, reputations and prospects (all of which were practically identical) would probably not otherwise have afforded them. The advantage lay not so much in having attended a lyceum, the benefit of which was not widely recognized before 1830, but rather, through the personal acquaintances and friendships which a teacher formed there. In addition to an incipient sense of professional kinship and some greater knowledge of teaching method, the lyceum bestowed that traditionally useful quality of American professional advancement—social connection. Alcott and his cousin by being brought into contact with the Friends of Education, many of whom were influential and widely respected, were drawn away from their native region of western Connecticut and steered to Boston where the high salaries of teachers made the city an index of New England's best teachers.

Although they were perhaps more fortunate than many young men who attempted to improve their work in teaching, the Alcotts' careers beyond the Brooklyn Lyceum and May's role in their advancement suggests the highly practical and personal benefit that teachers drew from the early lyceums. William Alcott's letter to May in 1826 reported the efforts which he and his cousin made in western Connecticut during the preceding ten years. May became sufficiently interested in their work that he invited Amos Bronson Alcott to his Brooklyn parish for a visit. This first visit developed into several during which Bronson Alcott gradually came in contact with some of May's Boston friends. The younger Alcott went on to Boston with high recommendation from May, and there established one of the early Infant Schools in the United States. Eventually he founded there the controversial Temple School, conducted with the assistance of Elizabeth Peabody, the sister-in-law of Horace Mann and Nathaniel Hawthorne. Soon Alcott was befriended by Ralph Waldo Emerson and the Transcendentalist group in Concord, Massachusetts, where he spent the remainder of his life as School Visitor and resident philosopher. His most educational experiment came with the founding of the utopian community, Fruitlands. Certainly his career was not hindered by the fact that in May 1830, shortly after his arrival in Boston, he had married the sister of the Reverend Samuel May and gave one daughter, Louisa May Alcott, the benefit of both family names.[41]

The Brooklyn Lyceum provided similar professional opportunities for William Alcott. Within a year or two after his attendance at this lyceum, he too traveled to Boston with letters of introduction from May to some of his influential friends, notably the Reverend William Ellery Channing.[42] When in 1830 the editorship of the only educational journal in the United States was transferred from one of May's close friends, William Russell, to William Channing Woodbridge, a cousin of William Ellery Channing, it was not mere accident that William Alcott became, first, Woodbridge's assistant and, later, editor of the retitled journal, the *American Annals of Education*.[43] While its responsibility was ultimately directed toward informing the public, the lyceum also served, therefore, to place teachers whose own preparation and qualifications would not readily suggest them to respectable and prestigious positions of instruction. For many rural New England teachers the lyceum became, if not a bridge to Boston, at least a bridge to better opportunities in other towns.

If both Alcotts experienced the advantages of Boston and uncommon professional opportunities, they also recognized the fortuitous quality of their opportunity. The professional contribution of both men subsequently reflected an attempt to make their own advantages not just accidents of circumstance but opportunities which the profession itself systematically provided to talented young teachers like themselves. They spent a substantial portion of their remaining work in education, but not as teachers of local or even city schools. By the end of the 1830s the Alcotts had committed themselves to writing and lecturing among lyceums, seeking to provide for many local communities the service May had provided for them.[44] While such full-time educational proselytizing, especially in the travels of William Alcott, was a novelty in the early 1830s, the Alcotts' work served as a precedent for much of the labor in behalf of educational reform carried out by Josiah Holbrook, the Reverend Charles Brooks and Horace Mann. In William Alcott's subsequent effort to render teaching a distinct and special profession, the education of the community and the contribution of the lyceum were neither abandoned nor ignored. Still, after the work of teachers like Alcott and men like May, the role of the community increasingly became a separate, though significant, aspect of the professional preparation of teachers. William Alcott's extensive travels to lyceums reflected also the increasing concern of teachers and the Friends of Education for specialized organizations, professional preparation and systematic procedures for selecting and improving talented young men for teaching.

The Alcotts had no better experience than their own lives to demonstrate the necessity of evolving institutions which would be wholly dedicated to the preparation of teachers. Talent, ambition, common sense, inventiveness, community trust, a sense of kinship with other teachers, career mobility and increased social status could carry a person just so far in approaching secure professional standards. As long as the only forum for teacher advancement remained the lyceum in its informal and unspecialized form, there would be something lacking in the teaching profession—namely, institutions for educating the educators.

CHAPTER II

From Consecration to Conversion:
Early Experiments in
Professional Preparation,
1825–1837

Only admit the importance of the object [a seminary for the
preparation of teachers], (and who can deny it) and it looks like an
impeachment of their Christian sincerity, to suppose that among those
hundreds of young men who are pressing forward into the ranks of
charitable enterprise, none can be persuaded to enter upon a domestic
field of labor, which promises so much for the advancement of the
Redeemer's kingdom. No, only let the project be begun, let the way of
usefulness be opened, let the countenance and support of even a few
pious and influential individuals be afforded, and I am persuaded that
agents to carry on the work, at least to commence it, will not
be wanting.
> —The Reverend Thomas H. Gallaudet, 1825

My preparation for school-keeping consisted, primarily in attending
the district school near my native home from three to four months
every winter, from the age of four to thirteen, and a few months every
summer, from that of four to eight. . . . For I scarcely ever had, in my
early life, notwithstanding my ambition, one serious thought of
"keeping school" myself.
> —William A. Alcott, 1839

The Unholy Waste of Young Men

From earliest times the education of American children had been within
the prerogative and power of churches and ministers. The evolution toward
recognition of a professional educational system in America as a consequence progressed only as rapidly as did recognition of the professional
status of teaching. Conducting elementary and district schools had been a
traditional attendant function of an American minister's duties, with clergymen conducting tutorials and small classes as an integral part of their

21

religious duties. During the eighteenth century, moreover, the instruction of youth provided men of God with a means of supplementing their salary. In both legislation and public opinion a habit of thought emerged which regarded the instruction of youth as a sacred responsibility. This habit perdured into the early decades of the nineteenth century, even as schoolkeeping became separated from a minister's numerous tasks. By 1820 instruction itself had become a full-time occupation, and during this period ministers increasingly left the actual teaching to others. The instruction of children became a work for persons undivided by other occupational loyalties.

This rearrangement of the minister's involvement in education set the stage for a broader educational development, the distinct forms of which began to take shape from the early 1820s to the Civil War. Whereas during the early part of the nineteenth century, the actual instruction of the young became less and less a specific part of the ministerial vocation, ministers did not simply abandon the education of the young. They insisted on preserving for themselves the role of advisers and overseers as members of the school committee in local communities. In such positions they did the important work of selecting those who actually taught. They also sustained their influence in the educational sphere by officiating as School Visitors, whose principal duty involved the semiannual inspection of the school committee's selection. Frequently the law designated several leading men in a community as visitors, but often only the minister performed this task with any regularity, thus providing the only continuity among the visitors. Finally, a number of ministers saw schoolkeeping as simply a social extension of the pulpit, an effective and distinct mode of implementing their sacred calling. Such men left the ministry in order to commit themselves wholeheartedly to what had been the irregular and subordinate function of their earlier profession.

Much of the actual schoolkeeping of this period, however, had little to do with ministers. The majority of persons in education were young men in need of temporary jobs to finance other aspirations. The influx of such young men sparked a crucial issue, the question of standards and needs in professionalizing teachers. Some very specific reasons engendered these discussions. The most fortunate communities of New England staffed their schools with young men who spent their winter vacations from college in their hometowns. Frequently the town fathers had to employ considerable persuasion with the young man and his parents in order to compel him to exchange private study or vacation travel for the instruction of a heterogeneous group of youth, most of whom were not much younger than himself. In addition, many citizens rebelled against the higher costs of maintaining a school staffed by college students; the salaries required seemed exorbitant for the service rendered. Not infrequently committees preferred young men who plied a local trade when not teaching school. When the ground was frozen, farmers often occupied themselves teaching in the district schools in lieu of handcrafting domestic objects for their families or for sale. In such a situation it was not surprising that men concerned with improving schools and education would soon raise questions about the suitability of such practices in so important and "sacred" an activity.

Professionally trained individuals, especially ministers, were the most frequent critics of the values and mechanics in the existing procedures for training teachers.[1] One of the earliest and most important of such statements was contributed by the Reverend Thomas H. Gallaudet. His newspaper articles, which appeared in the *Connecticut Observor* of Hartford in January of 1825, were soon republished in pamphlet form and later were reprinted in numerous educational journals. Undoubtedly he found this notoriety as gratifying as it was surprising, since in the early years of the century very little discussion had occurred about any educational topic, and no educational literature existed before 1827 to provide supporting authority. Not that Gallaudet needed substantial supporting authority. In the year of this publication, 1825, he was nearing the peak of his effectiveness in one of the most publicized philanthropic experiments of the day. Gallaudet was thirty-eight years old and had for the past eight years directed the American Asylum for the Deaf and Dumb, which he had founded at Hartford. At this time, too, he was sought after to assume the direction of several educational and benevolent organizations and was engaged in correspondence beyond the bounds of his native country.[2] In a word, he was a commanding figure for a number of charitable efforts, like the institution he currently directed, which had substantial investments in matters of education.

During the 1820s the recurrent theme of Gallaudet's articles centered on the need for a seminary, devoted exclusively to the training of teachers. His innovation of the proposal rested explicitly on the assertion that, if teachers were ever to achieve maturity and profitable training, the only way was by *"a diligent course of preparation and a long discipline in the school of experience."*[3] A special trinity of priorities informed this preparation. First, teaching had to be made a *"distinct* profession or calling."* Second, novices in the occupation must yield to those who have experience in the work, and finally they must *"devote* themselves to it, and . . . pass through all the *preparatory* steps which are necessary for the consummation of their acquaintance, both with theory and practice."[4]

Over and over again Gallaudet's articles focused on the needs, which would be met by his proposal, especially the need for young men to prepare for teaching careers through specialized training. Comparatively little discussion occurred about the mechanics of such an institution. Without "auxiliaries" like the seminaries, he envisioned individuals would be forced "to grope their way, through a long and tiresome process." Such institutions, he suggested, would "render a thousand times more easy, rapid and delightful," a course of strained and painful effort. The product of the seminary, the prepared teacher, would through his apprenticeship have enlisted an "entire devotedness," an "undivided consecration," and a fitness for success in his profession. The promise of the specified "terms of years" in the proposed training school would be an immediate and subsequent achievement of the highest and most positive sort. If one's qualifications were commensurate, any hesitancy to commit oneself to such a regimen could conceivably raise doubts about one's spiritual condition among prospective teachers. The absence of immediate "consecration" to this benevolent work, Gallaudet judged, "almost looks like an impeachment of their Christian sincerity." [5]

The primary dread playing through Gallaudet's writings was the fear that a particular kind of waste would be the by-product of this absence of formal teacher training, namely, the loss of potentially professional talent. The analogy of the teacher's plight to other professions which had achieved by 1830 tangible forms of social esteem and influence made this sense of loss particularly keen. Whether he discussed lawyers, ministers, physicians or even the mechanical trades, Gallaudet emphasized that the striving for qualitative workmanship in one's occupation was more than a service which the public aggressively sought and had a right to expect. The orderly production of such workmanship was a justification of "Christian sincerity," a virtue which could only be achieved by some form of specialized training. Even a gardener's task, he observed, must proceed upon "some matured and well understood plan of operation. On this subject I can hardly restrain my emotions." [6] And again:

> Here, as in everything else, *system* is of the highest importance. Nothing should be left to whim and caprice. . . . Then might we hope to see the heart improved, while the mind expanded; and knowledge, human and divine, putting forth its fruits, not by the mere dint of arbitrary authority, but by the gentler persuasion of motives addressed to those moral principles of our nature, the cultivation of which reason and religion alike inculcate.[7]

Arbitrary authority, whim, caprice and groping were somehow to be excluded in the operations of the teachers' seminary. By contrast with these evils, the matters of the heart paced themselves by moral principles, operated only with the indirect force of gentle persuasiveness and externalized themselves in the affairs of reason and religion. In Gallaudet's mind the seminary was directed against ills far broader than those which impinged specifically upon education and the occupations of teachers. It was, in short, a formidable counter to all forms of moral debility. The need to prevent moral debility in American society through the enlistment as teachers of inspired, though often professionally anxious, young men, was to Gallaudet a paramount need of the young Republic.

The public, Gallaudet asserted, could not accept an unsystematized preparation for any professional activity. Without structure and planning, proper qualifications were left to the determination of "solitary, unaided, unadvised, untaught, inexperienced efforts."[8] Gallaudet reinforced his relentless explicitness of this point by an appeal to general public values which, he assumed, disparaged any manifestation of disorder and waste in human affairs. He could as easily have dramatized these values by a description of his own experience, which probably hovered in his consciousness, as he wrote these pieces at the end of 1824.

After his graduation from Yale in 1805 Gallaudet arranged himself, as did the majority of his graduating class that year,[9] in a study of the law. His access to the library and office of the Honorable Chauncey Goodrich [10] was an uncommon opportunity. Yet after a short time a deterioration of health compelled his departure from that office. Apparently his health was not so severely impaired to warrant a refusal of Yale's offer to appoint him a tutor in the college. Before long, that occupation, too, proved somehow unworkable for him. Gallaudet then went west to try his hand as a merchant. This venture eventually returned him to New York, where he once again was unable to complete a basic apprenticeship. In 1811 he joined the Reverend Nathan Strong's First Congregational Church of Hartford. In the fall of that year he took up the study of theology at the recently formed seminary at Andover, Massachusetts. Within the next three years he received his education and a license to preach and returned to Hartford to await the call from a congregation.

In the period of months while he waited, Gallaudet occupied himself with experiments in educating the deaf and dumb daughter of his neighbor, Dr. Mason Cogswell. In April 1815, still uncalled, Gallaudet once again committed himself to a wholly new activity, which required a different preparation. A group of "benevolent neighbors" in Hartford, headed by Dr. Cogswell, offered to finance a two-year trip to Europe for him to study the methods of instructing the deaf and dumb. Gallaudet returned from Europe in April 1817 and opened the American Asylum for the Deaf and Dumb in Hartford.[11] The process of fitting himself for his profession had involved a dozen years since his graduation from college and four false starts, only one of which, the ministry, even remotely approximated the systematic preparation outlined in his articles on the seminary for teachers. Although Gallaudet's early experiences concluded more fortunately than those of other young men who shared his aspirations, the broad contour of this meandering was not uncommon in the period. Gallaudet's conception of the value of system and his personal erratic pursuit of a calling form the boundaries of one of the important social and moral problems of this period.

In the context of his own experience Gallaudet's seminary proposal became a specific antidote for the special dread which emanated from a young man's meandering and wasteful engagements. This real fear was the waste of a dozen prime years of a young man's life with the concomitant accusation, whether expressed or implied, that his "Christian sincerity" was wanting. This kind of waste implied a lack of interest in fulfilling moral obligations; it might also indicate a willingness to risk temptation and moral corruption. Too long a hesitancy to engage a calling raised questions about a young man's genuine fervor and Christian sincerity. If such sincerity were pure, Christian humility would qualify a young man's aspirations, and his goals would be conditioned to his abilities. In other words, proper preparation gave an individual a framework for self-understanding, an ability to commit himself wholly to a work of which he was capable. It acted as a caution to pride and kept him from overtaxing his abilities for the sake of ambition.

While engaged in his last preparation, Gallaudet's letters from Europe repeatedly described to his benefactor the intense nature of his commitment to the instruction of the deaf and dumb. The frequency and fervor of these descriptions seem more concerned with a verification of his benefactor's trust than with the communication of his thoughts and feelings to a respected friend. Quite likely this stress was a function of his previous failure to enlist his "entire devotedness" in any sustained, effective way. Precisely because his previous advantages for preparation had been somewhat exceptional, his sensitivity to this failure would have been more than just embarrassment. "I begin to think," he wrote Dr. Cogswell, "that one intention of Providence, in permitting some men to reach lofty heights of intellectual excellence while their hearts are strangers to the love of God, is to illustrate in the clear light of the approaching future world, how insignificant and worthless are the proudest requirements and efforts of genius, that idol of literary paganism, when contrasted with the silent and despised graces of moral worth." [12] Such passages suggest also the all-important feature of any course of preparation; they demonstrate that preparation provided an opportunity for manifesting a Christian sincerity by "professing" it. These professions gave a particular meaning to preparation and, to an extent, shielded a young man from the implication of insincerity and wastefulness during the time of study for his calling.

Thus only secondarily did preparation involve the training to a particular task or occupation; primarily it provided an individual conditioning which would apply to any worthy occupation. This conditioning—Gallaudet called it "training up"—did not circumscribe an individual's potential for good but shaped it, or aided in the shaping of it, in order to realize and mature one's latent powers. The auxiliary institution Gallaudet described was fundamentally unobtrusive; its positive effect upon an individual's moral character was indirect and subtle, if the seminary was conceived to have any measurable effect at all. In this context there emerged something of the difficulty men like

Gallaudet had in conceiving what the purpose and nature of the seminary was to be. Assessments of the institution's actual effect were couched in analogy and hyperbole rather than definition. A young man's groping, loneliness and awkwardness, for example, were not eliminated by seminary training. Rather, there the opposites of such ills became "a thousand times more easy, rapid, and delightful." The process of seminary preparation neither wholly created nor wholly removed any aspects of a student's character or commitment, at least not directly.

The more important factor in the training of talented individuals was their own consecration, their own devotedness and willingness to undergo some sacrifice for their aspirations, *their* personal profession. Paradoxically, the value of the institution of preparation was sustained only by a Christian assiduity, a sincerity which the student brought to the seminary and which was unaffected by the institution in any positive and direct manner. The *fact* of a sustained education in a seminary became almost as important as the *kind* of education a seminarian received. Particularly for ministers like Gallaudet a preparatory education seemed to be as important in manifesting his personal devotedness and consecration as the occupation which would logically follow as a consequence of preparation. Training and maturity were, in his own words, achieved by *"a diligent course of preparation and a long discipline in the school of experience."* [13] Still, in his concern for the early consecration of a young man's life, Gallaudet necessarily became less anxious about the particular, eventual manifestation of commitment—ultimately experience in work determined that—and more about the fact of being ready and qualified to do the will of Providence. School teaching was one of many occupations well adapted to a young man bent on serving Providence. The term "seminary" could refer to the preparation of more than one occupation. His particular emphasis upon the highly personal devotedness of an aspirant professional kept him from clarifying *how* an institution for preparation could engage a young man in a work of Providence.

The conception of a teacher's seminary responded to the need for enlisting the Christian sincerity of young men in benevolent enterprises. In the initial stages, however, such seminaries merely located the real ground of such men's fear, the limbo between college and personal calling. Increasingly the discussions of a professional preparation of teachers included an anxiousness over this period of a young man's life. This worry was as much a function of concern for the fate of young men as it was for the unworthiness of young men who misapplied their advantages. In this context, preparation itself came dangerously close to unworthy inactivity, needless procrastination and lack of Christian sincerity. As a state distinct from the activity requiring it, preparation interjected a qualification into the genuine concern for moral worth and Christian sincerity. The longer one remained patient in the limbo, the more one risked challenge to spiritual values, for such values were only sustained in a worldly context by activity in their behalf. While one waited for the opportunity decreed by Providence, one might waste substantial amounts of precious time.

Preparation precluded the simple polarity between worthy and unworthy activity, since it was pursued before one's calling was clear, yet it could not approach the dignity of that calling once engaged. It was a kind of worthy inactivity which demanded scrutiny lest one develop a habit of not recognizing opportunity, until (pridefully) a young man was convinced of his own readiness. Was there a way of working immediately for one's eventual, temporal work without complete devotedness but also without being accused of halfhearted consecration, which implied divided loyalties and insincerity? This implicit ambiguity about preparation reflected itself in the ambiguity of Gallaudet's conception of a seminary and a profession. In his attempt to conceive preparation as a worthy enterprise, Gallaudet filled his discussions with appeals to quality, with analogies to respected occupations and with hopeful prognostications. However, greater clarity could emerge only when an institution for instructing teachers was actually founded.

Public Instruction as a Lesser Ministry

Before 1830 the orientation of young men to teaching proceeded somewhat similarly to the ways in which ministers trained young men for their profession. Usually this preparation for the ministry included a few students working and studying in a minister's own home and parish. The discretion of the older man and/or the resources of the younger generally determined the duration and intensity of preparatory training. Virtually all the preparation was incorporated into the workings of an active church. The enlistment of pious young men advanced through study and the practical observation of parish work. Likewise in teaching, experienced schoolmasters took particular pains with a few selected pupils in the course of regular teaching. Proficiency coincided with one's degree of exposure to proven techniques observed in practice. Beyond these general similarities the development of training procedures for ministers and teachers reflected even more specifically common aspects. These resemblances were hardly surprising, since the earliest conceptions of preparation were advanced by ministers. The establishment of the first school for training teachers in 1823, for example, is generally attributed to the Congregational minister, Samuel Read Hall.[14]

Hall's own experience suggests how preparation for the ministry naturally grew into a similar training for an associated occupation. In 1814, at age nineteen, he began his own studies for the ministry with the Reverend Daniel Gould, who had succeeded Hall's father as pastor in the town of Rumford, Maine. The next year Hall began teaching winter schools in Rumford and neighboring Bethel in order to support his studies, since his father left no patrimony. The few improvements Hall introduced, especially at Bethel, achieved widespread public attention. When public appreciation expressed itself in a salary increase, he was able to finance study at an academy in North Bridgeton, Maine, under the direction of the Reverend V. Little. In the autumn of 1818 he entered the Kimball Union Academy at Plainfield, New Hampshire, where some assistance was offered to young men preparing for the ministry. For three years he remained there, teaching the winter schools in the nearby towns and developing a reputation akin to his earlier one at Bethel. His health, never strong, proved sufficient reason to abandon the academy and his intention of going to college. Still committed to the profession of the ministry, however, Hall went to Woodstock, Vermont, where he studied with the Reverend W. Chapin and a short time later with the Reverend W. Eaton in Fitchburg, Massachusetts.

While at Fitchburg several clergymen warned him of the dangers of deferring his entrance upon the actual work of the ministry. Unconvinced himself that his studies had been sufficiently advanced and thorough, Hall submitted the decision of embarking into ministerial work to the Worcester North Association, which licensed him. Soon after, he received a commission from the Domestic Missionary Society of Vermont to labor in Concord. Hall's first duties in Concord were those of a School Visitor. In this office he discovered that the conditions of the schools were far below his own standards. Within the year the public of Concord called him to be their pastor, a position he accepted upon condition that he devote the majority of his time to a special school for training teachers. The school he opened in March 1823 was the first normal school in America. It was to be his prime ministerial responsibility in Concord for the next six years. In the circuitous course of his early preparation, in his sensitivity to the unsystematic nature of that preparation (he called it "inadequate"), and in the comparatively late enlistment of a calling (he was twenty-eight), Hall's career paralleled that of Gallaudet. These similarities also suggest common conceptions about preparation and professionalization, and they can explain much about the similarities and differences between a minister's and a teacher's preparation.

For so many young men like Hall, teaching was an occupation by default. Initially his work in the schoolhouse simply financed his aspirations for another profession. His lack of physical and financial resources eventually caused some alterations in how he prepared for the ministry. The staggered order of his studies created some ambiguity, even in his own mind, about the degree of his preparedness. Even when he finally entered the ministry, Hall participated little, if at all, in the decision to conclude his preparation. His actual, ministerial assignment as a home missionary did not necessitate preaching of a scholarly nature, which was demanded by many established congregations. Nor did his eventual ministerial function as a schoolteacher presume a background of systematic theological study. In this respect the missionary and the schoolteacher were parallel works. Both were primarily concerned with aiding Providence's design; both had broad, unspecified duties to unstable communities; and, for men with Hall's aspirations, both permitted unscholarly forms of preaching. Nevertheless, Hall tried to give school teaching a dignity and system comparable to that of the ministry.[15]

During the early nineteenth century the use of institutions which were designed exclusively for professional training was in America a new means of elevating the prestige and effectiveness of certain occupations. The established professions had already begun to develop strategies which teachers, in turn, began to copy. Andover Theological Seminary, founded in 1808, where Thomas Gallaudet received his training, was the first institution of its kind in the United States. Physicians had something of a precedent for formal training, since the lectures in chemistry at the College of Philadelphia (later the University of Pennsylvania) had developed into a semisystematic preparation as early as 1768. Still, the establishment of a distinct school of preparation, a permanent faculty, a student body distinguished from the regular college undergraduates, laboratory practice and less arbitrary Europeanized standards did not occur at the University of Pennsylvania, Brown, Harvard, the College of Physicians and Surgeons of New York City or elsewhere until the early nineteenth century. In Connecticut, the Litchfield Law School, the first institution of its kind in America, began the training of legal minds and skills about 1784.[16] Hall's efforts in behalf of teachers simply reflected these broader experiments in professional education. For none of these professions, however, were the precedents sufficiently compelling to have determined in any rigid manner the character of preparation. Indeed the novelty or absence of such precedents in America played an important part in the sanction given to experimentation with the forms of occupational procedure at this time.

The incorporation of educational experimentation into the regular course of a community-supported school provided a natural means for improving the instruction of teachers and children alike. In Hall's early school at Concord, for example, the younger children were gathered together in order that he might demonstrate his methods and attitudes to the older students. Still, the number he trained for schoolkeeping, as he termed it, was apparently small. Nevertheless, the school was a means of publicizing the results of a successful experiment in awakening public interest in the status of teaching. In order to reach many who did not attend his school, friends in Boston encouraged Hall to commit his lectures on teaching to print. The highly successful volume which followed was primarily responsible for the offer he received in 1830 from the trustees of the Phillips Academy at Andover. The trustees of this old and respected institution intended Hall to take charge of the newly created English Department. This additional course of instruction would respond, they hoped, to the needs of those who intended to teach in the common schools and of those who did not pursue the classical course necessary for college. After a long correspondence with the academy's trustees in which he argued the inadequacies of his early education, Hall accepted the principal-ship of the new department or seminary, as it was variously called.

Andover was a logical location for the prototype teacher's seminary in several important ways. First, it met an important qualification which Gal-laudet himself had specified as crucial, namely, its healthy endowment. The Phillips Academy had been founded and directed by the wealthy family of Samuel Phillips since 1780 and was the first institution of its kind in America. Second, it had highly significant theological ties. Since 1808 and the founding of the first theological seminary in America on the academy's grounds, Andover had become the focal point for young men who wished to prepare for the ministry, but who preferred to avoid exposure to the liberal Unitarian teaching at places like Harvard. Third, the proximity to the theological seminary assured that the Teacher's Seminary or Department would be staffed by men, who, if they were not already properly prepared for such work, would at least be properly committed. Hall found such men in Frederick A. Barton and Lionel Tenney, who combined their studies at the theological seminary with their instruction of aspirant teachers.[17] Finally, Andover in 1830 possessed some of the strongest intellectual resources in America, not only with scholars like Moses Stuart, Leonard Woods and Frederick Emerson but also with one of the largest libraries in the country.[18]

The two seminaries at Andover dramatized the options open to a young man who wished to engage in a sacred calling. The prestige and twenty-two-year history of the theological seminary there—not to mention the tradition of the ministry in general—embodied a value which in 1830 did not need to be advertised. The Teacher's Seminary, however, had no such history or sig-nificance. Even though the director of the new institution sympathized with the sacred implications of an instructor's calling, ministerial control ensured a conception of school teaching as subordinate to a ministerial one. A young man's choice of either seminary implied certain things about the chooser, his talents and aspirations as the very structure and program of the Teacher's Seminary suggested. The school was separated into three sections: a Teacher's Department, which involved a three-year course of instruction, encompassing most of the English branches pursued in the colleges, together with special training in the art and science of teaching; a General Department, enrolling most of the students, which was shorter, more irregular and entered by those not quite equipped for the Teacher's Department; and, a Preparatory Depart-ment, essentially an English school for boys, which was usually taught by a separate instructor and was under the general guidance of the principal of the Teacher's Seminary.[19]

In general, an English school excluded the Latin curriculum studied by those who planned to enter college. Attendance, therefore, at the English school of the seminary implied a student was preparing for a trade or business. This implication of inferiority, or at least of disadvantage by comparison with the classical education in Phillips Academy, shortly transferred from the Preparatory Department to the upper two sections of the Teacher's Seminary as well. Initially, however, no subtle inequities between the preparation of future teachers and the preparation of future ministers, lawyers and doctors in the academy had been intended. The trustees of Phillips Academy had carefully invested between two and three thousand dollars in a prodigious set of school apparatus. In addition, they erected a two-story stone building, exclusively for the use of the Teacher's Seminary.

Despite all the preparation and Hall's enthusiasm, the experiment at Andover was somewhat less than successful. Students did not flock to the seminary, Gallaudet's "Christian sincerity" notwithstanding. Hall remained principal of the seminary for seven years and was succeeded by the Reverend Lyman Coleman, who in turn presided until November 1842, when the entire project was abandoned.[20] In the twelve years of the seminary's life approximately six hundred students attended. Of that number, however, less than one hundred completed the entire course. Though the experiment began hopefully with eighty students, subsequent enrollments of *continuing* students were always disproportionate to the student body as a whole. In the peak year of 1835, for example, the three departments of the seminary totaled 190 students. Only thirteen in the senior class of the Teacher's Department completed the entire course requirements.[21] The failure of the enterprise was attributed to a want of funds.[22] Initially the funds had not been lacking and had been invested generously in appointments and facilities. After two years, the trustees of the seminary, who were also the trustees of Phillips Academy, even instituted a policy of assisting indigent students as they had always done for financially strapped young men in the classical department at Andover. Financial aid was provided if the student in the Teacher's Seminary had completed one school term and was considered a proper candidate. This policy compelled the majority of students to attend one of the four eleven-week terms at the seminary according to their means. The large number of students who merely passed a term or so in the school and the difficulty of supporting indigent students [23] suggest that the few fortunate enough to complete the course of study had the advantage of either an uncommon amount of money or else an uncommon "consecration." Without one of these, proper preparation was impossible.

Under such conditions only an enterprise launched under the auspices of Phillips Academy and Andover Theological Seminary could have lasted even a dozen years. The ultimate survival of the seminary strategy, however, was not entirely predicated upon the planning and authority of prestige institutions. Even after the actual experiment at Andover had been suspended, the concept of a specialized institution for the instruction of prospective teachers remained. Hall and his associates elaborated the initial planning of the seminary and the changes they instituted gradually developed a more extensive and specific conception of preparation in the process of responding to the school's immediate needs.

The seminary's most pressing problem centered upon the difficulty of sustaining a student through the entire course of three years. One of the implicit assumptions of the seminary had been that they would receive properly devoted young men from all over New England. In fact, however, over half the students at the Teacher's Seminary came from the town of Andover itself and the nearby environs.[24] This situation, which was but a corollary to the inability to maintain a continuing student body, gradually developed into a larger question: was the seminary a service for the local town or an instrument for a wide dissemination of methods and standards of education by means of prepared teachers? What was required, Hall had come to believe by 1832, was a more hybrid structure than the Teacher's Seminary, one benefiting both the local community and the profession of teaching. As Hall would shortly recognize, such a structure already existed in the lyceum meetings begun in the late 1820s. By 1850 the evolution of professional teacher training in New England had shifted first to the lyceum and eventually to an important and indigenous American institution, the teachers' institute. These institutes spread quickly through New England, the west and the south, and in many rural areas of the United States survived the century itself.

Lyceums and Itinerants

The Andover experiment was important less for the seminary than for another organization, which Hall devised simultaneously to enlarge his scope of operations—the School Agents' Society. Initially his concern for stabilizing the students' residency imitated measures employed elsewhere. In the example of Marietta Collegiate Institute in Ohio, the more famous Oneida Institute in New York, the Lane Seminary in Cincinnati and Princeton College in Kentucky, Hall and his sympathizers perceived the effectiveness of self-supported manual-labor institutes.[25] A farm was purchased for the students attending the Teacher's Seminary, but it proved unsuccessful as had most of the other manual-labor schools by 1840. Most likely, the reasons were similar. Frequently very poor students had to work extra time to pay their way and were too tired physically to pursue their studies after a day in the field. Also the unpredictable fluctuations between productive and unproductive seasons precluded a dependable source of financial support. The farm often had to be subsidized, if funds were available, which meant that the auxiliary, employed to alleviate a student's expenses, became an added financial drain. The only other alternative which was tried for a while involved hiring a superintendent for the farm, someone with experience sufficient to ensure that the farm gave a reasonable return for the investment. But again, this procedure required an additional expense. Some institutions, like Andover's Teacher's Seminary, resorted finally to appropriating funds from time to time to meet students' needs.[26] Even if this measure had not been a mere stopgap and if a policy of support had been established, the fundamental problem still might not have been met. Unless the student's home or relatives resided within manageable proximity to the seminary, the expenditure for even one year of the three-year course of instruction away from home proved either prohibitive or wasteful, often both. Teaching was simply not an occupation for which sacrifices of that nature were made in New England society during the first third of the nineteenth century.

By the end of the 1820s individuals concerned with education had come to recognize that the problem of preparing teachers lay not with the cost necessarily but with the intensity of public interest in such training. Discussions of the problem frequently noted that money followed personal interests, and most locales did not see community welfare as bound up with the training of teachers. To a certain extent, some communities already had demonstrated this observation by competing aggressively for the few young men who graduated from Hall's seminary. Nevertheless, the majority of the public did not imitate this example. Many towns, educators agreed, acted contrary to their best interests, when current concerns did not include education. Hall himself had recorded the malady of public indifference in the first chapter of his influential manual, *Lectures on School-Keeping.* Whatever solution emerged from the difficulties of financing students and faculty at the Teacher's Seminary, intensive efforts had to be made to overcome public apathy toward education.

On July 13, 1832 Hall gathered at Andover a group of men and formed the School Agents' Society which would within two years be moved to Boston and renamed the American School Society. Almost all the officers and staff of the organization had strong ties with Andover. Of its seven directors four were immediately associated with the schools there, and a fifth was William C. Woodbridge of Boston, the editor of an important educational journal of the period, the *American Annals of Education.* Its corresponding secretaries were drawn literally from every state in the union and included such men as the Reverend President Edward Beecher of Illinois College of Jacksonville, Illinois; the Reverend George Gale of the Oneida Institute, New York; Professor Denison Olmstead of Yale College; the Reverend Benjamin O. Peers, soon to be president of Transylvania University in Lexington, Kentucky; and the Reverend Alva Woods (brother of the Reverend Leonard Woods of Andover and former president of Transylvania University), president of Alabama University in Tuscaloosa.[27] Such an assembly of distinguished men was indicative both of the broad geographical, social and religious influence

Andover exercised and of the growing interest in the improvement of teachers.

The most significant appointment in the new society went to a person whose background not only lacked association with Andover but whose aspirations and training had not been ministerial, namely, Josiah Holbrook. Indeed his pivotal position in the organization explains much about the extent to which Hall and his associates were willing to accommodate their efforts in order to train teachers properly. Holbrook chaired the first meeting of the society and served as the first corresponding secretary as well as treasurer.[28] By 1832 he had been involved in the work of education for more than ten years and had become, more than any other individual, the self-appointed missionary in the cause. In 1810 he graduated from Yale, having studied with the scientist Benjamin Silliman. His fame increased, as his writing and itinerancy in behalf of lyceums intensified. In 1826, at the age of thirty-eight, Holbrook had committed himself to this work, which he continued until his death in 1854. In the course of these years of championing lyceums, Holbrook advanced the professionalizing process of teachers one step further.

As Holbrook conceived it, the lyceum aimed to sustain communal interests in edifying and practical subjects. The organization depended for its continuation upon public-spirited citizens who gathered the lyceum members together as often as convenience allowed. The meetings varied in character, using conversation, illustrated lesson and lecture-discussion as methods of "mutual benefit." The best town lyceums collected a "cabinet, consisting of apparatus for illustrating the sciences, books, minerals, plants, or other natural or artificial productions."[29] Holbrook's presence in the School Agents' Society explains why Hall and his associates came to favor increasingly the lyceum concept. However, Hall's vision of the great need for massive teacher training would not be met simply by using Holbrook's example of establishing lyceums from Maine to Georgia.[30] Hall seized on Holbrook's boast that the lyceum, ideally conceived, adapted to any particular local and communal setting, and he presumed that his problem would be met by a lyceum with variations.

The actual conception of the nature and purpose of the School Agents' Society was as vague as Gallaudet's conception of the nature and purpose of a seminary for teachers. The service of the society, like that of the seminary, was indirect, suggestive and subtle rather than promotional, deliberate and efficient. Nevertheless, it is clear that the School Agents' Society attempted to cast a broader view of teacher training, a view which would integrate the benefits of an established seminary in a selected town with those of interim agencies in many towns. There was in the society's plans little that Gallaudet would not have willingly embraced. The purpose of the School Agents' Society was to implicate every community in its own educational affairs. To achieve this end, the society initially relied upon the personal attributes and reputations of the agents rather than upon the technical organization of lyceums. Largely through Holbrook's efforts the society gradually became more sensitive to the potential value of the lyceum concept. It was recognized not just as a teaching forum for agents and itinerant teachers, but as a means of sustaining within the community the benefits they received from the agents' visits. Apart from the exhortation of the public to its responsibilities and the dissemination of information, the society's constitution declared its intention "to procure and encourage the labors of school agents and circuit teachers." [31] Three types of agents worked toward these ends. First, the agents of the society were responsible for establishing a circuit, structured on lyceums in six to twelve towns in New England; second, those appointed as itinerant or circuit teachers would ride the circuit in exactly the same way Methodist circuit riders did (the society's example), the difference, of course, being that the circuit teachers would in all things be nondenominational. The third category of agents included the teacher of the local community itself. The circuit teachers operated the lyceums or circuit schools on varying schedules. At times they simply met for a few days to a week on those weekly, semimonthly, or monthly occasions, when circuit teachers appeared.

Even during the itinerant teacher's absence, however, the school was to continue as a lyceum. This eventuality, the society knew, depended upon the varying talents of teachers and influential citizens in each community. On the crucial question of preparing teachers, the society peculiarly enough was not entirely clear. The process of preparing teachers would emerge, they thought, from the actual experience which the agents received while actively disseminating notions of professional and educational standards. In part, young men who were exposed to such instruction might also "awaken" to the opportunity which teaching offered to his own "consecration." Finally, and on this part there was greater conviction, such activity would challenge public apathy which so often impeded educational progress and the elevation of the profession of teaching. Thus the lyceum or circuit school worked toward a threefold goal: education of the public, recruitment of teachers and development of methods for preparing teachers.

It is really not clear which of these three aspects of their activities the society's members deemed the most important. Discussions of the society and its aims did not go beyond locating these distinctive duties of the agents. For most of the men who established the School Agents' Society, as for Gallaudet, the actual operations of an organization with preparatory functions were matters of personality and circumstance, not matters of procedure to be set up by a central planning group. In this respect, Holbrook provided an important departure from his colleagues in the society. His own preoccupation with technical considerations introduced a new stress into the discussions of educational institutions and teacher preparation. A "brief sketch" of the necessary accommodations for an instructional facility went as follows:

1. A tract of land, with a naturally fertile soil, in a good state of cultivation, and fitted for a variety of plants, and different kinds of husbandry.
2. Water power sufficient to move a moderate quantity of machinery.
3. Buildings fitted for dwellings, studies, and lecture rooms.
4. Farm-houses and workshops, sufficient for all the agricultural and mechanical operations in which it might be necessary for the pupils to engage.
5. Apparatus, collections in natural history, and books for scientific and literary exercises.
6. A supply of appropriate implements for agricultural and horticultural exercises.
7. Tools for mechanical operations in all the arts capable of being conducted in such an institution.
8. Animals necessary to stock the farm and conduct the agricultural and domestic operations.
9. An able mathematician and thorough teacher in the exact sciences and in drawing.
10. A naturalist, and practical teacher of agricultural and domestic operations.
11. A teacher of the English language, elocution and other English branches.
12. A practical farmer and gardener.
13. A practical and scientific mechanic.[32]

These accommodations, Holbrook imagined, would result in an institution which he called a Lyceum Seminary. In spite of Holbrook's technical specificity this conception of a proper instructional facility was so broad as to cover everything from a single manual labor institute to a unit as complex as a whole town. Precisely how such an institution would achieve his goal of "self-education" and "self-improvement" was as ambiguous in Holbrook's writings as other previous conceptions of preparatory institutions. Ultimately the mechanics of the Lyceum Seminary were subordinated to the aim of *impressing* a self-sustaining quality upon any educational achievement. Nevertheless, Holbrook's concern for the long-range thrust of an educational enterprise and his affinity with the technical aspects of the society compelled him at infrequent intervals to reflect upon the procedure of the organization, upon *how* the agents were to acquit their responsibilities while on circuit.

The Lyceum Seminary and Holbrook's concern help explain not only the shift of the early 1830s to an emphasis upon procedure in teacher preparation but also the sense of immediacy which pervaded the activities of the School Agents' Society. The Lyceum Seminary, which Holbrook estimated would cost thirty thousand dollars (the precise cost of the Teacher's Seminary at Andover), never materialized. Still, the very specificity of the long-range goal intensified the society's immediate efforts and bore witness to the overriding seriousness of their fervor. There was now a clear blueprint in terms of which they could fix their zeal.

In the early months of 1833 lecturers of the society traveled to 150 towns in New England and set the stage for the work of the agents. By April 1833 Hall had drawn together fifteen men to act as the first agents of the society. Of these, four including John Adams, the recently retired principal of Phillips Academy, departed for parts of New York and Ohio; nine, including Hall and his Andover assistants from the Teacher's Seminary, covered all of New England; the remaining agent was given Illinois as a territory. In fact, the society saw its own purposes as approximating those of a "missionary" organization: ". . . this Association may act as a Lay Education Society, a Foreign and Home School Society, which shall supply destitute portions of our own and other countries with the blessings that follow in the train of our free schools." [33] Their fervor affected not only the agents' missionary zeal but their style and purpose of instruction. In particular, their purpose was "to direct their efforts to the improvement of common schools during the operations of the present season. To secure this object, it is expected that they will present such improvements, and illustrate them in such a way, that every lady and gentleman who witness them, can introduce them *immediately* into their schools, and for the benefit of everyone of their pupils." [34]

Both Hall and Holbrook agreed that an agent's apparatus—his globes, maps, orreries, blackboards, etc.—were necessary and distinctive elements of his occupation. Teaching like other professions required its own special tools. The apparatus of the teacher enabled him to communicate with impressive and lasting illustrations. The cultivation of heightened interest became in Holbrook's mind the proficient teacher's special function. All the agents and circuit teachers of the society relied heavily upon such apparatus. In October 1832 Holbrook stated, "Instead of depending upon a course of lectures given once a year, from fifty to a thousand miles from them [aspirant teachers desiring a professional preparation], they are provided with the same means of meeting once a week for instructing each other, and for carrying information to their firesides and tables." [35] By May 1833, not quite a year after the founding of the society, Holbrook indicated the extent to which the agents of the society relied upon teaching aids.

It is the opinion of those interested in the Society, that a more direct process may be taken to get access to mind and heart, and to produce intellectual operations and improvement, than the circuitous course of books—the two or three years process of learning letters, syllables, words, sentences and volumes. They [agents of the society] believe that such objects may be presented even to the most untutored mind, as to elicit thought and feeling the moment they are presented.[36]

The implication of such a view, the replacement of books with a more direct procedure of instruction, qualified the stress of a Teacher's Seminary upon a sustained process of discipline through intellectual study.

This dangerously antischolarly stress upon teacher preparation and methods of instruction may well have been the cause of the society's removal from Andover to Boston, where its direction was assumed by men of a decidedly scholarly bent, men like the Reverend Francis Wayland, president of Brown University; the Reverend Heman Humphrey, president of Amherst College; William C. Woodbridge and William A. Alcott, editors of the *American Annals of Education;* and Professor Bela B. Edwards, who was a Hebrew scholar, Andover graduate and afterwards the editor of the *American Quarterly Register* of the American Education Society. Many of the other godly men who joined at that time, like the Reverend Thomas H. Gallaudet, had demonstrated by their careers their concern with the intellectual character of a young man's preparation.[37] Not long after its relocation, the society waned. A final circular in August 1834 simplified the objects of the reformulated organization. First, agents would explore and make known the state of common education in the country; second, they would engage in organizing local associations for the same purpose; and finally, they would excite the interest of the citizens and legislators in the subject.[38]

Shortly after, the American School Society, as it was last known, came to the same end as would Hall's Teacher's Seminary at Andover, and officially for the identical reason, lack of funds. It is likely, too, that the society's demise was assisted by a shifting trend in conviction among its members toward Holbrook's orientation, the cultivation of the nonacademic as well as the academic procedures in education. When in 1832 the Reverend Samuel Hall published a fourth edition of his influential teacher's manual, he added a lecture entitled, "On the importance of establishing a lyceum among the members of a school." The significance of the lyceum had not been lost upon him. "Popular education," Hall observed in that lecture, "is exciting new interest in the country; and many, who once looked upon themselves as having outlived the time of improvement, are now learning that they may, by efforts which are easily made, retrieve some of the losses they have heretofore sustained." [39]

sense of devotedness had been created by any human agency. Among
teachers as well as ministers the necessary temper for committing oneself
wholly to godly work involved a gradual and natural process, through which
God's design was made known to man. It was necessary that human agencies
pace God's work without interfering directly with it. Nevertheless, the itinerancy of teachers whose purpose was to provide public excitement about
educational matters dramatically debased consecration based upon systematic study. Even though the conception of "awakening" was explicitly no
more than the invigoration of an already existing potential, the aim of itinerancy was to mobilize and activate that potential. From itinerancy emerged
the realization that, as Holbrook asserted, an agency could be fashioned to
produce and not merely *affect* improvements in education. By implication, the
consecration of teachers could be similarly produced.

If the use of itinerants as instruments of preparation implied a qualification
of the systematic discipline inculcated during a seminarian's usual tenure of
study, the same methods which excited the general public to their educational obligations were to be used to arouse the teacher, or the potential
teacher, to a concern for constructive alternatives in schoolkeeping. In addition, the limited exposure to each community or lyceum prevented an itinerant from achieving any precedented standard of intellectual preparation.
The very nature of his riding circuit fragmented the systematic character of
education associated with conceptions of seminaries like Gallaudet's. The
circuit teachers were responsible for encouraging public support of students
who were inclined to the profession of teaching. Where teachers' seminaries
were unavailable, preparation and consecration, if they were to be had at all,
could come only from what had been an unsystematic arrangement, namely
the lyceum. In such a view, the admission followed that in some adequate
fashion they both could be achieved more quickly than previously
anticipated.

In addition to discipline and long study, consecration gradually implied
also a condition which could be managed by effective, impressionable instruction in a short period of time. Gallaudet had assumed a close, if not a
causal, connection between study and strengthening of character. The introduction of nonintellectual elements into teacher preparation complicated
the meaning of consecration. Since it was no longer an entirely academic
responsibility, consecration became susceptible to cultivation by nonintellectual procedures. Gradually the preparation of teachers assumed both the
older and the newer kinds of consecration. On the one hand, a student could
bring a Christian sincerity, an entire devotedness, a consecration which
emerged slowly and naturally over many years. On the other hand, equally
acceptable, a student could undergo a kind of conversion experience which
was produced in a short period of time by someone other than himself, like
agents and itinerant teachers. Similarly the institutions which sustained and

cared for this consecration could as well be the seminary as its less scholarly companion institution, the lyceum or even the home (Holbrook's "firesides" and "tables").

Before 1830 young men considered the professional preparation for school teaching only after college, as with Gallaudet, or after college became an impossibility, as with Hall. The broadened sense of consecration for teachers awoke young men to the possibility of considering such a preparation earlier than was customary. This consequence did not settle the problem of preparation, that is, of engaging one's calling with minimal waste, so much as it made the task more individually manageable. In this regard, the use of itinerants was significant, even though not entirely new. There were, of course, appropriate religious precedents for this activity in the circuits riders. In the process of professional preparation, however, the employment of itinerants was new. More and more proper preparatory procedure aroused young men to an awareness of the moral usefulness of school teaching. Eventually professionals accepted the responsibilities for conducting awakenings as something more than a prerequisite to systematic preparation. By the 1840s this awakening was the central activity in professionalizing schoolmen.

During this early stage the process of professionalization eliminated both formal, academic preparation and the most privileged supporters of the new profession. The new rituals, however temporary and unsystematic, contained their own rigidities. Younger professionals saw the circuit and the home, if not as schools themselves, at least as contexts for professional instruction. The influence of such agencies was thought to be as great morally speaking as the more traditional seminaries once were. During the 1830s the proliferation of lyceums was but one manifestation of this growing confusion between educational and social institutions. The newer and ostensibly more professional institutions, like the younger professional teacher, had to account for less academic procedures for preparation. The Teacher's Seminary at Andover itself established the Holbrook Association of Teachers in order that informal conversation would occur about professional matters.[43] These and similar reorientations resulted in various dislocations between and among the advocates of the new profession. In 1837 Samuel Read Hall retired from the charged intellectual atmosphere at Andover and returned to the less academically inclined New England towns, where he continued to train teachers as he had done earlier in Concord, Vermont.[44] It may well have been as much a sign of the change as anything else that, when the trustees of the Teacher's Seminary offered the post vacated by Hall to Thomas H. Gallaudet, he refused.

CHAPTER III
The Dynamics of Career Choice

I must be a fluid sort of man. . . .

—Horace Mann, June 29, 1837

The Strategic Necessity of Preparation

After the 1820s the growth of public education became increasingly feasible because the American public and educationally interested groups finally reached agreement on a few basic aims of education. From the 1820s to the end of the century the fundamental goal of educational improvement was, in their terms, the inculcation of character. During that time two generations of schoolmen successfully shaped a profession of teachers and a variety of educational systems in the name of character-formation.[1] Near the end of the century schoolmen still reiterated the clichés associated with this goal of education: "The real end of all education is to produce morally trained *men* and *women*, rather than, except in special cases, scholars. Unless this point is kept in mind by the teacher throughout his school-life experience, the professional element of his chosen vocation fails utterly of its chief end, and the pedagogue places himself in the same class as the mechanic, producing things instead of creating characters." [2] Not only did the creation of characters become the primary undertaking of the public classroom, but also schoolmen esteemed this end as the indispensable prerequisite in the formation of a professional teacher. The very adaptability of this goal to such different forms of instruction explains its long service in the educational discussions of the nineteenth century.

"Character" always referred to the moral potential of each individual. It varied broadly according to assumptions about the extent and degree of its improvement or degeneracy. Only in the most general sense did its inculcation predict the patterns of postschool behavior and ideas.[3] Educational discussions employed the term as synonymous with a discipline of mental faculties,[4] with the ideal Christian gentleman,[5] and with the necessary power in creating other men of character.[6] Nowhere did any examination of this idea become so specific that it implied deterministically or even probably a man's later occupation, political affiliation, economic advantages, domestic values, etc. The failure to define character more specifically did not connote to schoolmen an absence of parameters to the thought and action of educated men. One of the principle clichés of character was that it did produce a proper, genteel and harmonious style of life. The chief function of character formation, one begins to sense, was its service as a goal whose functional implications need not be sharpened.

The invocation of character was a clear separation from earlier traditions of education. The longest tradition of instruction began in Massachusetts with its seventeenth-century legislation providing for the basic skills of reading, writing and ciphering. The striking feature of this legislation was its repeated endorsement of the provisions for basic instruction.[7] Progressive historians have interpreted this repetitiousness as evidence of America's early and firm commitment to notions of public education. As likely, the necessity of passing virtually the same laws over and over indicated the practical frustration of those notions, if not the success of another, more exclusive educational tradition. The continued emphasis upon minimum public training marked an ongoing disagreement over the practical application of the laws favoring public literacy. The indifference to and nonenforcement of these laws has been as much a characteristic of prenineteenth-century education as its supposed "democratic" assumptions.[8] If it existed at all in the early periods of American history, public education usually conjured up all the awkward and invidious associations exploited by the fictional image of an Ichabod Crane.

The cultivation of character also assumed another duty, other than merely overcoming these debilitating assessments of public education. In addition, schoolmen employed it to appropriate the more academic tradition of the college and academy. While they did hope to raise the level of instruction at the earliest possible stage and to give public education a minimal intellectual rigor, schoolmen wanted the academic tradition most for its supposed social rather than its intellectual consequences. The prospectus of many an eighteenth-century academy and college testified to the belief that education refined the rude and uncouth bearing of students.[9] Often these publications made forthright claims that this training readied young men for the higher pursuits and positions of the country. When men of this tradition discussed how education produced gentlemen of knowledge and virtue, few misunderstood the connotations of special social advantage.

The graft of these two traditions began with certain fundamental notions about the relations between education and social opportunity. Families and communities whose low economic status ensured at best minimal instruction in public schools continued to shift between a latent and explicit hostility to public education throughout the nineteenth century.[10] By the 1820s, however, other groups well served by the academies and colleges began to discard their earlier preferences and look to the common school as a means of creating a safe and rational society.[11] In its initial stages Whigs and Democrats alike participated in the new educational orientation, although the Whigs generally assumed major responsibility for the work of improvement.[12] This cooperation among rival political factions illumiated the complicated strategy supporting the educational goal of character. Public education became safely open to all by putting sharp political and sectarian views outside the classroom. Although infringements upon this tacit arrangement occurred, nineteenth-century schoolmen made the inculcation of character coincide with apolitical notions of social development.

The new public education would broaden the privileges of academic study by muting the explicit connections between instruction and economic or occupational preferences. A devotee of this new educational slant put it carefully: "The child is to be educated, not to advance his personal interests, but *because the State will suffer if he is not educated."* [13] Ideally the state would benefit, but these benefits could be neither planned nor predicted within any given social or communal structure. Schoolmen were confident, however, that the state would be well served.[14] As a consequence, the opposite of service to the state, that is, service to oneself, indicated serious flaws in one's character and in one's ability to benefit from education. Rarely in the educational literature of the nineteenth century can one find discussions which broach the relationship between education and social problems like career-planning. To deal with such issues too directly and specifically opened one to charges of fomenting controversy and divisive political contentiousness. This divorce of politics and education was the first major ramification of a new education committed to creating characters rather than producing things. It is significant that neither the first nor any subsequent generation of schoolmen have conceded that this divorce was itself a political act.

The cultivated distance between education and social opportunities decidedly affected the contours of professional teaching careers. Training a staff of professional teachers for this new education dramatized how social realities continued to impinge upon education's new apolitical goal. The process of admission to professional training and rank necessarily avoided all suggestions of privilege, although the professional curriculum often contained academic and even classical studies. The demand for a training equal to instruction received in the established professions ensured a prominence to many practicing teachers. However, the profession of teaching could not comply with demands of character formation and at the same time permit successful schoolmasters to impose their methods or their judgments upon the body of professional teachers. Similarly the broad assurances of peaceful social growth, attributed to character, precluded on the professional level the admission of anyone and everyone who aspired to the moral work of public instruction. To be democratic in some feasible sense the profession of education could become neither as selective nor as uniform in its criteria as the established professions, and yet to ensure a distinctively moral style they could hardly trust each member of the profession to deal properly with his fellows, his students and even himself in all cases.

The cultivation of character intimated an educational process that was discriminating though not wholly formal, moral though not unduly coercive, individuating though not selfish, socially responsible though not politically biased or partisan. Moreover, it produced neither a scholarly nor a mechanical frame of mind. In its early formulation this educational aim became an effective weapon in prying finances from tight-fisted school committees and support from affluent citizens who possessed genuine alternatives to the public schools. The awakening of the public in the 1820s and early 1830s was largely a victory of words. By the end of the third decade of the century schoolmen found themselves in the difficult practical position of having to implement their notions. They had to create not only characters but the agencies which would ensure that creative process. Schoolmen began to see the difficulties of making education appear socially beneficial to the public and attractive to ambitious young men without discussing its immediate, special advantages.

The subsequent reformulations of moral character never extended to a repudiation of its early apolitical implications. Instead, schoolmen began to associate character with a range of special motives rather than with a series of special consequences. An intermediary stage emerged for professional instructors, a stage intimately connected with lofty principles and private aspirations. Such motives never produced professional teachers, but professional training of them made their development near-predictable. (Had they been wholly predictable, the sphere of moral and professional choice would have been forfeited.) "Indeed, I have observed," Horace Mann had insisted, "that acts emanating from worthy motives have almost invariably yielded me an ample requital of pleasure; while those which sprung from selfish motive, however intellectually judicious, have, at least in their connections and remoter results, ended in annoyance or injury." This symmetry was not accidental but "an adamantine law of necessity," and for Mann was a "revelation." "This species of revelation," he explained, "cannot be gainsaid. It does not depend on historic proof. It was not designed to be transmissable from one generation to another. It had a higher design—that of being personal, and therefore indisputable to each and all." [15] In this context the training of professional teachers became a curious creative process. The prerequisite of a successful career implied, first, a recognition of larger principles of the Republic and, second, an inner submission to them. Schoolmen fashioned thereby a preparation for professional teaching that made self-conscious choices concerning careers largely unnecessary.

The preparation of professional motives intended to reduce career crises and their attendant delays, doubts and disruptions. Because character formation could not become political, such crises would best be addressed in their most nascent stages, that is, before motives were translated into explicit action. The training of teachers implied a habituation of external and internal responses which muted precarious choices. Schoolmen never presumed to intrude upon an individual's choice or to preempt choices altogether. The exercise of professional volition was a self-evident fact of nature.[16] The new style of the professional instructor, affecting both thought and manners, proposed to anticipate difficulties, not to regiment subtly the values of professional teachers as a whole. Many consequences might ensue from any given motive. Cultivating motives did not determine consequences. Yet, through their cultivation schoolmen could affect the shape of their profession without denying the importance of voluntary action on each member's part. In this manner character, once inculcated, set up its own particular dynamic and became attractive to different groups within both generations of professional careerists.

The new intermediate stage of the profession—preparation—proposed to ensure a voluntary yet professional connection between motives and their consequences. Professional teaching focused on the highly tenuous relation between motives and consequences when they explored practical matters. The success, for example, of Horace Mann's career was in their eyes a more precarious affair after it was assured than before. Similarly motives and connections became most deterministically linked when schoolmen faced the future.[17] Their most practical assertions concerned the pitfalls of the profession; their most theoretical statements assured positively the irrepressibility of principled motives. Together the two tactics reflected an orthodox evangelical style of argument—fearful dangers and bold promises. This peculiar mode of preparation never admitted as a problem the confusion between inward moral power and a quasi-irrepressible social improvement. Instead, they worked the more hypothetical aspects of this assumed connection, dwelling far more on the motives than on their consequences. The very insistence upon professional preparation moved the center of professional activity away from instruction itself and toward the mental conditions for teaching and learning.

Their patterned argumentation, no less than their creation of embryonic models for public schooling, bear witness to the early schoolmen's appreciation of the structures necessary for any serious social purpose. (They would have been shocked to hear later historians accuse them of anti-institutional, impractical and even antisocial sentiments.[18]) Although enemies of mechanized forms of education which produced things rather than created characters, they recognized that education was a formal affair. Horace Mann himself had insisted that public education was "the balance-wheel of the social machinery." [19] And more, Mann knew that the school functioned within a larger network of social institutions: "If there must be institutions, associations, combinations, amongst men, whose tendency is to alienation and discord, to transmit the contentions of the old to the young and to make the enmities of the dead survive to the living—if these things must continue to be in a land calling itself Christian, let there be one institution, at least, which shall be sacred from the ravages of the spirit of party, one spot in the wide land unblasted by the fiery breath of animosity. . . ." [20] Their effort in the design of educational institutions paralleled their evangelical rituals of thought. Their structures would be fashioned by avoiding the pitfalls of other extant institutions. The dynamics of the schoolman's early thought and action left them intolerant of precise definitions and heedless of the actual demarcations of their work. If it gave them rhetorical and inspirational leverage in their claims of a novel profession, their own apolitical image of the professional schoolman hampered them severely in discussing the actual mechanics of becoming a professional teacher.

As a result of their own historical choices, nineteenth-century schoolmen forced themselves to explain the new advantages of character training without any specification of how, when or who would be particularly benefited. How much education did a prospective teacher need, was college essential, what towns were educationally enlightened and open to the new professional, were certain special advantages more advantageous than others, what schools, meetings and associations were most useful, and a host of similar questions were never put in professional circles. The ubiquitous teachers' manuals dealt thoroughly and exclusively with the governance and discipline *within the schoolroom.* Education and especially professional education prepared one for life and a worthy career but not for "career-planning." They skirted such issues by dwelling on motives, first in the name of phrenology and then psychology. However, they could not avoid the controversial consequences of moral character indefinitely. Even in their earlier discussions schoolmen had to deal with that sensitive area where motives ended and consequences began. One such area was the moment of career choice. How they dealt with this crucial problem in the lives of professional teachers explains much about those notions which directly shaped the contours of their careers.

The Mechanics of Professional Preferment

The actual choice of career was predominately an individual rather than an institutional responsibility for American schoolmen. Throughout the century public and private schools never intended their actual service to be a direct or programmatic interference in the moral realm. Schools inculcated character to prepare rather than coerce career choices. The choice of work was serious and depended upon a host of specific factors which no institution could anticipate. In that sense both formal, permanent seminaries shared a common aim with impermanent and less formal lyceums, associations and institutes: their benevolent conditioning of minds had to terminate before individual choices were actually made. The actual point at which institutional power ended and individual choice began, of course, remained itself discretionary and murky. This dilemma was not restricted to the teaching profession in the nineteenth century, but there it put special pressures on both institutional and individual development. In the special context of the professional schoolman career choice became at once one of the most creative and decisive moments within an individual's control and also a choice which his institutional experience had taught him to see as highly precarious. The later discussion of these institutional experiences in this study will be more understandable if now we restrict examination to the experience of an individual actually making a "successful" career choice.

The career of Horace Mann is particularly instructive in understanding how and what schoolmen learned about the mechanics of professional preferment and choice. Mann's own experience was not in any literal sense representative of the profession, though it did reflect some of the significant characteristics of nineteenth-century careers in the work of education. Like Mann, prospective schoolmen usually had pursued several occupations before appreciating the merits of public instruction as a profession. Such careers generally began late by comparison with the established professions. Once in education, even successful schoolmen rarely held the same position all their lives. (The professional idea of a permanent position became a possibility in public instruction only in the graded systems of the cities and originated as an administrative rather than as an educational objective.) The most powerful positions did not pay salaries competitive with other professions (or even with many of the manual trades) and were never held by women or seldom by men without college degrees. Though common to both Mann and other nineteenth-century schoolmen, these outward features do not grasp the dynamics of educational careers in this period. By contrast, Mann as a case study offers the advantage of following a career's sequence which alone illuminates the relative place and meaning of formative educational and social values. Mann's own place in the larger sequence of the schoolmen's profession warrants his selection over other schoolmen.

The life of Horace Mann was a part of the lore of the professional educator—then and since—and this lore gives his career a particular pertinence. Looking backward, the second generation of professional teachers (1860–1890) saw in mentors like Mann men *destined* to be heroes and martyrs in a great cause.[21] One serious account offered this version of Mann's entry into educational work. "He heard the call and turning his back on the brilliant opportunity of a great professional and political career, stepped upward into the little office room in Boston, not under the statehouse dome, where for three years he lived and slept, working sixteen hours a day on a salary of $1,500, with no official assistance, that the common schools of his beloved Commonwealth, attended by what he called his '80,000 children,' might be rescued from the decline into which they were falling. . . . And the more intelligently and broadly the educational affairs of that period are studied, the more clearly it appears that this man was one of the providential makers of American history." [22] This rather florid account intended no overstatement with its summary sentiment: "Here were a character and a career which have never been quite appreciated and never sufficiently honored by those who, by their position, and culture, would be expected to hail his coming as 'a man of God sent from heaven.' " [23] Although this view reflected certain ministerial preconceptions of its author, the ingredients of the characterization—a divine call, a lack of appreciation in his own country, a self-sacrifice to his flock in spite of themselves—did capture the schoolman's evangelical assumptions about saving decisions like career choices.

Most biographies of nineteenth-century schoolmen were interlaced with accounts of meager education, relentless farm routines, heroic mothers, stern Calvinism, severe climate, etc.; they sustained notions of a stereotyped adolescent adversity which most successful professionals had to overcome.[24] Horace Mann's boyhood burdens were invariably repeated by his biographers who merely transmitted uncritically Mann's own conception of his early experiences. "I believe," Mann had said, "in the rugged nursery of toil, but she nursed me too much." [25] The more popularized biographers of Mann also continued to stress upon the hardships of his youth. Frequently educator-biographers commented freely and moralistically upon the values of this type of early experience. One popular volume, Albert Winship's *Horace Mann, the Educator* (1896), tried to improve upon Mann's own version of his early days as irreparable loss. It is an open question, Winship advised, "whether he [Mann] did not owe more to the first twenty years of his life in which there was *developed* hunger for knowledge, craving for opportunity which necessitated his reading histories and other works adapted to men rather than children . . . than he could have owed to any method of instruction that would have monopolized his thought, or rather, have diverted his mind to books or even to nature through these years." [26] Winship enlisted Mann's own testimony to support the stereotype of childhood development.

The "rugged nursery" of childhood was not all loss; it trained one's later reactions to the conditions of life. "I know not how it [his craving for education] was," Winship quoted Mann, "its motive never took the form of wealth or fame. It was rather an instinct which impelled towards knowledge, as that of migratory birds impels them northward in springtime." [27] Even when edited and reinterpreted, later schoolmen simply wished to underscore Mann's own formulations. For them education became inevitably a compensation for early discontents. At no point was its long-term advantage clearly perceived at the time one first craved education. Particularly important, education was never seen as something Mann chose for himself. It was, rather, an instinctual change.

This instinctual process was not wholly involuntary, yet the instinctive cast of this formulation put ambitious young men at a disadvantage. Were they to make their aspirations coldly explicit, they would have provided by that very fact evidence against their own professional potential. Their option for the role of a professional teacher could not be their whim but needed, as the metaphor of migratory birds implied, the backing of larger, natural forces.[28] Whatever other circumstances of birth, geographical locales and institutional affiliations, these biographies took pains to document this natural "aptness" as a professional prerequisite. (In fact, some accounts, Mann's included, exaggerated the fact of their actual case to dramatize how their early adversities conditioned their later professional fortunes.[29] Thus, the particular mechanics which a given schoolman employed to enter teaching were never held up for literal imitation.) To establish a paradigm of individual steps to success risked the imposition of a crudely mechanical and characterless design. The promotion of instinct over discretion gave schoolmen an added incentive to reject "emulation" at both the elementary and the professional levels of instruction. If then professional education or any education for that matter, could be neither mechanical nor wholly voluntary, what did these biographies tell a young man about the workings and advantages of education for a professional career?

In the eyes of Mann, the adverse conditioning of youth stereotyped the larger problems of careers; it did not stamp a uniform model upon individual successes. In fact, the biographies of successful schoolmen savored the uniqueness of each man's trials. The more unprecedented the early burdens the more dramatic became later achievements. Having omitted discussions of unsuccessful careers, biographers intimated rather easily that the endurance of hardship rarely went unrequited. Thus, the preoccupation with the adversities of youth carried vague assurances that character was being properly developed by such trials. The individuation in the biographical literature mirrored a personal fortitude more than a shrewd management of opportunities. This stress upon individual determination underscored the importance of self-control rather than career choices made within a given social or institutional structure. In their eyes the development of character and career proceeded more often than not without institutional backing, social aids, often without the succor of friends and family.[30] "I had no protector," Horace Mann asserted. "I had none of those adventitious aids of wealth or powerful connections which so often . . . supply the deficiencies of merit." [31]

Alongside accounts of grinding poverty, hardship and loneliness encountered by schoolmen, this literature also recounted a series of mitigating conditions. As frequently as poverty was grinding, there were descriptions of angelic, supportive mothers, sizable homes, influential clergymen with city and collegiate contacts, access to private libraries of affluent townsmen, and leisure time for travel and study. Stress upon those conditions would likely have changed the tone of these biographies, making them imply less that success depended upon individual virtues and manners. Nowhere are these counter features more apparent than in the sketches of Horace Mann's life. Although Mann lived in a rural farming section of Massachusetts, his home had been one of the most commodious in the community for several generations. Similarly he entered Brown University at an early age. Not only did this in itself imply an uncommon advantage, but his acceptance immediately into the sophomore class belied his later claims of a meager basic education.[32] The lesson of all this literature drove home the point that perseverance overcame impeding circumstances. This fortitude always appeared as a reward for personal resolution rather than an opportunity contingent upon class arrangements and the current social order.

Schoolmen found it very important to see professional careers as gradual acquiescence in the larger patterns of educational improvement rather than as a series of discrete individual choices. Indeed they hesitated to credit individuals with initiating changes themselves as much as they avoided stamping a particular man or method as a model for others to emulate. Particular appointments or positions were never seen as coveted by professional teachers. Principalships, superintendencies and secretaryships were always properly bestowed, usually by consensus of committee or voters, never as an outcome of reasonable calculations by perceptive and ambitious young men. While most of these accounts describe one or more false starts in the pursuit of other nonteaching opportunities, these detours are treated most casually, neither desired, nor expected nor representing social dislocations. The idiosyncrasies of personality are rounded off in favor of those traits which best illuminated the subject's professional life. One autobiographer put it explicitly: "This book [his recollections] is not an autobiography. Its aim is to be pedagogical and historical. . . . I have not cared to give to the public my autobiography, but a long life of nearly four-score years has furnished sufficient material to build a scaffold upon which may be displayed to a large extent the pedagogical methods of the past and the great changes which have been made in our schools and processes of education." [33] So long

as this sublimation of individual choices could be maintained, the profession
as a whole did not risk its nonpolitical version of moral character.

Actual career choices became professional problems because schoolmen's
choices dramatized whatever differences existed between individual motives
and occupational requirements. Discrepancies here were serious so long as
undergoing professional instruction involved moral overtones. Like other
occupations which strove for professional status, teaching was considered
something more than breadwinning. Professional work reflected, the literature asserted, the moral character of the man; such activity, in turn, illuminated the quality of his motives. In spite of the risks of reputation and
character, the force of these moral pressures was acknowledged more after
the fact than in the anxious throes of decision-making. After establishing
himself in education, Horace Mann could exclaim: "How perfect the change
that may be wrought in us by new fortunes, new circumstances, and new
views, leading to new pursuits! What a topic of moralization is the change, of
which I am now conscious, between my present and my former self! Memory
alone connects the two together!" [34] Again the important changes are
wrought, not chosen. Nor does Mann's enthusiastic sentiment represent
superficial satisfaction with any improved material prospects. It is, rather, an
expression of relief after the fact that his risks were not proved imprudent
and irresponsible, a relief that no disparities appeared between his own
aspirations and the general image of the profession. His choice was professionally sound because his actual choice of position appeared as fortuitous
circumstance, as evolutionary rather than designed by self-interest, however
enlightened.

The conceptual ambiguities of character alone put special pressures upon
rational choices of a serious nature. As a moral problem, career choice
harbored an important operational ambiguity: it cautioned self-control to
young men at the same time that it prodded them to self-improvement. This
ambiguity did not deny that existing professional schools and teachings
conditioned careers; it ensured, however, that the efficacy of such conditioning received less emphasis than the opaque qualities of a young man's
character. Even though it carried serious professional and moral responsibilities, career choice became functionally a matter of private discretion and
chance. This nineteenth-century notion of character, lodged especially in
their many voluntary associations, restricted career choice as much as the
impersonal and specialized professional goals which followed later in the
twentieth century. For all the supposed loosening of social patterns in nineteenth-century America, there were also corresponding routines of thought
and behavior, routines which fixed life-chances just as firmly as the norms
and processes of modern industrial and urban life. Nineteenth-century careers were not chosen as freely and easily as the rhetoric of individualism
implied. The restrictions upon them had in a sense been set much earlier in

the ante-bellum period by schoolmen's efforts to create a new kind of education.

The conditions affecting professional opportunity in the nineteenth century generated their own peculiar pressures and limitations. Not the least of these essential conditions was the stereotyped image of the professional teacher, which dramatically affected the acceptable limits of all teachers' discretions and careers. This image made no effort to deal with the profound unsettlements of serious choice. In fact, it ensured these dislocations by distracting young men from the examination of the social factors affecting their careers. Thus opportunities always seemed too great and too elusive to young men starting out; they were difficult enough to understand, much less choose with reasonable certainty.[35] Instead of refining his opportunities in terms of institutional and functional consequences, a young man preparing for teaching gave his best energies to the curtailment of his ambitions. He was never more sure of the purity of his motives than when he refused alternatives which appeared to be obvious, personal advantages. When opportunities appeared personally rewarding, prudent professionals appeared self-effacing. "There is," Horace Mann claimed the day before his most significant career shift from politics to education, "but one spirit in which these impediments [bad motives] can be met with success: it is the spirit of self-abandonment, the spirit of martyrdom. To this, I believe, there are but few, of all those who wear the form of humanity, who will not yield. I must not imitate. I must not humble. I must not degrade anyone in his own eyes. I must not present myself as a solid body to oppose an iron barrier to any. I must be a fluid sort of man. . . ."[36] Whatever his real aspirations, professional deportment demanded a conciliating demeanor. The price of moral improvement was a pattern of self-denial and self-control; it was a flexibility that bore little reference to the circumstances of the social and political structure. Instead of assessing the varied forms and channels of power, Horace Mann offered a more fundamental truth, that the "great secret of ensuring the voluntary obedience to duty consists in a skillful preparation of motives beforehand."[37] The beginning of a successful career depended most importantly upon a special preparation, one which trained the will not to will.

This pedagogical intent did not presume to monitor choices so much as to condition motives, thereby skirting the obvious pitfalls of professional teaching. Rather than offering a strict paradigm, the biographies of successful schoolmen recounted unique situations and particular examples where actual choices had already occurred. Any practical inferences or analogies were the responsibility of the prospective teacher. Ultimately however, this preparation of motives made professional choice appear to be a highly introverted affair, more concerned with the preparation for choice than with choice itself. The essence of this preparation led to a peculiar self-effacing and genteel style. At the point of abandoning his promising career in law for a problematic one in education, Horace Mann pleaded in his diary: "God grant me an annihilation of selfishness." [38] At all those junctures where choices could not be avoided, one generally finds an overwhelming sense of risk and anxiety. Maintaining one's self-possession, enduring the adversity, outlasting problems, all became "choices" far more realistic than conscious decisions to rearrange one's life or one's society and inquiring where to begin.

The Snares of Voluntary Maneuver

The new educational goal of the nineteenth century, the creation of character, did not eliminate from the profession of teaching all considerations of politics and free choice. Schoolmen did, however, give far more attention to a teacher's responsibility to moral principles than they ever did to the teacher's responsibility to the state. The two obligations were intimately related for them, but few ventured to say exactly how. They trusted the inward force of moral character to deal with external difficulties, large and small. This set of assumptions did settle a host of problems of the early part of the century but created others equally formidable. If the older problems addressed essentially social questions—particularly what kind of education can be democratic—without fomenting further social divisions, the newer problems responded to more individualized dilemmas—particularly what kind of education prepares for a moral life if instruction fails to detail the specific contours of moral choice. Teachers served as stewards of the social order in the nineteenth century by tending their own vineyards. Professional schoolmen of that era generated neither a distinct asocial attitude nor any conscious social or political philosophy.[39] Their strategic use of character as a goal kept education and professional training nonpolitical and noncontroversial and gave the impression that true teachers confronted the essential moral facts of life.

These moral concerns of professional schoolmen determined which issues were necessary to confront. In the educational literature public issues emerged out of the natural course of events or out of selfish designs. Schoolmen never prepared themselves for specific public problems but, rather, for life. In any given dilemma social forces for both change and retrenchment always *overtook* men of character who were seen as having to respond to rather than anticipating and meeting such issues. In both success and failure private initiatives were desperate measures. The major restriction then on matters like career choice became the schoolmen's own self-designed hesitancy to heed their own instincts. Their dilemma was quite severe: they doubted their own drives and could not adopt uncritically the laudable drives of established teachers. Their apolitical assumptions reinforced this dilemma, for, had they let themselves examine the specific consequences of these drives, they might have permitted schoolmen to rank and prefer some over others. In lieu of this alternative, social issues became moral problems easily. In the language of moral responsibility schoolmen dealt with political questions. Having to settle political issues in nonpolitical ways, schoolmen developed an ingenious negative style. They understood practical problems by exhausting the dangers associated with them. They were always more certain of what occupations or roles a young man dared not choose than what he dared chance.

Out of a political necessity to avoid controversial issues in the act of instruction, schoolmen developed their own rituals of moral inquiry and proper maneuvers. The moral sphere dealt primarily with motives which were treated both as aspirations and as embryonic consequences. When actual consequences were called for or questioned, as in the case of career choice, moral character as an educational aim showed its starkest limitations. In the nineteenth century the ambiguities surrounding this goal did mitigate some divisive class distinctions and actual obstructions to the democratic hope for public instruction. It did not replace the older tradition with an alternative equally class-bound but it did fail to substitute an equally clear educational and social framework. Schoolmen continually groped for some workable coherence with a variety of arguments and styles of professional behavior. They ended their activity in the nineteenth century still repeating their desire for a professional yet voluntary norm of behavior, not because the few clear patterns of their labor had reflected the practice of free choice within the profession, but because their version of character training made it impossible to tell exactly how voluntary their professional labor could have been.

During this period the very synonyms schoolmen employed for career put notions of free choice at a disadvantage. A career was an orientation, a competency, an aptness, a hold, a balance, to use just some of their terms.[40] "Is there a spectacle," Horace Mann pondered in his *Thoughts for a Young Man* (1848), "fairer and more enrapturing to the sight than that of a young man . . . surveying and recounting . . . the mighty gifts with which he has been endowed, and the magnificent career of usefulness and blessedness which has been opened before him; and resolving with one all concentrating and all-hallowing vow, that he will live, true to the noblest capabilities of his being, and in obedience to the highest laws of his nature!—If aught can be nobler or sublimer than this, it is the life that fulfills the vow." [41] The implementation of this balance of capabilities and natural laws followed a ritual of thought rather than a program of action: "In selecting his vocation," Mann continued, "he abjures every occupation, every profession, however lucrative they may be, or honorable they may be falsely deemed, if with his own weal, they do not also promote the common weal; and he views the idea with a deep religious abhorrance, that anything that advances the *well*-being of himself which involves the *ill*-being of others." [42] The social implications of balance as a synonym for career were, as always, a social awareness by default. Their primary aim was for a training which turned men to a more abstract order of moral principles. These synonyms recognized indirectly the actuality of social and political institutions. Their vagueness muted the question of *how much* the new educational idea of character would change existing institutions and improve conceptions of education; it did put the burden of awakening all manner of changes on the individual professional. In a sense, the best professional choice connoted a compensating and restorative function.

Career choice became dramatically freer and more independent the more involuntary it was made to appear. In an often repeated sentiment in his journal, Mann rehearsed his reaction to the offer of the new office, the secretaryship of the Board of Education of Massachusetts: "For myself, I never had a sleeping or a waking dream that I should ever think of myself, or be thought of by any other, in relation to that station." [43] Mann's own work in designing and engineering the necessary bills for the secretaryship through the state legislature put that sentiment in a peculiar light. Moreover, in the larger pattern of his life, this sentiment is repeated in different ways.[44] He was always reluctant to appear other than indifferent and passive about his hopes and aspirations. This attitude was widely admired for reasons Mann applauded, namely that without such diffidence in the face of opportunity, men took great risks with their professional potential.[45]

The moral ambiguities associated with career choice regulated the self-consciousness rather than the achievement of nineteenth-century schoolmen. While almost overwatchful about their prospects, schoolmen did not become introspective like their Calvinist forebears. Their autobiographies read no differently than their biographies, and together they form a single genre.[46] Their moral soundings gauged not their own inner dispositions so much as their fit within a given professional perspective. At times Mann's own political success seemed to be the very reason he abandoned it.[47] Early success and the wide acclaim of his promising talents removed much of the sense of arduousness from his work and gave him pause. Indeed William Ellery Channing almost alone sanctioned Mann's shift to education as a wise move. Channing's rather exclusive support more than balanced the numerous other reactions of his many friends who openly asserted that his resignation of law and the position of president pro tem of the Massachusetts senate was precipitous. Moral judgments of the turns of fortune did not rely on popular judgment or majority rule within the profession. In a sense, Mann's full prospects for a professional career and the prospects of more disadvantaged young men gravitated toward education for equally desperate reasons. Neither could assess the moral differences between promising and unpromising professional careers. Early successes and late beginnings in careers both drove men on to ever greener pastures and other occupations, explaining much about the nineteenth century's indifference to the social instability of careers composed of several completely different kinds of work.

The low profile of education as a professional career in the nineteenth century permitted schoolmen to exploit the obvious analogies between instruction and missionary work.[48] Both required rather profound material and personal self-sacrifice. In addition, as schoolmen like Mann developed the institutional forms for this unsung work, they made their organizations contribute to this professional style of self-effacement. Mann explained the nature of the new State Board of Education and its secretary in terms which enabled both agencies to avoid unworthy political intrigue and temptations of coercive power. Existing political realities do not explain Mann's detailed insistence upon the office's powerlessness: "To accomplish the object of their creation," he stressed, ". . . the Board are clothed with no power, either restraining or directory. If they know of better modes of education, they leave no authority to enforce their adoption. Nor have they any funds at their disposal. Even the services of the members are gratuitously rendered. Without authority then, to command, and without money to remunerate or reward, their only recourse, the only sinews of their strength, are their powers of appealing to an enlightened community, to rally for the promotion of its dearest interests." [49] If schoolmen tried to make their organizations proper channels of self-sacrifice, they also made departures from education more difficult than entering teaching in the first place. Young men were never as anxious about their careers as they were when their individual (read "selfish") preferences argued exit from a work undertaken and sanctioned originally for reasons of "moral usefulness and blessedness." Hence in a lifetime of several occupations the numerous shifts from one to another were most commonly preceded by illnesses and other rituals which made the shift appear involuntary. Recovery of health and reassignment were usually surprisingly rapid.

For nineteenth-century schoolmen the peculiar separation of politics and education did not imply a forfeiture of social and political influence. Indeed this distinction attempted to clarify a more independent and moral method for improving the course of human events. At the heart of this effort was the creation of a work equal to but outside the established professions of medicine, law and the ministry. The important choices of this work were negative ones, principally those of avoiding traditional options and procedures. Functionally education became concerned more with the inner working of man's ideas and aspirations than it did with arranging for needed skills, subsequent appointment, placement or salary. The new education implied a necessary barter. It was necessary since men with professional prospects seldom pursued education as a professional work. The great majority of men without clear professional prospects sought the larger and more tangible remuneration of the manual trades. For a host of reasons men from both these different classes became professional schoolmen in the nineteenth century. Whatever their private reasons the explanation in the professional parlance for both college-trained and farming youth was the same; it insisted that the shift to education implied a self-selection of men of character. Paradoxically the rhetoric of moral choice resulted in a profession whose choices shied away from politics in the hopes of trading some social power for an educational style which eschewed precise assessments of its actual significance.

CHAPTER IV

From Awakening to Self-Discipline: Later Experiments in Professional Preparation, 1838–1860

Revivals of Education

During the 1840s and 1850s the transformation of schoolkeepers into a professional corps of educators hinged as much on the efficiency of contemporary revivalist strategies as on any conception of scholarship or systematic pedagogy. Previously theories and ideologies of instruction offered only supplementary argumentation to justify immediate practices and experiments. Little educational activity seems to have been inspired directly by any ideological treatises on learning, although professional schoolmen of the ante-bellum period freely invoked Pestalozzi, de Fellenberg, Rousseau, Lancaster, and the European educational systems as models of various educational practices. In New England the effective plan behind the call for professional educators came not from adaptations of foreign instruction but, rather, from already proven measures which had been applied and perfected by religious evangelicals of the 1830s. The major institution for educational improvement in the ante-bellum period was the teachers' institute which operated as a kind of revival agency. The origin, spread, and eclipse of this institution for professional teachers, both in its conceptual and institutional features, illuminate the shifting contours of educational policy and practice in New England before the Civil War.

Before the 1840s and 1850s, popular and professional discussions of pedagogy described the educational processes and goals in vague, poorly defined terms. The educational literature stressed the importance of a teacher's moral character in producing desired changes among his students, but at no point did they explicate the full complexities of the learning process nor did they discuss the nature of moral character. The rhetoric of the time attributed any change of mind, any alteration of moral conviction, any development of social consciousness in a student, or, in a word, any educational experience, primarily to the moral and personal qualities of the instructor. This assumption about the pivotal role of a teacher's character reduced the technical aspects of pedagogy to a subordinate position. This subordination produced a vague criteria for evaluating proper instruction and the qualifications of teachers and, at the same time, sanctioned the failure to confront the pedagogical problems involved in shaping the moral development of students. While most schoolmen of the period agreed that moral character was the primary end of education, not until the late 1830s were they challenged to determine precisely how character was also the primary means of instruction. This challenge was reflected most dramatically in institutions for preparing teachers.

In the context of confused descriptions of the educational process, several experiments developed to train teachers especially for the publicly supported elementary classes called common schools.[1] There was no one model or rule by which institutions for preparing teachers could be designed or evaluated. For example, in the ante-bellum period, the state-supported normal school, the most durable of these experiments, did not function as an efficient state institution nor did it become a model of a specific professional pedagogy. The absence of a commonly held set of techniques or a discussion of the nature of the normal school apart from the character of its principal made this potentially special school merely one more institution in the educational spectrum. In addition to problems of conception the normal school faced other significant impediments in these years. In spite of large enrollments of any given class—usually women—the normal school graduated very few who had passed through its three-year course of study. Even cumulatively over the ante-bellum period no professional corps of normal school teachers emerged to orient the process of education. Few young men who might have been attracted to normal schools could afford the expense or time away from family farms or businesses. Nor did the schools compensate with scholarships or financial aid until the 1850s, though the first state teacher-training school began in 1838.[2] All of these obstacles prompted state legislatures to withdraw or try to withdraw their support from these schools. Only after the Civil War did the normal schools flourish.

The major institution for preparing young men for a worthy profession in education, for heightening their own awareness of themselves and of their talents for instruction, or to borrow the schoolmen's own term, for" awakening" aspirant professionals, was the teachers' institute. For the first generation of professional educators this institution made explicit, more than any other educational agency, how determined schoolmen were to equate professionalization with "awakening" of moral character rather than with the training in communicable skills and the standard techniques of teaching. "Awakening" arranged the inspiration of the inner man; training assured at least minimal competencies in actual classroom performance. Professionals employing numerous individualized strategies to inculcate character in these early years always discussed their techniques in nonmechanical terms, as emanations of moral character. Competence and effectiveness were measured intuitively and impressionistically, never precisely by common rules or authorized standards. However, by the 1850s the next generation of professional teachers had begun to alter the purpose of their training institutions and their views of effective professional preparation. Most significantly, they attempted to delineate specific measures for training all professionals. The essential professional contribution of this second generation came with their separation of "awakening" from professionalization. Their transformation of the teachers' institute documents in concrete form the significance of this separation and explains the importance of the normal school in postwar America. The work of these two generations active before the Civil War changed the conception of a teacher from something akin to an evangelical minister into a professional with technical training in pedagogy.

The significant reorientation of educational ends and means suggested by this generational difference emerged historically through the growth of the teachers' institute. The man most responsible for the origin and development of this educational agency was Henry Barnard, whose educational career began as the first commissioner of education in Connecticut in 1838 and ended after the Civil War as the first commissioner of education of the United States.[3] In 1839 Barnard, having failed to gain state support for a normal school, circulated an advertisement for a "Teachers' Class" in Hartford County, Connecticut. In his official capacity as state commissioner he placed this pilot project under the general charge of the principal of the Hartford Grammar School, T. H. Wright.[4] Several weeks of meetings concentrated on lessons in mathematics, reading, composition, geography and lectures on the theory and practice of teaching. Visits were made to local Hartford schools to observe the quality and techniques of instruction currently employed. A portion of each day was devoted to emphasis on subjects of current interest to teachers, such as relationships with parents or modes of conducting teachers' associations. Twenty-six young men answered Barnard's call to this conference which proved to be the prototype for subsequent teachers' institutes. So familiar did this institution become after 1839, that in 1851 the Reverend Cyrus Peirce, whom Horace Mann had hand-picked to be principal of the first state-supported normal school in America, could describe the normal school as a "kind of standing Teachers' Institute."[5]

The success of this first experiment encouraged Barnard to expand his proposals and to advocate similar programs for other states. He insisted that such classes be conducted twice a year for three years, a proposal that in 1842 Barnard felt was an adequate substitute for normal school preparation.[6] Even the elimination of his state commissionership by political fiat in 1842 and his dismissal from Connecticut's service did not dissuade Barnard from pursuing the implications of his early work with teachers' institutes. That same year he fashioned with Emma Willard, the principal and founder of the Troy (Female) Seminary, a more ambitious plan for a "permanent Normal Institute." [7]

The Normal Institute, conceived by Henry Barnard and Emma Willard, was another effort to develop a New England version of the normal school. The espoused aim of the institute was the improvement of young people in the teaching skills; the instruction centered on lectures, observations of experienced teachers, and practical experience by the aspirant teachers. Barnard's own "teachers' class" seems to have served as the referent point for this model. Their combined vision, however, extended beyond the Hartford experiment. The students, Mrs. Willard explained, would attend the Normal Institute for a month twice a year and return for four consecutive years in the intervals between actual teaching in elementary schools. After four years, Mrs. Willard concluded, the students would be adequately prepared for the classroom. The institute, moreover, would group its student body into four levels according to each applicant's previous experience. In the Willard-Barnard plan, the timing of these classes assumed crucial importance. By scheduling them for April and October immediately before the summer and winter schools began, they used the actual preparation to best advantage. Teachers would have ample opportunity for immediate experimentation with their new skills. In addition, by constant correspondence with and visits to the practicing teachers of the institute, Mrs. Willard intended to provide suggestions and minor alterations of technique during each school term.[8]

The institute's conductor, the agency's teacher, was central to the careful planning of this educational institution. The moral character of each experienced teacher determined how effective and impressive was the image of superior instruction. The actual teachers of the first teachers' institute in Hartford in 1839 reflected the importance placed upon the character of the teacher. Including Barnard, at the time head of the state educational system, seven educators had been invited to lead the experiment: three long-time teachers of unquestioned reputation, like T. H. Wright of Hartford; two ministers with unimpeachable educational credentials—the Reverend Frederick A. Barton of Teacher's Seminary at Andover, Massachusetts, and the Reverend Thomas H. Gallaudet, most famous for founding and directing the American Asylum for the Deaf and Dumb in Hartford, the first school of its kind in America; and one college professor of mathematics, Charles Davies of West Point, whose mathematics textbooks had already established his serious concern for upgrading education.[9] In the earliest years of the institutes, conductors were men whose professional reputations were often made in other professions or in semieducational work. Institute activity was largely a sideline rather than a full-time responsibility.

Throughout the next decade, teachers' institutes developed along the general lines suggested by Barnard and Willard in the early 1840s. Quickly the teachers' institutes became accepted as more than experiments or temporary substitutes for normal schools in professional training and spread throughout New England. In 1843 Henry Barnard replied to a call from Rhode Island and shortly after became state superintendent of education there. He immediately succeeded in having legislation passed that required institutes to be held in each county annually. In Massachusetts in 1844 Horace Mann found teachers' institutes so effective that he began, as he had done for normal schools, to solicit private contributions which he hoped would be matched by state subsidy.[10] Mann's campaign to accumulate greater financial support for teachers' institutes succeeded as remarkably as his work for normal schools. Where no state subsidy was possible, some institute conductors charged tuition, and still others, to lessen the financial burden on underpaid teachers, only agreed to hold institutes if townspeople boarded the student-teachers free of charge. This latter arrangement ensured also that the town became involved in educational improvement through discussion with student-teachers at fireside and table. Many institutes set aside their evening exercises for lectures of a more general nature to which the public was invited.[11]

The success of this conception of institutes rested entirely upon the personal character and reputation of the conductor. Emma Willard could declare confidently "that no other person but myself could put in practice the plan to be proposed, I would by no means assert! Yet I would not hold myself responsible for its success in any other hands." [12] Concerned educators assumed that they could feel sanguine about the subsequent and ultimate consequences of educational development, so long as their own moral vision informed the nature and direction of the earliest stages of instruction. Even when instruction was most systematic in normal schools and colleges of the 1840s, educators were less preoccupied with the orderly diffusion of information—an educational ideal of Jefferson's generation—than they were concerned about the capstone of all instruction, the senior-year course in moral philosophy taught by the principal or college president.[13]

Just as the moral character of an institute conductor was something of a known quantity due to his educational interests and occupational reputation, the moral character of an attending student was equally important. The students, however, usually possessed neither educational reputations nor formal credentials, letters of recommendation nor academic degrees. Teaching had never attracted young men into common schools or academies on a

full-time basis if they had the glimmer of a prospect for decidedly professional work in law, medicine or the ministry. It was almost a resignation to
necessity when Emma Willard judged the most promising institute students
as those "youth who have not wealth, but who have an ardent desire for
education and are willing to labor to obtain it." [14] In another light, however,
her comments were not entirely a resignation. The formation of moral character headed the aims of all educational institutions. The significance of the
institute was not entirely the provision of philanthropic service to young men
whose own resources did not lead to professional work. More important, and
more reason for predicting extraordinary success by this agency, was the
assumed equation between "ardent desire" and poverty. The poorer boys
would have to work uncommonly hard and have to possess a readier disposition toward moral training than their more fortunate fellows.[15]

The nature of the education provided by teachers' institutes was not
conceived in strictly intellectual or academic terms. The fundamental distinction was not between the ignorant and the informed, or, if such terms
were used, their reference point was not the command of useful information
in a given subject or set of subjects. The Normal Institute of Henry Barnard
and Emma Willard would separate students "sound in mind, in manners and
in morals" from those who were "dull and unworthy." This screening
process remained a moral affair of which intellectual training was but one
part. The institute provided a medium for selection of potential professionals, although its formal operations generated no distinctions or gradations
among student participants. If an institute scholar labored through the course
for the specified time, its founders anticipated, his "will and ability to learn
would be manifest." The result, Mrs. Willard continued, "could be no in-
considerable solid acquirement." [16] The institute experience set the stage not
merely for knowledge but also for wisdom; it presumed to lay a foundation
not only in particular skills but in a social department which always signified,
however obliquely, the man of upright character. At the very least, attendance at an institute meant that a pious young man's desire to cultivate moral
discipline had been certified by the conductors, successful men of unquestioned character. Though not a degree-granting agency, the institutes
provided an informal professional credential which testified to a young man's
awakened character.

Although they laid particular emphasis upon this special "awakening" as
an indispensable prerequisite for professional success, Barnard and Willard
did not hold a mystical conception of the teacher as a member of an elite and
restricted corps. Accompanying the emphasis upon "awakening" was the
notion that *everyone* was capable of professional improvement and would
profit from attending an institute. The necessary "awakening" and "quick-
ening" of moral sensibilities were accessible to all who aspired to educational
improvement provided they were receptive to the institute's conductors.

Once this moral development was thought to have begun, the work of the institute was finished. Apart from attendance at later institutes, an aspirant professional generated from himself all subsequent control and development of his moral character. Moral development was seldom qualified by any consideration of unforeseeable circumstances or the idiosyncrasies of personality. Indeed, subsequent difficulties were thought to be like the fires to steel in a forge; they were trials that hardened or softened one's resolution but could not alter substantially the basic structure of moral character once awakened.

In 1859 Barnard voiced his clearest, if somewhat defensive, statement about the nature of the institute, that it was an "educational revival agency, of the most extensive, permanent, and unobjectionable character." [17] This categorizing of the teachers' institute as a revival agency made explicit the nature of many measures which conductors commonly employed in this professional activity. First and foremost, both teachers' institutes and religious revivals were planned as a chain of temporary meetings, located in different towns to which their organizers went as circuit riders. Like the earlier "protracted meetings" of denominational revivals, institutes were advertised far in advance and timed to avoid or override competition with ordinary town activities devoted to similar purposes. Conductors often planned institutes during vacations when common schools were not in session or else during college commencement exercises to take advantage of educationally oriented crowds. Visits of conductors to homes that boarded students served as preliminary or supplementary measures to actual institute exercises, much like the religious revivalists' "anxious meetings." Prayers and hymns not only were incorporated into the actual proceedings but usually began and concluded the main exercises and lectures of an institute. It was often more than a matter of convenience that institutes were held in churches.

As with the more conservative sectarian revivals of the 1830s, women attended but did not participate publicly in teachers' institutes of the 1840s. Also, extemporaneous exhortations to the institute attendants were common, though once again, like the more conservative revivals of the later 1830s, individuals were not singled out for special praise or chastisement in these inspirational efforts. Numerous expressions, such as "filled with the spirit," "the holiness of the work," the "vocation" of teaching, being "called," "fixing attention," and, of course, "awakening" itself, bore striking similarities to the rhetoric of the religious revivals. Most of all, the institute, like the revival, proposed to transform a congregation of individuals into a conscious moral body with its own special tone and spiritual goal, the two essential elements of awakening and professionalization.

Several important historical factors explain how this institution for professional teachers took on revival techniques rather than modeling itself upon existing educational structures like the American college or the European normal school. By 1839, when Barnard conducted the first institute, the religious revival had become a rather commonplace and noncontroversial measure for ministering to a congregation.[18] The controversies that revivals had caused through the 1820s and early 1830s, especially the rude, emotion-charged camp meetings of the Reverend Charles Grandison Finney, had abated. Not only had Finney himself tempered his revival measures but his former antagonists, the more tradition-bound ministers like Lyman Beecher, Joel Dawes, and Nathaniel Taylor, had incorporated revival practices into their own work. By the late 1830s many members of conservative Congregational cartels, ministers like Charles Brooks, Noah Porter, Merrill Richardson, Horace Bushnell, as well as Beecher, Dawes, and others, served as itinerant agents for or participants in teachers' institutes. The ease with which such men passed back and forth between the ministry and education suggests as much about changes in the ministry itself as it confirms how profoundly moral and spiritually regenerative education was thought to be. This interprofessional mobility also indicates how subordinate institutional measures were in both professions to the moral character of the minister or the teacher and also how easily education could commandeer institutional measures from its sister profession, the ministry. Within three decades the structure of both occupations narrowed and became more exclusive, rendering this mobility and this borrowing of techniques impossible.

In the late 1830s, at precisely the moment when revival measures were becoming socially acceptable and when they no longer threatened accepted denominational orthodoxy, men like Barnard required effective measures for improving the occupation of teaching. Efficiency, however, was colored by two considerations. On the one hand, the short duration of the institute necessitated measures that were extraordinarily efficient. The institute had to condense the inculcation of character, which permanent schools, committed to long-term study, could do more gradually. At the same time institute measures could not appear extraordinarily efficient without suggesting that something other than character was the basis of proper, morally informed instruction. Conceptually the major strategy schoolmen employed was the stress upon moral character. Their insistence upon character controlled every effort to dispel the ambiguity about precise measures of awakening potential professionals; it made diverse procedures appear equally legitimate and equally efficient. Functionally they endorsed the acceptable means of persuasion and inspiration which evangelical ministers had earlier developed on circuit in the face of a very different set of moral problems. The vagueness that shrouded the process of professionalization in the ante-bellum period permitted equivocation on the very issue which quite likely would have spawned disruptive controversy. In this context ambiguity and a semblance of neutrality were quite self-consciously cultivated to stabilize the profession of instruction. Professional schoolmen truly believed that education was a moral process. Conveniently the moral value they espoused gave them a leverage they would not have had were they more demanding technically or more exact conceptually.

The revival background of the institute and the vagueness of professional procedures suggest, moreover, why in education there was so little controversy before the 1850s over education in general and pedagogical techniques in particular.[19] In education as in the ministry technical devices became controversial only when they got out of hand. One of the educator's and minister's working assumptions, too, was that technical devices could get out of hand quite easily. Moreover, the problem with controversy was that it was a form of disorder, and disorder was a moral not a technical problem. To lose control was to doubt the efficacy and self-sufficiency of moral character; to lose control was to believe that techniques were somehow unrelated to the technician, hence morally neutral. Only in controversy apparently did schoolmen draw distinctions between the technical and moral power of instruction. When such distinctions could be drawn, they were never academic, but always rapidly became boldly personal. The close association between morality and technology gave ante-bellum education its peculiar strength: it permitted schoolmen the belief that individual character, as irregularly moral as it was, was the source of any school's stability rather than its preeminent weakness. It was this assumption that made professional teachers chary of sanctioning rigorous criticism as a part of legitimate instruction. Controversy and criticism could never locate problems or weaknesses without implying individual reprehensibility. Could morality ever be divorced clearly from techniques of instruction and could individuals be awakened and converted by devices rather than by the force of moral will, the pivotal role of the schoolmaster, the institute conductor, or the minister would have lessened in importance. In such an event moral character would have been relegated to an auxiliary or secondary power in any educational or regenerative process. Up to the 1850s an uneasy truce existed between the conception of moral character and the specific means for inculcating it. Upon this truce schoolmen fashioned an ambiguous sense of professionalization which made morality and pedagogical technology mutually reinforcing. A major product of this ambiguity was the avoidance of gradations or distinctions between the various titles: schoolmaster, schoolkeeper, teacher, educator, or Friend of Education.

Institute conductors of Barnard's generation rarely questioned the use of revival techniques in awakening teachers. In fact, there were remarkably few innovations in procedures for conducting institutes. For all the potential leeway and experimentation that their moral view of education might have endorsed—morality possessing at all points a highly individualistic dimension—Barnard's generation varied technical procedures only slightly from institute to institute. In some measure the lack of variety was a function of detailed preplanning and precise scheduling. Planning committees sought to provide for every eventuality—advertisement, seating, censorship and pub- lication of lectures, registration of participants, enrolling local support, electing officers, etc. Many institutes appointed monitors to ensure absolute conformity with a prearranged timetable. One institute manual, William Russell's *Suggestions on Teachers' Institutes,* describes this obsession with efficiency and precision in a sketch of the monitor's duties:

> It is the duty of the monitor to ring the signal for commencing and closing all lectures, general exercises, and recesses. The monitor of time is expected to be perfectly exact as to the moment for ringing his bell, even if it is to interrupt a lecturer in the middle of a sentence, and after the recess, to ring his bell at the entrance door, as well as within, to recall the members to their class duties.[20]

While such preplanning may have hindered technical innovations, a more important limitation was the professional uncertainty within which all in- novations operated, an uncertainty reflected by the discrepancy between the imperative tone of the quotation above and the cautious title of the manual itself, *Suggestions on Teachers' Institutes.* Russell's manual makes clear how easily institutes could get out of hand without strict control. His remarks consequently fluctuate between suggestion and insistent strictures like the following: "Disorder otherwise [without the monitors of time] becomes in- evitable. If a lecture overruns its hours, it cuts off some important part of other business, and disturbs the regularity of the day. A public body without order becomes an unwieldy mass, and, sometimes, an unruly mob."[21] Between the polarities of success and failure no gradations existed for de- termining the worth of a particular innovation or how a particular measure might have affected the proceedings of an institute as a whole.

Just as a successful institute, like a successful revival, transformed a gath- ering into a moral entity, a failure of organization impugned the characters of conductors and attendant students alike. Such evaluations of institute proceedings established not procedural limits but ambiguous dangers which undermined all but the efforts of the most confident and venturesome teachers. For very particular reasons the institutes of Barnard's generation attracted young men whose prominent virtues were neither intellectual self-possession nor professional daring.

While the technical procedures varied only slightly from institute to in- stitute, the styles of conductors, the content and duration of institutes, and the role of institutes within particular states did vary. The idea from the very first had been to retain a flexibility so that the institute in each community would be pertinent to local conditions and heterogeneous audiences. "Exactly how much," Mrs. Willard had originally declared, "and what could and should be taught during each of these terms, it would not now be worthwhile laying down." [22] This emphasis upon flexibility was simply another variation on the insistence that the institutional structure of any school extended rather than constricted the moral power of the leading teacher. So long as technique was viewed as an emanation of moral character, flexibility and rigidity were differences in emphasis, not in kind.

By the late 1840s institutes were the most prevalent teacher preparatory agency in America and touched the lives of more teachers than any other educational institution.[23] Their mobility ensured that their importance would vary from state to state, depending upon the relative significance accorded to them by leading educators. But by 1860 the complex institutional system of a state rather than individual educators began to determine the number and nature of teachers' institutes. Their flexibility, once a central virtue, began to connote the weaknesses of instability and inefficiency. In the 1840s, however, no one intended disparagement by reference to institutes as "traveling teachers' Seminaries."

The institutes continued to receive widespread support from educators of the same generation as Henry Barnard, men like Noah Porter in Connecticut, the Reverend Francis Wayland in Rhode Island, Horace Mann in Massachusetts, the Reverend Nathan Lord in Ohio and Samuel Sweet in New York.[24] The Reverend Barnas Sears, the superintendent of the School Fund in Connecticut in 1848, reported enthusiastically that "institutes, or schools for teachers, should be regarded as a part of our system of common instruction." [25] The editor of the first educational journal in the English language, William Russell, went even further than Sears in asserting, "Institutes are not superceded by Academies or Normal Schools." "Professional schools," he continued, "do not do away with their [teachers' institutes'] existence." [26] In 1859 Barnard himself expressed the reigning sentiment:

> During nearly a quarter of a century's study and observation of schools, school systems, and educational agencies, in different states and countries, I have tried, seen or read of nothing so universally applicable or so efficient in awakening and directing rightly both professional parental interest in the broad field of popular education, as a well-attended and wisely conducted teachers' institute.[27]

Such statements, endorsing the institutes' peculiar value and role, increased in clarity and in quantity by the late 1850s. Such endorsements reflected the confidence of professionals who had worked in teachers' institutes from the earliest years; they revealed also the attempt by older professionals to stem the increasingly potent challenge from younger professionals who had already begun to alter the original use and service of institutes. From its origins and through the 1840s, all assessments of the institution had been somewhat reserved and tenuous, since the institute was conceived as an experiment. Even after it became a permanent feature of a state's educational apparatus, schoolmen hesitated to discuss the nature of the institute and satisfied themselves with assertions of its effectiveness and efficiency.

By the 1850s some teachers began to criticize the confusion about the nature of the institute: was it an essential or subordinate part of state educational systems? were they temporary or permanent agencies? were they practical schools or informal meetings and conventions? The questions themselves indicated the shifting assumptions about the institutes. Younger schoolmen were beginning to view the institute as a functional part of a larger administrative complex and not, as Barnard's generation saw it, as a moral entity in itself.

Teachers recruited through the institutes provided the largest percentage of professional instructors in the generation succeeding Barnard and his contemporaries. Although their work altered the institute and significantly changed basic educational assumptions, the second generation of professional educators effected this transformation largely without systematic planning or deliberation. They advertised no educational ideology nor did they levy broadsides against the work of their predecessors. Alterations of policy and practice were usually justified in terms of changing times rather than new assumptions about education. Criticism of previous measures and conceptions virtually crept into the profession of teaching and emerged with extraordinary indirectness. The change worked in such low-keyed fashion largely because young men entering teaching in the 1840s and 1850s accepted the moral rhetoric of their forebears and conceived of themselves as carrying on their work.

Even if some of these second-generation professionals harbored differences over pedagogical and institutional ideas, they faced the tactical difficulty of discussing them without also seeming to disparage the character of the teacher who employed them. This difficulty remained, so long as such measures were accepted as emanations of the moral character of a particular teacher. The acceptance of this version of moral character by both generations of professional educators ensured that criticism was also at the same time a personal attack upon a fellow teacher. During the entire ante-bellum period such criticism, indeed any rigorous criticism, was considered a breach of professional decorum and was simply not countenanced.

Evangelical Professionals

By the late 1840s many factors had begun to put new pressures on older attitudes toward teacher training. In part, the writings of Russell, Sweet, Barnard and others in praise of teachers' institutes at this time seem to be attempts to assert and to solidify the educational gains of their generation in the face of an increasingly significant challenge by younger professionals. During the 1850s professional institutes began to take on greater responsibility for the standardization of training and not simply for the initial awakening of teachers. Gradually educators relied less and less on the awakened character of the teacher to bear the brunt of professional and educational change. Experienced teachers began to assume that the profession was advanced not by each individual improving himself at his own pace; rather, they began to establish minimum standards for professional efficiency through new state officers and new professional organizations such as the superintendency and the teachers' associations.[28] This broad shift occurred as a consequence of several important historical developments.

By the mid-1850s the profession of teaching had added substantial numbers to its ranks to keep pace with a population that had nearly doubled in a decade and a half. Educationally advanced states like Massachusetts and Connecticut established teachers' associations and state education journals in order to study, fashion and publicize educational standards and to ensure a more distinct and less personalized arrangement of professional affairs. Professional aids like the anecdotal manuals of "hints" and "suggestions," such as Samuel Read Hall's *Lectures on School-Keeping* (1829), were replaced by highly simplified and systematic guides like Norman Calkins' *Object Lessons* (1860).[29] Moreover, substantial raises in salaries for teachers accompanied public willingness to invest in normal school training. In the 1850s alone these institutions doubled in number and were founded as far from New England as Minnesota. Most important, perhaps, states established laws of certification.[30]

These aspects of professional change also affected the pivotal role and conception of a teachers' institute. No longer did superintendents pride themselves on holding more institutes than legally required. In some states where two institutes per county had been required, the number was even reduced to one. The duration of an institute, moreover, became shorter. By the end of the 1850s a typical meeting began on Monday evening with an address by some educational official of the state and closed with prayer and song the following Saturday morning. Instead of four weeks or even two weeks, five days now sufficed. Booksellers, once considered a disruptive influence because salesmanship competed with conductors for class attention, were now admitted as a professional service. By 1862 teachers even began to abandon the policy of living in local homes while attending institutes; they preferred hotels and boardinghouses. In many cases, this preference required that the institutes be transferred to larger towns which had demonstrated a substantially enlightened educational view. Towns that held institutes during the 1850s had populations between twenty-five hundred and three thousand, considered a professionally manageable number.[31]

Whereas institute conductors in the 1840s had felt an obligation to bring their message to as many towns and locales as possible, after 1860 professional teachers abandoned this goal and relegated institutes more and more to agricultural areas. As appendages of the state educational system, this foreshortened form of the institute was but a shadow of its former self. Nothing demonstrates this distillation of the institute's original scope and purpose more clearly than the fact that educators ceased to refer to themselves as missionaries and pioneers and toned down their rhetoric of religiosity and self-conscious moral reform.

As the creator of teachers' institutes, Barnard did not abandon his original conception, but over the years he clarified and refined his view of it. As they moved west in the 1850s, the institutes remained remarkably faithful to Barnard's original model. Indeed Barnard himself articulated his clearest conception of the institute as a "revival agency" only after 1859, when he arrived in Madison to become chancellor of the University and of Normal Schools in Wisconsin—at that time as much an educational backwater as Connecticut and Rhode Island had been two decades earlier.

In the east, meanwhile, concern for experimentation with professional preparation and educational change, begun at Barnard's Teachers' Class in 1839, had undergone drastic alteration, even among educators who had been formerly Barnard's closest colleagues. Both in Connecticut and Rhode Island, Barnard gathered about himself young men of kindred spirits, many of whom would later revise and reinterpret their teacher's dicta. One such was David Nelson Camp, one of the twenty-six students in attendance at the first teachers' institute in Hartford. Barnard had accurately recognized in Camp the potentiality for a particular kind of professional educator. In less than a decade Camp became one of the leading teachers of his state, the first officer of the Connecticut State Teachers' Association, and a professor in the state's Normal School in New Britain. Appointed as associate principal of the school in 1855, two years later he was elevated to principal and became state commissioner of schools. Camp held the statewide post until 1866, when he moved to a professorial chair at St. John's College, in Annapolis, where Barnard himself was the newly inaugurated president. In 1867 when Barnard became the first United States commissioner of education, David Camp went to Washington as his assistant. In 1869 Barnard entrusted Camp with complete editorial responsibility for his *American Journal of Education*. Upon his return from Washington, Camp continued his educational work as principal of the New Britain Seminary in Connecticut.[32]

While he was the kind of young man in whom Barnard saw potential as a teacher and fellow professional, in 1839 Camp did not possess qualifications like those Barnard and his generation brought to their work in education. Barnard and his colleagues had usually trained themselves in one of the established professions—law, medicine or religion. Commonly they had completed a full course of collegiate study. Moreover, between college and their emergence as educators, men like Henry Barnard and Horace Mann had distinguished themselves as vocal proponents of social and political reform. Mann and Barnard commanded influential positions as prominent Whigs in their state legislatures, positions through which they became acquainted with their states' most influential citizens.[33] Most important, these prospects and connections permitted Barnard and Mann to view educational work as a benevolent activity which they freely chose.

By contrast, Camp in 1839 was a young man of modest means. In that year at age nineteen he was somewhat anxious about his prospects for a career that had not yet clearly begun. His interest in teaching as a permanent occupation seems to have developed more by circumstance than by choice. Only during the course of the winter preceding his attendance at Barnard's first institute did Camp take his first teaching post in a local district school. "I knew nothing of the place or of the school," Camp glibly explained much later, "but it seemed an opportunity for some good to others and perhaps to myself. I accepted the proposition and became a teacher."[34]

Previous to this work Camp's credentials invited no immediate associations with influential persons who might have assisted his ambitions. Nor were they, in fact, credentials with which he could realistically entertain the possibility of traditional training in a profession. The major obstacle to such opportunities was in part the fragmentary nature of his own schooling. He had attended a total of five schools before his eighteenth year—a district school, two academies, a grammar school, and a private school conducted by a local dame. Apart from this unsystematized training he received tutoring from his mother, who was formerly a teacher herself, and from the family's pastor. Without some form of higher study or extraordinary good fortune, Camp was effectively blocked in this period from imitating Barnard's own professional pattern or from entering teaching as if it were the proper outlet for his talents.

Camp's education was not uncommon or so fragmentary that he could not enter college. Indeed he had planned for some time to enter, first, college, then the ministry, but illness stifled both aspirations. Still, he seems never to have forgotten his sense of ministerial calling. Throughout his autobiographical reminiscences Camp discussed the spiritual and religious aspects of his career as much as those of professional teaching. He provided extensive descriptions of his family's religiosity, of his own conversion experience, of his dutiful attendance at all functions of his church (Congregational), of his favorite books—the Reverend Jacob Abbot's *Young Christian* and John Bunyan's *Pilgrim's Progress*—of his lifelong activity in Sunday school instruction, and preeminently of his work with the American Home Mission Society. In a discussion of this last organization Camp took pains to specify the many ministerial luminaries with whom he came in contact in this enterprise, men like the Reverend Nathaniel Taylor, the Reverend Noah Porter, the Reverend Horace Bushnell, and the Reverend Merrill Richardson. Significantly, in his autobiography as in his life, Camp treated separately his two avocations, teaching and the ministry. His uneasy fluctuation between them itself intimated the distinction that his generation began to fashion between professional and moral activity.

For Barnard in 1839, Camp's distinguishing feature quite likely rested upon his pursuit of a professional career in spite of poor academic credentials. Indeed the selection of Camp offered Barnard the luxury of ignoring the two basic personnel problems of professional teaching. On the one hand, he no longer needed to coax young men from college to sacrifice vacations or temporary periods after graduation to common school instruction; and, on the other hand, he might avoid haranguing local communities for hiring young men with neither the competence for nor the commitment to teaching. A partially formed and somewhat desperate ambition provided a third alternative and was retrospectively the most successful basis for a corps of professional teachers in the ante-bellum period.

In 1839 Camp's distinguishing feature, this particular aggressiveness, seemed characteristic of "institute professionals." This quality resulted not merely from his attendance at the teacher's institute, nor from his frustrated college plans nor from his inability to shake his ministerial aspiration. All together, however, pointed toward a specific quality of professional activity: the manifest willingness to have this ambition tutored in behalf of a worthy cause. Barnard intended his Teachers' Class in 1839 to be more than an experiment in professional preparation or a form of intellectual instruction; it was an "awakening" which committed a young man to a life of self-examination and self-preparation, no less strenuous than the life of the ministry. "The rising generation of teachers," Barnard had remarked, "are the chosen priesthood of education—they must bear the ark on their shoulders." [35] With some justification in the association Camp viewed teaching as a quasi-religious function and the teacher as a surrogate minister.

The subsequent career pattern of David Nelson Camp crystalized in its basic contours the occupational characteristics of Barnard's successors. Perhaps the most important factor of this pattern was the difference between the service rendered them by the teachers' institute and the use to which they put that educational facility once they controlled policy-making positions in education. The institute offered Camp and his compatriots their only formal opportunity for professional preparation. It exposed young men at once to the prerequisites for professional development in condensed form. The institutes inspired as well as drilled young men in the skills of their trade, and through associations with experienced teachers and respected citizens, it provided the sense, if not the reality, of social service and status accorded to the professional work to which they had originally aspired.

Camp could not afford a long period of training but required a substitute. He had become interested in the new profession of teaching at an age when young men usually were finishing college in order to begin a professional apprenticeship with a lawyer, doctor, minister, or merchant. At such a late date, the leisurely pace and familial tone of college life was too costly in its informality and lack of specialization for Camp's purposes, apart from considerations of money which alone would have undermined his aspirations. The flexibility of the institute in dealing with the diverse backgrounds of men like himself and the speed which its specialized purpose implied met Camp's needs rather neatly. Camp was not uncommon among the men who eventually became prominent institute conductors and trainers of common school teachers in the 1850s and 1860s. Charles Northend in Connecticut, William Fowle in Massachusetts, William S. Baker in Rhode Island, James B. Thomson in New York, and Asa Lord in Ohio all fit this mold in significant ways.[36]

In spite of the benefits that men like Camp obtained from the institutes, they eventually deemphasized the importance and desirability of institute preparation. In the 1850s, ironically enough, Camp's own educational labors circumscribed the institutes' usefulness when he argued the merits of a more explicit professional selectivity by means of normal school study. This preference by a later generation of teachers for long-term study contrasted markedly with Barnard's intention. Unlike Camp, Barnard wished to improve whatever talent a young man brought to the institute rather than to eliminate all those who could not give evidence of a capacity for professional development. The difference ultimately represented an important shift in the conception of moral character. Furthermore, because of this difference awakening and professional training in pedagogy became further and further separated, though at no point did these features of preparatory instruction become fundamentally antagonistic to each other. The teachers' institute dealt with the inculcation of moral character consistently throughout its history. For Camp, however, its moral purpose no longer made it the educational equal of the normal school.

During the first years of their association, Barnard and Camp organized the institutes, and their common enthusiasm for this new project cloaked incipient differences between them. Barnard's all-encompassing view of the teacher as the "chosen priesthood" of society contrasted with the image which Camp updated two decades later. In one of his early reports as superintendent of Connecticut schools, Camp distinguished two important types of professional teacher:

There are now employed in some of the Common Schools of the State, persons of *high scholastic attainments*, who have chosen teaching as a profession and bring to the daily work of the schoolroom the right treasures gathered from years of study in our highest colleges . . . there are others still who have never enjoyed the advantages of a Collegiate or Normal course, yet have secured for themselves, in the experience of several terms in the schoolroom, accompanied by constant *self-culture*, a well-earned and deserved reputation.[37]

The significance of this divergence extends beyond the single careers of Barnard and Camp, but through their careers one can perceive clearly how this distinction implied a wide-ranging set of assumptions about the training of a competent teacher. Barnard never explicitly tied collegiate study to teacher training. The normal school for him was not a college with variations. Still, Barnard easily recognized a particular kind of commitment in a young man who aspired to college study. He could readily agree to Camp's distinction between professional types, but for Barnard this observation accounted for two kinds of equally valid credentials for professional work. For Camp's generation these two categories of teachers attained professional success differently and thereby implied qualitatively different alternatives. Nevertheless, Camp did not conceive these two types as competitive nor did he rank them in his reports as superior and inferior. Their different views of how character is best inculcated became manifest in the varied uses to which both men put teachers' institutes and normal schools.

Beginning as it did with the first teachers' institute in 1839, Camp's own career gave him a genuine authority to review in 1860 the twenty-year history of this educational agency. Significantly his 1860 report as superintendent of common schools in Connecticut began without sketching clear institutional lines which invited judgment or preference for one of the two agencies, the institute or the normal school, over the other. Each of the state's eight counties, he said, held at least one teachers' institute each year, as they had for the past ten years. Through this frequency, professional schoolmen in Connecticut maintained the tradition, customary since 1850, of reaching from one-third to one-half of all the state's teachers annually. With only brief mention that the teachers' institutes were becoming more frequent in agricultural districts than in populous towns, Camp proceeded to give the appropriate statistics for the more specialized normal school. In its first decade of existence (1850–1860) the state-supported normal school in Connecticut had enrolled 1,744 students. By 1860, of the approximately four thousand (3,917) teachers active in Connecticut, some 580, or one-third of the normal school enrollees of the first decade, continued to teach in the state. Camp left the impression that the cooperation of these two distinct agencies warranted no significant change. Quantitatively the institute appeared to be the more effective.[38]

Camp's subsequent comments, appended almost as an afterthought to his discussion of normal schools, provided a rationale for the institute's decline in professional significance after 1860. The focus of his postscript fixed upon the peculiar failure of practicing teachers. Ambitious young men used brief attendance at both institutions to feign qualifications, and overanxious School Visitors hired them without proper scrutiny. The major professional problem of his report involved the presumption of professional responsibility by immature young men attending institutes. As early as 1850 Camp had already begun to worry less about providing a kind of credential and commitment through the institute and more about strengthening the lax standard which enabled poorly prepared youth to pass state examinations. How much time one was willing to spend, not how one spent it, signified for him whose individual character was ultimately capable of professional development.

Camp felt that institute activity and brief attendance at normal schools alone were insufficient bases for professional recognition. Young men of fourteen, fifteen, or sixteen could appear qualified after such a smattering of preparation only while competence coincided with superficial intellectual polish.[39] The problem existed, of course, because more young men now were turning toward teaching as a career. Barnard perceived the popularity of teaching as a vindication of the institute's efficiency; Camp, however, viewed the lack of discrimination among applicants as a loss of control over admission to the career of teaching. Behind this judgment lay the seeds of a very different meaning of professional control. In the 1850s, as Camp's contemporaries began to assume responsibility for major principalships, presidencies, and directorships of training institutions, the process of professionalization itself reflected this basic shift of authority within the occupation of teaching.

In spite of the institute's service to Camp, several factors from his own experience and career persuaded him eventually of the agency's inadequacy. Camp traced the intellectual agility of immature teachers to their exclusive reliance upon the formal instruction of an institute or a normal school. This rendered them shallow, since they had never undergone the tempering influence of actual professional apprenticeship. Camp himself had entered upon studies of educational technique only after a period of one year of actual teaching. He viewed the lack of such experience, however minimal, with great skepticism. By contrast, Barnard, though he would perhaps have objected to enrolling fourteen-year-olds, would have been quite willing to grant a position to a teacher oriented toward a college training but prepared only through an institute. Second, one should recall that in 1839, when Camp entered the Teachers' Class in Hartford, he was nineteen, the age when professional maturity began, according to his later view. As early as 1851 Camp wondered in print whether the teachers' institute, which had been established to ensure among other things the maturity of teachers, were not counter-productive. "Teachers' Institutes," he admitted, "will tend to the improvement of those who labor in our schools by disseminating information of various subjects connected with their duties. But nothing except months and perhaps years of close and earnest study and training, with practice in teaching, can make true and successful teachers of some who claim that name." [41] This perception placed Camp in a peculiar position. At the very moment he succeeded in becoming a leading educator in Connecticut, he began to eschew the agency which made his success possible. Instead of bringing the institute to the forefront of the state educational systems as forcefully as Barnard had done, Camp began to insist, in effect, on extensive systematic training in a normal school along with actual teaching. In a curious way, his image of professional competence through a normal school combined the scholastic training to which he once aspired and the lengthy experience in practice upon which his professional credentials were actually based. The awakening to a calling was no longer a highly personal process carefully tutored in mutual instruction; it had become a private experience which preceded professional preparation.

By the time that Camp's generation assumed control of educational policy in the 1850s, moral character had become less and less a professional quality which experienced teachers intuitively tended in mutual instruction. Professional institutions now nurtured the "aptness to teach" as it appeared in long periods of behavior which could be measured by standards of time and actual service positions. Camp took awakening for granted and restricted professional training to matters of technical skills and intellectual lessons.[41] He was no less concerned than Barnard for moral commitment and indeed paid theoretical homage to the importance of moral character at all points. The distinction is simply this: the actual origins of voluntary commitment for Barnard could be engineered, while for Camp they did not result from individual choice and began apart from institutional manipulation. In Camp's eyes institutional activity did not initiate fundamental change or awaken benevolent energies; it merely prevented professional backsliding and it distinguished, as it were, the educational elect from professional hopefuls.[42]

The shift of generations bore with it a different set of assumptions about the means of certifying a teacher's competence. If Barnard discerned character as self-sacrifice and a freely chosen commitment to a holy cause, Camp perceived character as self-discipline and a dutiful acceptance of natural talents. The two dimensions of character were not mutually exclusive during Camp's generation, though they would begin to be one generation later. The nature of the difference, even in Camp's time, determined the fate of the teachers' institutes. Barnard tended to imply that formal classes and exercises in an institute provided a context for the initial inspiration to character development. Camp, on the other hand, considered that the highest achievement of an institute was practical training in technical skills. Only years of slow maturation and acculturation in a teaching milieu, Camp felt, would mold a man as a professional educator: "It is not to be expected that a few weeks or a few months or even years will make a competent teacher of everyone. There are some whom no influence of a normal school or any other instrumentality will make efficient teachers." [43] Implicitly Camp questioned Barnard's assumption that every aspirant teacher would profit to some extent from professional training, that anyone could be remade through an educational institution into an efficient teacher, that awakening could occur in an institute. One had to admit, Camp suggested, that there were people patently unsuited for this profession, for whom no amount of training would avail. "Application and perseverance will do much," Camp asserted in 1860, "but certain God-given qualifications are indispensable, the want of which, no amount of human effort can supply." [44] Moreover, Camp expressed greater skepticism than Barnard concerning the efficacy of formal training. He was not as willing as Barnard to substitute lengthy academic preparation for zeal, enthusiasm and strenuous activity.

Distrustful both of untested training and untrained zeal, Camp preferred to stress natural rather than volitional qualities as the prerequisites of professional teaching. If one possessed a natural disposition to teach, one could easily be instructed in technical skills, become imbued with professional ardor, and be entrusted with a classroom assignment. Camp attributed the crucial advantage of this disposition to its very naturalness, i.e., its lack of either academic dexterity or artificial zeal. This conception of the suitable teacher represented a significant, if subtle, shift in orientation from Barnard's views of the late 1830s and 1840s, and it fairly reflected the new generation of professional educators to which David Camp belonged. The shift toward a greater insistence on the necessity of innate qualities and dispositions which slowly matured in a natural fashion would find great favor with the third generation of professional educators (in their prime during 1890–1920), men like G. Stanley Hall and William Torrey Harris.

If in Camp's mind the sources of professional awakening had changed, so too had the technical means for nurturing this commitment. While working with both educational agencies, he gravitated more toward the normal school than to the teachers' institutes. Over the issue of matriculation the full implications of the new orientation can be seen. Camp would have preferred stricter requirements, both personal and pedagogical, and a more careful screening process carried out by the normal school itself. Significantly, if these injunctions had been carried out by Barnard in 1839, Camp might well have never entered the Teachers' Class in Hartford or have tried to realize his professional aspiration in education. During the late 1850s and 1860s, however, admission to normal schools was the prerogative of local school districts whose visitors nominated candidates. The normal school had to accept all officially recommended students, the caliber of whom was frequently below Camp's standards. As principal of the Connecticut Normal School, Camp attempted to counter this custom by adopting a regulation, stipulating that each pupil had to attend for at least one full term. This ploy, he hoped, would discourage the transiency of appointees who did not remain a full term. It was also an indirect effort to effect a greater discrimination among students in normal schools. If positive admissions requirements and regulations on enrollment were impossible, due to prerogatives of local school districts, prescriptions such as lengthening required attendance would, Camp hoped, serve the same end, namely, the deterrence of students not possessing strong innate qualities of perseverance and self-culture.

Over and above such strategies Camp assured the preeminent role of the normal school by clarifying the distinction between it and the teachers' institute. What he accomplished, in fact, was a fundamental circumscription of the institute conception. In 1860 he remarked, "Teachers' Institutes, to some extent, will meet the wants of those who would attend the Normal School for a few weeks, so that the short term has been abolished and pupils will only be received at the beginning of the terms, and are required to remain at least one term. The trustees strongly recommend all whose talents and attainments are sufficient to pass through the entire courses." [45] No longer was it possible for Camp to subscribe to the concept of William Russell's and Henry Barnard's generation that the teachers' institute was a central and permanent part of a state's educational system. By 1860 Camp and other educators of his generation had come to envision the institutes as merely taking up those students who for any reason were unacceptable or unsuitable for the normal school. Institute conductors resorted more and more to lectures and exhibitions rather than drills and practice teaching. Abandoning the countryside, institutes gradually functioned jointly with state teachers' associations in the larger towns of the state. By the 1860s and 1870s young men were no longer invited to participate with experienced professionals for "mutual instruction"; now they were simply exposed to the attributes of *esprit de corps*, an idea expressed again and again in institute lectures of later years. After the Civil War educators transformed the institute from an itinerant school, dominated by a single personality, as Emma Willard and Henry Barnard had conceived it, into two institutional devices. Professional schoolmen of David Camp's generation specialized the institutes' earlier and broader responsibilities into the professional convention, on the one hand, and, on the other, into educational agencies like the Martha's Vineyard Summer Institute, one of the first summer schools in America.[46]

After the Civil War professional conceptions of education modified the inculcation of character and the training of the will as the primary goals of teaching. They concentrated upon the development of uniformly effective measures of instruction rather than morally informed personal styles, upon the exercise of skills rather than the strength of commitment to a cause. More and more teaching coincided with the transfer of technological knowledge, which had been but one component of the earlier ideal, the inculcation of character. Instruction stressed methods rather than the mastery of a subject or a set of subjects. Through the process of mental discipline, it was thought, young men acquired the means for providing for their own needs and deficiencies, be they physical, intellectual, or moral. Professionalization and education generally came to mean a compensation for native talent and insight, not a means of transforming and improving native ability. The second generation of professional educators provided the specific bridge by which students of moral philosophy in the ante-bellum period would after the war turn to moral science and experimental psychology. Because of the changes of the 1850s and 1860s successful educators became neither distinctly self-disciplined nor especially competent scholars. Nevertheless, due to the careers and professional experience of men like David N. Camp, these two images—the self-made man and German scientific methodology—functioned as the most satisfactory expressions of professional and educational ideals until the 1890s.

CHAPTER V

The Creation of
the American Institute of Instruction

The Scholarly Science of Education

If there was a common feature to all experiments for educational improvement and professional preparation of teachers during the early nineteenth century, it was their ephemeral quality. The rapidity with which organizations were formed and dissolved in this period was a fact in the general social history of the Republic, of which the fate of educational organizations was but one manifestation.[1] Several private endeavors, like those of James Carter and the Reverend Samuel Read Hall, were ambitious attempts to create an institution whose sole purpose was the special, professional preparation of teachers. In addition, academies and colleges broadened and enriched their programs with prospective teachers in mind. Almost without exception, the teachers' seminaries and special programs failed within a decade. The educational journals fared no better, and even the normal schools, which represented the best-designed instrument for the establishment of a genuinely professional corps of teachers, underwent substantial changes, unforeseen in the original conceptions of Mann and Barnard.

The informal and at times wholly unspecialized structure of the lyceum usually kept alive communal interest in education when energetic and influential citizens participated, but the leading spirits of the lyceum were not those primarily concerned for directing education. If the ability to survive the shifts and tensions of personalities and circumstances marked a rare characteristic of organized efforts for social improvement during the nineteenth century, then the American Institute of Instruction, which began its eighty-six-year history in 1830, deserves special attention.[2]

Despite individual preferences for one or another of the various institutions concerned with the work of experimentation and teacher training, nearly all New Englanders and nearly all major American figures interested in educational reform from 1820 to 1860 shared membership in the American Institute of Instruction. In the long run it was the one society which tried to mold itself to all segments of educational opinion and activity and thereby to provide a context for informal association and exchange of views among men of varying opinions and convictions concerning specific strategies for educational reform. The result was an extraordinarily eclectic society—a hybrid rarely at peace within itself—but one which in its own history mirrored most of the shifting currents and directions discernible in the history of American education before the Civil War.

Although from its inception in 1830 the American Institute of Instruction proclaimed its interest in a broad and diversified membership, for its first seven years the association bore the stamp of its founders. It was learned, affluent and oriented toward Boston and the Boston intellectual establishment. Its founders remained its guides during the 1830s, and they showed great similarity in social and professional status. Their papers and lectures were the mainstay of the Institute's meetings. Moreover, they shared to a much greater extent than any other group in the association's history common concepts of education and convictions concerning educational reform. In part, this broad ground of agreement may well have been the product of the independent experimentation in educational improvements in which many members of the Institute had indulged before 1830.[3] One of the most prominent of the Institute's early members was the Smith Professor of Romance Languages and Literature at Harvard, George Ticknor, whose own élan reflected the founding spirit of the American Institute of Instruction.

As a lecturer before the American Institute of Instruction, George Ticknor appeared with a long list of educational activities and reform ideas behind him. In 1826 Ticknor himself had established a short-lived association of teachers and the Friends of Education, which proved to be prototype of the American Institute of Instruction. Even before that, however, he had pioneered in advocating collegiate reforms at Harvard and changes in the Boston school system. In a sense, Ticknor had been born and bred to the pursuit of educational reform. His father, Elisha Ticknor, had spent a considerable part of his life in behalf of educational improvement and had made this activity something of a family tradition. After beginning his career as a schoolmaster, Elisha Ticknor left schoolkeeping during the 1790s and entered the mercantile trade in which he became wealthy.[4]

Although his business interests consumed his attention until his retirement in 1812, the elder Ticknor never lost his interest in education and became especially active after 1818. The general economic crisis of 1818–1819 caused a crisis in Boston society as a whole and in the city's schools in particular.[5] As money became tight, the tuition of private schooling became a burden which many families could not bear. Parents who had intended private schooling for their children now began to transfer them to common schools. This shift plus the increased population of the city underscored the need for adequate yet inexpensive instruction. In 1818 Elisha Ticknor and a close circle of friends turned their attention to the work of the Boston School Committee. Their principal contribution was the organization of a number of primary schools, which attempted to garner public funds so that all children would be assured of at least the rudiments of an education in preparation for their entrance into existing grammar schools. George Ticknor shared his father's view that education should be extended to children from all segments of the population. Both Ticknors subscribed fully to the idea that social harmony was a function of the degree of intellectual discipline which public education should impart. Family interest in education played a large part in George Ticknor's decision in 1816 to abandon the legal career he had just begun in favor of several years' study in European universities.[6]

Ticknor returned from Europe with admiration for the intellectual discipline and methodology which was a hallmark of the German university system. In 1819 he arrived home to assume his duties as Harvard's first Smith Professor of Romance Languages and Literature. Throughout the next decade Ticknor took up his father's struggle to reinvigorate the Boston school system through improved facilities and extension of the time a student spent in college preparation. Throughout all his efforts Ticknor never questioned that college matriculation should be the goal of all preparatory education, although he gradually came to realize that in many cases it would remain an unattainable one. During the 1820s Ticknor's zeal for public school reform was directed principally against the 1823 Massachusetts education act, which permitted any town with less than five thousand inhabitants to eliminate its grammar school. Ticknor used his favorable review of James Carter's controversial *Letters to William Prescott* (1824) to protest this educational disfranchisement. Unless grammar schools were provided by each town, Ticknor argued, many able students, particularly "the gifted children of the poor," would not have access to instruction in Greek and Latin and would thereby be unable to meet the prerequisites for college. The effect of this legislation, Ticknor declared, was "to reduce the general tone of intellectual improvement throughout the commonwealth."[7]

On several occasions George Ticknor was asked to serve on subcommittees of the Boston School Committee, an experience which provided him with substantial information about the status of the school system.

Throughout this work he was a staunch advocate of the extension of this system to less advantaged young men. In 1821 Ticknor lent support to the establishment of the English Classical School, the first high school in America, under the direction of George Emerson. This facility endeavored to give education beyond the elementary levels to young men whose financial circumstances restricted them to the business trades rather than to the professions for which college training was a prerequisite.[8] Although he remained faithful to the ideal of collegiate training as the capstone of an individual's education, Ticknor recognized the economic pressures which made this impossible for many Bostonians. Two years later he was instrumental in gathering a group of sponsors for William Fowle's Boston Monitorial School for Girls, which served as the prototype for the first public high school for girls, begun in 1826 under the direction of Ebenezer Bailey.[9] The greatest single service Ticknor rendered to the Boston school system came in the 1850s when he gave a portion of his fortune for the founding of the Boston Public Library and later donoted his own extensive library.

Ticknor's most important work in educational reform came with the attempt to render the education of Harvard College more germane to the needs of its enrolled students as well as more accessible to young men who ordinarily might not attend college at all. Ticknor's residence at the University of Göttingen had made Harvard seem parochial to him. In large part, the limitations of the institution seemed a function of its isolation from the actual needs of Boston and society in general. In part also the parochialism of Harvard, he believed, emanated from the actual process of instruction employed in the college. Ticknor's aim throughout was to extend and systematize the process of education at Harvard in order to make teaching "thorough" and "useful." His *Remarks on Changes Lately Proposed or Adopted at Harvard University* (1825) suggested Ticknor's preeminent concern that all able young men be educated to the full extent of their talents.

Since it was obvious to him that Harvard had not the stature of the University of Göttingen, Ticknor suggested that the first step toward achieving such a preeminent position would be to form Harvard into "a respectable high school in which young men might be safely sent to be prepared to the study of a profession." [10] Some of his proposals for reforming Harvard were clearly variations on German themes, particularly the call for departmentalization of subjects and faculties and for greater choice by students in selecting their studies. His stress upon adapting instruction to a particular student's degree of preparation and capacity compelled Ticknor to pare his own educational models for Harvard to the immediate environment and needs of Boston's youth.

Because the Boston School Committee grew increasingly reluctant to implement reforms which he had suggested for primary and secondary education, Ticknor believed that Harvard must accommodate itself to the educational backgrounds, deficiencies and needs of academically disadvantaged youth. Ticknor suggested that Harvard open its classes even to students who did not wish a degree. Indeed, his primary interest was for Harvard to accept its responsibility to initiate social changes and, more specifically, "to extend effectual instruction to portions of society that now never resort there." [11] Unlike Harvard's president, John T. Kirkland, who obstructed the realization of such proposals, Ticknor did not feel that the admission of normally unqualified young men would deemphasize the "thorough" teaching which as a scholar he demanded from Harvard, and as a citizen he expected. The crux of his proposals both for extended public education and for reorganized collegiate education rested, as the final pages of his *Remarks* indicated, upon his particular conception of the teacher and upon the necessity for thorough instruction.

His studies in Germany left Ticknor with a high regard for the importance of the teacher in the process of education. He asserted that the idea of making the commentaries of teachers as important as recitations from a book was relatively unknown in this country. He assailed the style of instruction which he found most prevalent in American education as one in which the mechanics of learning tended to dull or substitute for mental vigor. In his writings Ticknor frequently referred to the phenomenon of proper instruction as "bringing the minds of . . . instructors to act directly and vigorously on the minds . . . of pupils, and thus to encourage, enable, and compel them to learn what they ought to learn and what they might easily learn." [12] In Ticknor's view the prerequisite of a good and effective teacher was thorough scholarship, a detailed familiarity with a given subject. Ticknor did not confine the role of scholarship to academic pursuits alone but assumed that scholarship and social responsibility were intertwined. To develop the mind of any young man and, by extension, to strengthen the social and political fabric of society, a teacher had to know his subject in detail so that he would be able to communicate it effectively. Even when Ticknor restricted his own activities to the study of Spanish literature, he assumed that his research at home and abroad was actually preparing him for social obligations as a responsible citizen.

Such thoroughness of instruction, no matter what the subject, was for Ticknor the teacher's prime obligation in the classroom. Whether in a primary school, a high school or a college, it was a teacher's duty to impart as thorough a knowledge as the students were able to receive. Without ensuring thoroughness in education, Ticknor believed, a society ignored its obligations to the present and its responsibilities to the future, since the proper discipline of intellect fundamentally affected the entire fabric of a community. Ticknor was far from sanguine about the contemporary pursuit of thoroughness in American education. "Nay, who has been taught anything at our colleges," Ticknor asked rhetorically in his *Remarks*, "with the thoroughness that will enable him to go safely and directly onward to distinction in the department he has entered without returning to lay anew the foundation for his success?" [13]

Though Ticknor was able to achieve only modest success toward educational reform in Boston and at Harvard, he resolved to seek other means for implementing his conception of the social and instructional responsibilities of the teacher. This abortive reform experience and the undoubted frustration consequent upon it were not uncommon phenomena during the late 1820s. In his travels in America several years later Alexis de Tocqueville noted "a curious thing" concerning public attitudes toward education:

The enlightened classes of the population feel the need for public education and work ceaselessly to spread it. But the people who still do not see the need to give their money to attain this object, does not reelect to office those who thus work for their welfare in spite of themselves.[14]

In the absence of public, popularly supported educational endeavors a group of individuals gathered in George Ticknor's study in the autumn of 1826 to discuss educational reforms through alternate methods. Among those in attendance were Thomas Wait, the Boston publisher of the *American Journal of Education* and William Russell, the *Journal*'s current editor. These men resolved to initiate an informal association for the improvement of education.[15]

As chairman of a committee appointed to draft a statement of purpose, George Ticknor subsequently published in Russell's *Journal* his proposals for this association. Its general aims were to implement "a combined and concentrated effort . . . of men eminent and active in literature, in science, and in public life," in order to ensure the progress of enlightened educational ideas. Through this loose alliance of influential men Ticknor and his group hoped to avoid the "temporary results" and "restricted spheres" which had caused problems with past reform efforts.[16] Among the specific objectives of the society were Ticknor's most favored reforms: the establishment of infant schools, aid to instructors in the discharge of their duties, a school or college for teachers, a library of useful words on education, a uniform set of school books designed to overcome the deficiences inherent in books stressing "local peculiarities" and "local custom," and finally "a central committee for managing the concerns of the society" and its affiliated branches which were to be formed in every town and rural district.[17] The group who had originally met in Ticknor's home soon expanded to some fifty members who assembled weekly for a period of several months. This promising beginning ultimately failed since, apart from William Russell, no individual could be found to act as "agent" (executive secretary) for the society.[18] There were several capable individuals interested, but the diversity of the group seems to have prevented their agreement upon any one name. Sometime between the middle of 1827 and late 1829 the association dissolved itself.[19] Shortly after the dissolution the nucleus of the group, according to William Russell's account, regrouped and formed the American Institute of Instruction.[20]

Ticknor was central to this process not so much because of his personal contribution but, rather, because of the imprimatur his social station placed upon educational reform. His personal values and experience forced him away from the official and more established means of educational policy-making represented by the Boston School Committee and Harvard College. These bodies did not lend themselves to Ticknor's preferred aims. Whether through social class suspicions, their own traditions, or both, these bodies sustained organizations which kept separate the existing class stratifications of early Massachusetts society. In spite of the political forces which frustrated Ticknor's aims, neither his educational "salon" of the mid-1820s nor his support of the American Institute of Instruction in the early 1830s implied new political alliances. Nevertheless, Ticknor and other members of his privileged station catalyzed a new multiclassed cooperation in the Institute, a cooperation which did contain new political and social possibilities. Ticknor's original intentions had been social and benevolent. He wished to extend his ideas of pedagogy and educational quality beyond their traditional scope to improve schooling. By historical default these initiatives led to new organizations, to new purposes for older organizational formats, to new centers of educational power. At the very least Ticknor's work for educational reform illuminates the historical course by which an association of teachers, unprecedented in its educational and social diversity,[21] became an efficient focus for professionalizing teachers in the early nineteenth century.

The specific origins of the American Institute of Instruction occurred early in 1830 with a call for a "general association of persons, engaged and interested in the business of instruction." [22] At a convention on March 18, 1830 nearly three hundred teachers and friends of education from several eastern states gathered in Columbian Hall, Boston. The meeting was well attended primarily because of the assistance given by the Boston Lyceum then under the direction of Ebenezer Bailey and of other lyceum activists like Josiah Holbrook, who possessed contacts throughout New England. A committee, comprised of Ebenezer Bailey, George B. Emerson, B. D. Emerson, A. Andrews, and Gideon F. Thayer of Boston, Henry K. Oliver of Salem and J. Wilder of Watertown, was appointed to arrange an organizational meeting for the following August. Further, they were directed to see that a constitution for a permanent association was prepared for that later meeting.[23]

Owing to the frequent conferences which laid preparation during the summer of 1830, the convention held on August 19 successfully gathered hundreds of teachers and friends of education from all over New England into Boston's State House and there formed the American Institute of Instruction. President Francis Wayland of Brown University, soon to be elected the institute's first president, gave the introductory discourse, and other subjects were assigned "to gentlemen eminent as teachers, or in professions, who had given to the subject special attention." [24] The selection of these gentlemen was significant, since the delivery and publication of lectures on all aspects of education was the Institute's principal function, and the reputation and erudition of the persons chosen to speak gave the society its distinctive character. During the early years there were few district or common school teachers actually lecturing to the Institute. Most were of Ticknor's privileged station. Of the fourteen lecturers at the 1830 meeting, six taught private academies, four were college presidents or college faculty, two were private scholars. Like Ticknor, eleven of the fourteen were in their thirties and twelve were actually college graduates, six from Harvard.

In the early years of the Institute's work nearly all the men chosen to advance the educational literature and the professional knowledge of teachers were remarkably similar to Ticknor in terms of their personal background, their education and educational values and their history of benevolent efforts for social reform. Even more, a substantial number of these lecturers were among Ticknor's most intimate friends and some had collaborated with him in several efforts to improve the educational processes of Boston and Harvard. Among these early lecturers, in addition to Ticknor himself, were John C. Warren, a prominent doctor and later founder of the Massachusetts General Hospital; James Walker and Cornelius C. Felton, the one a well-known Unitarian divine and the other soon to become an outstanding classicist, both eventually presidents of Harvard College; George B. Emerson, Harvard graduate and tutor in mathematics there, first principal of the Boston English High School and founder of the Boston Natural History Society; William Russell and William Channing Woodbridge, the first a graduate of Glasgow University and the second of Yale, both editors of the first journal of education in the English language, the *American Journal of Education* (which under Woodbridge became the *American Annals of Education);* William Sullivan, Boston lawyer and author of school texts; Joseph Story, who had served many years as a justice of the Supreme Court of the United States; and Francis C. Gray, a learned and wealthy merchant whose talents were frequently devoted to public service, as in his representation of Boston in the General Court.[25]

The variety of content among the lectures plus the reputation of the lecturers in the Boston community suggests the two basic duties which the American Institute of Instruction conceived itself as fulfilling. On the one hand, the association attempted to become a learned society and, on the other, an agency for elevating the public understanding of education in all its varied facets. With but nine exceptions in its entire eighty-six-year history the Institute published an annual volume of lectures which its censors considered of sufficient propriety and erudition for wide circulation. From among those lectures chosen for the annual volume the directors of the Institute at times ordered that exceptional essays be printed as pamphlets and distributed either gratuitously or at reduced rates.

There were, moreover, associated functions by which the Institute sought to enlighten its members and the public. During the several days which occupied its annual meeting special committees arranged for visits to Boston's Atheneum, its libraries and its schools. In addition, they encouraged correspondence among members and appointed officers to gather information from other educational societies, school committees and individuals. On two occasions, in 1837 and 1838, the Institute petitioned the Massachusetts legislature in regard to two problems of pressing concern: first, the creation of a Board of Education and the office of secretary or superintendent for the carrying out of the state's own aims with regard to education, and second, the establishment of state-supported normal schools. In both of these ventures the American Institute of Instruction achieved striking successes.[26]

In case the authority of their proceedings and publications did not give firm legitimacy to their work in the public's eyes, the Institute in its early years bestowed the office of vice-president upon educators and nationally prominent citizens whose work in behalf of educational improvement and public service was unimpeachable. The office had no defined responsibilities and served in later years, even for active members at the annual meetings, as an honorary position. The vice-presidents during the early years rarely attended the Institute's proceedings, but their appointment as officers reflects further the founders' sense that professionalism in education would be advanced by association with distinguished educators and respected public figures. Among the early vice-presidents of the American Institute of Instruction were Benjamin O. Peers, a prominent Kentucky educator and soon after president of Transylvania University; Nathan Lord, president of Dartmouth College; Roberts Vaux, wealthy Quaker philanthropist of Philadelphia; Thomas H. Gallaudet, the well-known Connecticut minister who founded the American Asylum for the Deaf and Dumb in Hartford; John Adams, former principal of the old and respected Phillips Academy, Andover, Massachusetts; Theodore Frelinghuysen, United States senator from New Jersey and later president of Rutgers University; and William Wirt, prominent Maryland Lawyer and later to become a United States presidential candidate.[27] In addition to the cultivation of these men for their reputable work, especially in higher education, this office represented the aspirations of the Institute for national prominence.

Side by side with this effort to give their lectures a wide public distribution, the work of the Institute for the advancement of the professional teacher developed with equal fervor. While several lectures in the early years explored the more abstract and theoretical implications of education, more commonly the directors of the Institute seemed to have preferred those essays which discussed educational experiments undertaken by the most enlightened private schools. Practical means of teaching rhetoric, linear drawing, grammar, music, languages, the principles of physiology and other subjects were presented. The merit of various modes of school government such as without emulation, with monitors, without the rod, and with manual labor, as well as desirable school architecture and judicious classification of students were all covered by Institute lecturers. Initially the lecturers were drawn from professional experts in fields outside teaching and from the most prominent of the private school teachers. Increasingly, and particularly after 1837, the Institute drew from the ranks of actual teachers in a variety of schools for consideration of topics in the light of their current experience.

From the earliest sessions of the Institute the founders, who so carefully shaped its early direction, examined education from a particular viewpoint. More and more assertively they stressed that education was a subject with scientific properties. The ultimate effect of the American Institute of Instruction, it was claimed, "will hardly fail to show that education is a science, to be advanced, like every other science, by experiment; whose principles are to be fixed, and its capacities determined, by experiment; which is to be entered upon by men of philosophical mind, and pursued with a philosophical spirit." [28] The founding members of the Institute, like George B. Emerson, believed that through a gradual, cooperative deliberation among the practicing members of the profession, education might become a subject which at least the public would consider as scientifically exact and prestigious as medicine, law and theology.

The solicitation of scholars like Ticknor, Story, Sullivan and Wayland was not simply a design to give the Institute an aura of respectable determination in the interests of educational instruction:

> The society ought not to restrict its attention to instructers [sic] of any order, but should endeavor to embrace the service and duties of all, from the lowest to the highest in the scale of advancement; and the mutual understanding and the universal co-operation thus secured in the business of instruction, would probably be one of the greatest advantages resulting from the society.[29]

Coming as it did from Ticknor himself, this statement demonstrated that even those "highest in the scale of advancement" did not intend the Institute to reflect a uniform set of educational values. Still, the very familiarity of the founders, the Friends of Education and early Institute lecturers with the scholarly overtones of the established professions ensured a tacit harmony of opinion about the means for establishing the teacher as a true professional.

While the earliest notices contained unqualified invitations to all instructors whatever the grade or level of their school and to all "gentlemen of good moral character," the annual meetings, nevertheless, were not open to the general public during the first years of the Institute's history.[30] In spite of the founders' desire to cast a wide net, they made clear that the establishment of a professional educational association would not be achieved without a kind of indirect discrimination. Officially the constitution of the American Institute of Instruction admitted all teachers and Friends of Education who agreed to sign the charter and pay the annual dues of one dollar. Considering the salaries which district schoolmasters were paid, particularly in common schools outside Boston, this statute indirectly barred a number of New England teachers whose seriousness about their occupation was not yet sufficiently confirmed to warrant the expense of membership or travel to an annual meeting.[31]

The constitution's preference for "gentlemen of good moral character" focused on a quality of behavior and individual personality which Ticknor had extolled a few years earlier as a state where physical, intellectual and moral development had been "regulated by good instruction." [32] Although good moral character and gentlemanliness were vague terms for the Institute in this period, they were usually employed to indicate those who possessed an advanced degree of education, usually at the collegiate level. Here again it was evident that the founders of the American Institute of Instruction, most of them college-educated, retained a subtle bias in favor of college graduates as the most promising teachers. Although attended by hundreds of teachers, many more than the actual membership, the Institute's early meetings were directed in fact by a comparatively small group of its founders who shared common values of education and common conceptions of the professional teacher. Without a conscious elitism the work of the association's first group of officers shaped the Institute into a restrictive coterie whose educational standards were impractically high.

By their very knowledge of other professionals and their experience with good instruction, the planning and efforts of the founders misconceived the status and resources of most of the New England teachers outside Boston, who were sufficiently serious about their work to attend the early meetings of the American Institute of Instruction. The surprising number of teachers who traveled to Boston in the 1830s introduced a wholly unexpected element into these early professional gatherings. At the association's first meeting in 1830 116 teachers and Friends of Education from Massachusetts alone journeyed particpate in the proceedings of the Institute. Out of a total membership of 256 who signed the constitution, only sixty-five came from Boston.[33]

The desire of all the founders for a diverse membership led to enthusiasm for this great number of teachers from outside Boston who underwent the sacrifice and inconvenience of travel for the sake of education. Early accounts claimed that some participants had come over five hundred miles. The implication was not lost on the Boston members that these teachers had great seriousness of purpose for advancing education and the teaching profession. What was less clear to the founders of the Institute was the fundamentally divergent conception of the "professional" teacher held by these non-Boston schoolmen. For the schoolmaster in a country district whose annual income was equal to the salary of a manual worker or a farmer, whose school teaching was restricted to a period from two to four months in the winter, and whose own academic qualifications for teaching often did not excel those of his most promising students, the view of a professional teacher as a scholar with broad social and benevolent obligations remained but a remote ideal. The majority of New England teachers could not undertake any additional study away from home, and many could scarcely afford the expense of travel to the Institute's meetings in Boston, much less time away from the duties of their farm or trade which they pursued during that part of the year when not teaching. Moreover, further learning apart from what he could obtain through books of other teachers had not become even an aspiration for the district schoolmaster in the 1830s. Nor did school committees insist on erudition; they barely accepted responsibility for examining a teacher in rudimentary subjects.

In the 1830s as more young men in district schools became interested in pursuing teaching as a permanent occupation, they realized that if they were to seek further educational improvement for their careers, it would have to come not from special seminaries or colleges but only through experimentation in their own communities and schools. When they looked beyond their own community to Boston and the American Institute of Instruction, they sought not recondite discourses from well-known personalities but discussions of more effective pedagogical techniques and modes of governing classes which they could adopt themselves without additional preparation. Their special concern became less a furthering of their own formal education, a goal patently beyond their reach, and more the long process of self-improvement through actual teaching. They recognized that, apart from brief attendance at institute meetings or perhaps a local lyceum, their claim to professional recognition would have to be founded upon expertise gained through years in the classroom rather than by that immediate professional recognition which came with college study. While they favored the extension of educational facilities and hence professional opportunities, the great majority of non-Bostonians who came to the early meetings of the American Institute of Instruction were interested less in the philosophical and quasi-scientific aspects of education and more in immediately applicable procedures which would enhance their professional standing.

For the first twenty-five years of the Institute's history Boston men directed the organization, yet accommodations to members from outside Boston began in the earliest meetings. The continued existence of any professional agency or learned society in the nineteenth century was a function of its ability to maintain an expanding membership. Almost immediately after ts inception the American Institute of Instruction was hit with a serious crisis as new membership not only failed to appear in anticipated numbers but actually fell off sharply from 1830 to 1836.[34] This failure to attract new members at a significant and steady rate was a problem which demanded accommodation and imagination. Apart from drawing its lecturers from a broad base of teachers and shaping the topics more to the circumstances of practicing district school teachers, the officers of the American Institute of Instruction debated among themselves and finally resolved to open the meetings to the Boston community without charge. Even this did not solve the problem, and in 1836 the Institute adopted a constitutional amendment which permitted meetings to be held outside Boston. In retrospect, this amendment proved to be the first major step in the reformulation of Institute policy by a group of members not so intimately tied to the Boston milieu and who held a new conception of the professional teacher. In 1837 the Institute met at Worcester, Massachusetts and experienced the first significant increase in membership since its initial meeting in 1830.[35] From 1837 to the broad changes in the organization during the 1870s the American Institute of Instruction shifted its meetings to the smaller towns of New England and New York. The Worcester meeting in 1837 indicated that a new type of teacher had begun to modify the organization and indirectly to challenge the educational views of the Institute's founders, who cherished an image of the teacher which the careers of men like Ticknor reinforced.

For the first decade of the Institute's activities the presidents of the association continued to reflect in the persons of the Reverend Francis Wayland, The Honorable William Calhoun and James G. Carter the principles upon which it was founded. Until the election of George B. Emerson in 1841 no practicing teacher had entered the institute's highest office, and not until 1849 with the election of Gideon F. Thayer, himself a founder and practicing teacher, did the majority of New England teachers find their own class interests directly represented in the presidency. After the tenure of John Kingsbury, also a founder and successful teacher, the office passed in 1857 to an entirely new generation of professional teachers.[36]

During the 1840s the Institute attracted new members in an erratic and haphazard fashion. Since new members were expected to attend the annual meeting the year they joined, the great fluctuation in recruitment was contingent upon many variables, including the nature of the towns where the meetings were held, the modes of transportation to these communities, their facilities for board and recreation and not least their education interests. In part, the great advances in New England transportation alone in these years explains the rise in membership and attendance from the 1840s to the 1850s.[37] But even more important this rise was a function of the individuals who superintended the preparation and proceedings of the annual meetings. During the long presidential tenure of George B. Emerson between 1841 and 1848 there was little expressed concern for wide publicity or the employment of sophisticated techniques for drawing a variety of teachers to the annual meetings. In attitude and aim Emerson's tenure looked back to the initial impetus of the Institute's founders who wished to grow slowly, stressing the scientific aspects of education. The presidency of his successor, Gideon F. Thayer, turned to different attitudes and different achievements. The first meeting of Thayer's presidency was marked by the highest increase of new members between 1830 and the Civil War.[38]

Besides the large number of new members, there were other differences in the Institute's annual proceedings between the 1840s and 1850s. During these decades the scientific orientation of the association began to combine with procedures whose inspirational qualities resembled the local teachers' institutes as they had developed under the direction of David Nelson Camp, himself an officer of the Institute during the 1850s.[39] Particularly in the decade before the Civil War the lectures of the Institute became less detailed, less specialized and less thorough than those of the 1830s. More and more the increasingly diffuse and exhortative addresses were directed to topics like "Earnestness," "Self-Reliance," "The Dignity of the Teacher's Office," "The Essential Elements of Education" and "The Duty of the American Teacher."[40]

The American Institute of Instruction grew gradually in stature so that by the Civil War nearly anyone entering responsible offices or reputable school appointments felt bound to join its ranks. When Horace Mann and Henry Barnard accepted their respective offices in the emerging state educational systems, they felt obliged at the same time to take up membership in the Institute. Such a pattern became customary for state educational officers after 1840, even outside New England. As the organization reached the heights of its effectiveness in the 1850s, more and more teachers of district schools flocked to its meetings, too, as soon as they became aware that teaching offered them a permanent professional career. By the 1850s the changes from the early viewpoint of the Institute were recognized as fundamental, and founders like William Russell called in vain for measures which would restore the association to its original program for developing education into a scholarly study and a worthy science.[41]

The Importance of Being Courteous

As a professional association of teachers, the American Institute of Instruction provided a medium for discussion and examination of all the significant experiments and viewpoints which emerged from the numerous efforts undertaken for educational improvement between 1830 and the Civil War. Its service as a clearinghouse for divergent educational opinion bestowed on the Institute the principal role of maintaining a kind of continuity and harmony among educational views and practices before 1860. Had it conceived of its goals in more specialized terms—had it, for example, advanced more controversial policies than it did, had it been less pliant than its founders actually made it, it is likely that the American Institute of Instruction would have dissolved as did the only other associations remotely similar to it in structure and purpose, namely, the Western Literary Institute and College of Professional Teachers in Cincinnati and the American Lyceum in New York.[42] While these organizations began auspiciously in 1829 and 1831, only the American Institute of Instruction survived the far-reaching ramifications of the economic crisis of 1837 and 1838.

The deep-seated economic strains of the late 1830s at first caused a reformulation of the organizational procedures of the Institute. The most dramatic of these alterations emerged from a sustained agitation for constitutional changes which would not only permit public participation in the proceedings of the annual meetings but which also ensured the greater involvement of the smaller towns about New England by actually taking the Institute's annual meetings to the New England towns themselves. The immediate result of this change lessened the participation and lectures of Boston's talented citizens, like George Ticknor and his circle. Indeed the activity in the association of the Friends of Education in general became less prominent. When it requested the services of the Friends of Education during the later decades of its history, the Institute invited the dignitaries of the smaller New England towns—an eminent minister, the mayor or notable state officials from the area—to deliver official greetings to the annual gatherings and at times to give the introductory address. The admission of the public, the planning of meetings in the more rural areas of New England and the solicitation of local dignitaries indicated as much a shift in orientation for the Institute as it did for the profession of teachers and education in general.

Between the 1830s and the 1850s the Institute was not alone in reevaluating its responsibility to back-country New England and to young men who ordinarily could not finance an education at the seaboard colleges. Indeed these very colleges—Harvard, Yale, and Brown—served less and less the major proportion of young men attending colleges than they had in the past. Newly created back-country colleges like Amherst and Wesleyan and older institutions like Bowdoin, Williams and Union all experienced in this period an upsurge in attendance, if not in quality.[43] Moreover, as institutes for the education of educators came to be established in the 1840s and 1850s, they too favored locations nearer the homes of those most likely to attend. Consequently normal schools were founded in Lexington, Westfield, Framingham, Barre and Bridgewater in Massachusetts and New Britian in Connec-

Table 2

The Annual Meetings of the American Institute of Instruction:
Locations and New Members, 1830–1918

Number	Year	New Members	Location
1	1830	256	Boston, Massachusetts
2	1831	68	Boston, Massachusetts
3	1832	58	Boston, Massachusetts
4	1833	32	Boston, Massachusetts
5	1834	33	Boston, Massachusetts
6	1835	34	Boston, Massachusetts
7	1836	38	Boston, Massachusetts
8	1837	40	Worcester, Massachusetts
9	1838	31	Lowell, Massachusetts
10	1839	36	Springfield, Massachusetts
11	1840	19	Providence, Rhode Island
12	1841	7	Boston, Massachusetts
13	1842	20	New Bedford, Massachusetts
14	1843	10	Pittsfield, Massachusetts
15	1844	43	Portland, Maine
16	1845	27	Hartford, Connecticut
17	1846	17	Plymouth, Massachusetts
18	1847	13	Concord, New Hampshire
19	1848	15	Bangor, Maine
20	1849	73	Montpelier, Vermont
21	1850	50	Northampton, Massachusetts
22	1851	47	Keene, New Hampshire
23	1852	36	Troy, New York
24	1853	43	New Haven, Connecticut
25	1854	65	Providence, Rhode Island
26	1855	28	Bath, Maine
27	1856	24	Springfield, Massachusetts
28	1857	39	Manchester, New Hampshire
29	1858	35	Norwich, Connecticut
30	1859	28	New Bedford, Massachusetts
31	1860	80	Boston, Massachusetts
32	1861	23	New Bedford, Massachusetts
33	1862	24	Hartford, Connecticut
34	1863	23	Concord, New Hampshire
35	1864	30	Portland, Maine
36	1865	52	New Haven, Connecticut
37	1866	35	Burlington, Vermont
38	1867	108	Boston, Massachusetts
39	1868	22	Pittsfield, Massachusetts
40	1869	67	Portsmouth, New Hampshire
41	1870	24	Worcester, Massachusetts
42	1871	89	Fitchburg, Massachusetts
43	1872	54	Lewiston, Maine
44	1873	40	Concord, New Hampshire
45	1874	57	North Adams, Massachusetts
46	1875	228	Providence, Rhode Island

Table 2
The Annual Meetings of the American Institute of Instruction:
Locations and New Members, 1830–1918

Number	Year	New Members	Location
47	1876	233	Plymouth, New Hampshire
48	1877	456	Montpelier, Vermont
49	1878		Fabyan's White Mountains, New Hampshire
50	1879		Fabyan's White Mountains, New Hampshire
51	1880		Saratoga Springs, New York
52	1881		St. Albans, Vermont
53	1882		Saratoga Springs, New York
54	1883		White Mountains, New Hampshire
55	1884	[269]	Cottage City, Massachusetts
56	1885		Newport, Rhode Island
57	1886		Bar Harbor, Maine
58	1887		Burlington, Vermont
59	1888		Newport, Rhode Island
60	1889		Bethlehem, New Hampshire
61	1890		Saratoga Springs, New York
62	1891	121	Bethlehem, New Hampshire
63	1892	31	Narragansett Pier, Rhode Island
64	1894	68	Bethlehem, New Hampshire
65	1895	51	Portland, Maine
66	1896	54	Bethlehem, New Hampshire
67	1897	49	Montreal, Province Quebec
68	1898	63	North Conway, New Hampshire
69	1899	116	Bar Harbor, Maine
70	1900	42	Halifax, Nova Scotia
71	1901	14	Saratoga, New York
72	1902	85	Burlington, Vermont
73	1903	Joint Session, NEA	Boston, Massachusetts
74	1904	235	Bethlehem, New Hampshire
75	1905	75	Portland, Maine
76	1906	81	New Haven, Connecticut
77	1907	23	Montreal, Canada
78	1908	67	Burlington, Vermont
79	1909	—	Castine, Maine
80	1910	—	Providence, Rhode Island
81	1912	—	North Conway, New Hampshire
82	1914	—	Cambridge, Massachusetts
83	1915	—	Cambridge, Massachusetts
84	1916	—	?
85	1917	—	Cambridge, Massachusetts
86	1918	—	Boston, Massachusetts

ticut. This pattern too was followed by many private academies.[44] The Institute's decision to move provided but one example of this general attempt to furnish educational opportunities for talented young men as well as for the public where they lived rather than expecting them to travel to a central location like Boston. The Institute's shift from Boston (Table 2) symbolized the growing strength of rural and non-Boston teachers within the association and the growing professional awareness of district and village schoolmasters in general.

While the principal offices were held by college-trained men, many of whom were not actually engaged in common school instruction, and while the lectures were dominated by subjects belabored with detail and presented by recognized experts, there was little in the early proceedings of the American Institute of Instruction to appeal to the rural teacher. As the meetings moved out into the country, their content underwent a gradual alteration. Since no assumptions could be made about the audience's level of education and since abstruse educational expertise could not command wide attention,

Table 3

Membership Distribution of the American Institute of Instruction, 1830–1908

1830s	1840s	1850s	1860s	1870s [a]	1880s [b]	1890s [c]	1900s [d]
626	244	395	464	1,184	269	553	622

Total [e]

4,357

[a] In the 48th volume of the *Lectures and Proceedings of the American Institute of Instruction* there is a cumulative list of the preceding years. Further research has revealed many inaccuracies in this list. Some members who were actual founders of the association are identified on the 1877 list as joining first in the mid-1830s; some members are listed more than once. Also, this cumulative list omits any membership increases which occurred in 1878 and 1879. Newspaper reports, for example, announced an attendance figure of over 2,500 at the 1878 meeting. Some schoolmen appear in the *Proceedings* but not on the 1877 list.

[b] This figure represents those new names which appear in the annual volume of *Proceedings* and elsewhere.

[c] Beginning in 1891 the annual volume contained the names of all members in good standing that year. Those annual lists duplicate names from the 1877 list as well as from other years between 1891 and 1908, when the institute published its last annual volume. The figures for 1890s and 1900s represent my own compilation without duplications.

[d] Although the Institute continued to meet until 1918, the last list of members appeared in its last annual volume, 1908. Consequently this figure represents only those new members who can be identified as joining between 1900 and 1908.

[e] In the context of the previous notes the total must be taken as definitive as far as it goes. However, the real membership of the Institute was considerably larger. A. E. Winship, the institute president in 1897, claimed that over 2,000 joined that year (my figures document 49!). George Walton claimed 2,054 for 1878, 1,029 in 1883 and 2,234 for 1897; William Mowry boasted 1,000 enrolled in 1877. See "Reminiscences," *Journal of Education*, 64 (June 28, 1906): 6-8.

the lectures gradually shifted to topics of more immediate concern to the common school teacher and to reflections on the values and importance of the teaching profession. The shift seems to have had results, since after the late 1840s the Institute's membership increased (Tables 2 and 3), drawing especially upon the rural areas of New England.[45]

While the impact of this change produced no direct confrontation of interested parties, the Institute's membership and organizational shifts did carry divisive implications. Neither the Friends of Education nor the teachers themselves were willing to forgo their claim of professional status for teaching. At the same time, if professional status were equated with advanced academic study, the majority of New England's teachers would be considered amateurs. Although these implications reflected a latent split among the Institute's members, the directors of the association seem to have effectively prevented an explicit controversy over the issue. As in so many other educational problems, the Institute sought to work out its differences with more regard to existing realities than to achieving uniformity. Nevertheless, it is not surprising to find in the educational literature of this period as a whole as well as in the Institute's own publications increased emphasis after 1837, not on professional preparation in special institutions and normal schools, but on expertise derived from actual practice and aided by attendance at a lyceum or teachers' institute.

As population growth put increased pressures on conscientious school committees and boards of education, educational policy-makers were forced to seek and employ committed teachers with long and reputable service records, if their schools were not to be left poorly staffed or understaffed. In rural areas especially, this development meant that experience alone was increasingly regarded as the professional equivalent of "thorough" training, a development of which the American Institute of Instruction had to take notice. These experienced rural teachers, once admitted to its ranks, began to change the structure, goals and orientation of the Institute.

These changes within the American Institute of Instruction were not dramatic. The founders, who continued to direct the association, tried to appreciate and serve the broad differences among the membership. In a sense they arranged the significant shifts themselves, since in the 1840s and 1850s practicing teachers alone and not professionals from other occupations assumed full responsibility for the planning and lectures of the association. After 1841 the presidency and vice-presidencies of the Institute (Table 4) were no longer held by national dignitaries and less and less frequently were offered to college presidents. With the election of George B. Emerson in 1841, members filled the highest office in their association with a practicing teacher. Emerson's tenure (1841–1848) in particular ensured that the Institute's transformation would be gradual, since he endorsed so completely the educational views of men like Ticknor. Yet he served throughout the 1840s

Table 4
First- and Second-Generation Presidents of the American Institute
of Instruction, 1830–1886

Name	Life Dates	College	A.I.I. Dates	Professional Position While President
Rev. Francis Wayland	1796–1865	Union	1830–1832	University President
William B. Calhoun	1795–1865	Yale	1833–1839	Friend of Education
James G. Carter	1795–1849	Harvard	1840	Friend of Education
George B. Emerson	1797–1881	Harvard	1841–1848	Academy Principal
Gideon F. Thayer	1793–1864	None	1849–1852	Grammar (pvt.) School Principal
Thomas Sherwin	1799–1869	Harvard	1853–1855	High School Principal
Rev. John Kingsbury	1801–1874	Brown	1856–1857	Academy Principal
John D. Philbrick	1818–1886	Dartmouth	1858–1859	Superintendent of Schools
Daniel B. Hagar	1820–1896	Union	1860–1861	High School Principal
Admiral P. Stone	1820–1902	None(xDart.)	1862–1863	High School Principal
Charles Northend	1814–1895	None(xAmh.)	1864	School Visitor [Asst. Supt.]
Rev. Birdsey G. Northrup	1817–1898	Yale	1865–1866	Agent [Asst. Supt.], Board of Education
William E. Sheldon	1832–1900	None(xMidd.)	1867	High School Principal
John Kneeland	1821–1914	(Bridgewater N.S.)	1868–1869	School Supervisor [Asst. Supt.]
Samuel S. Greene	1810–1883	Brown	1870	University Professor
Abner J. Phipps	1816–1886	Dartmouth	1871–1872	Agent [Asst. Supt.], Board of Education
Rev. Milan C. Stebbins	1828–1889	Amherst	1873–1874	High School Principal
Merrick Lyon	1815–1888	Brown	1875–1876	Grammar (pvt.) School
Thomas W. Bicknell	1834–1925	Brown	1877–1878	Editor, *Journal of Education*
Issac N. Carleton	1832–1902	Dartmouth	1879–1880	Normal School Principal
William A. Mowry	1829–1917	None(xBrown)	1881–1882	Academy Principal
George A. Walton	1822–1908	(Bridgewater N.S.)	1883	Agent [Asst. Supt.], Board of Education
Homer B. Sprague	1829–1918	Yale	1884	High School Principal
J. W. Patterson	1823–1893	Dartmouth	1885–1886	Superintendent of Schools

while the forces in American education which would eventually modify his views gained strength.

When Emerson left office in 1848, the members elected an active teacher more sympathetic to the plight of teachers without traditional professional advantages. At the same time the dramatic significance of the election of 1848 was somewhat mitigated by the fact that the Institute's new president, Gideon F. Thayer, was himself a founder of the association and had served with George B. Emerson on the Constitutional Committee which wrote the association's charter in 1830. Nevertheless, Thayer had merited the election by the membership through his successful sponsorship of the resolutions to admit the public without charge to the Institute's meetings and to take the annual meetings outside Boston. A comparison of the occupational patterns and professional advantages of these two men clarifies much about the subtle but significant differences which developed within the American Institute of Instruction from the era of Ticknor to the 1850s.[46]

Under the direction of his father, a doctor by profession and a scientist by inclination, George Emerson pursued a course of study which from his earliest years prepared him for college. In fact, his father's tutorship compensated for the deficiencies of the winter schools he attended in his native town of Kennebunk, Maine. Throughout his father's life this tutorship supplied constant stimulus to Emerson's scientific and mathematical interests.[47] For six months before his matriculation at Harvard College in 1813, Emerson studied with Benjamin Allen, L.L.D., the able master of Dummer Academy at Byfield, Massachusetts. When he left home for college, he was sixteen. Although his family was probably well able to finance his Harvard studies, Emerson occupied his winter vacations by keeping schools in various districts near his home. Like so many other young men during this same period, Emerson suffered a deterioration of health during his college years. Upon graduation in 1819 he sought to continue schoolkeeping as a means of diverting himself while he recovered. He accepted employment in a private academy in Lancaster, Massachusetts, where the duties were not especially taxing.[48]

In 1819, the same year Ticknor assumed the Smith Professorship, Emerson joined Harvard's mathematics faculty as a tutor, and at times also offered instruction in Greek. While a tutor, at age twenty-two, Emerson began to fashion his educational ideas and to take a teacher's responsibility more seriously. His cooperation with Ticknor's efforts to refurbish Harvard's organization, teaching procedures and hence the quality of education may have stimulated Emerson's deliberations. In 1821, with the support of several influential Boston citizens, Emerson became principal of the English Classical School, an experiment which eventually became the first public high school in America. His success there foreshadowed his second equally important educational undertaking. In 1823 Emerson took charge of a private high school for girls at a salary of three thousand dollars a year, an amount which made him the highest-paid schoolmaster in New England. He remained principal and instructor in this institution until his retirement in 1855.[49]

Emerson's early and extraordinary advantages resulted in his dramatic and quick success as a professional teacher. In turn the authority he derived from his teaching gave him contacts with many Boston citizens whose assistance permitted him to make equally important and serious contributions to other educational and benevolent enterprises. In 1827, through the formation of the privately sponsored Mechanics Institute in Boston, Emerson became acquainted with prominent Bostonians like Daniel Webster and Nathaniel Bowditch. When the Boston Society of Natural History was founded in 1830, Emerson shared the founder's honors with Walter Channing and became acquainted with well-known scientists like Edward Hitchcock. At the state's request the society appointed Emerson to direct the botanical and zoological surveys of Massachusetts. His own report on trees and shrubs was described at the time as a "classic in scientific literature." [50] Among other honors and recognitions for his educational scientific labors Emerson was elected to the Boston School Committee, Massachusetts Board of Education, Phi Beta Kappa and the American Academy of Arts and Sciences. In 1858 he received the degree of L.L.D. from Brown University, and in 1859, from Harvard.[51]

In contrast to Emerson's college preparation, his early educational opportunities, his comparatively quick success in his chosen occupation and his influential educational acquaintances and scientific friends, the experience of most New England teachers seemed quite foreign. The majority of New England schoolmasters, lacking such qualifications, were kept from two of the more important characteristics of a professional career—the opportunity to prepare for professional work while still young and the stability of a permanent position. Since teaching was popularly considered only temporary work, undertaken to support other occupational aspirations, schoolmasters themselves often had taught from four to six winters before they became impressed with the professional potential of instruction. Before a young man could establish himself with a degree of permanence in a single community, several more winters in schoolkeeping had passed. By the time they committed themselves to teaching, therefore, most New England schoolmen, especially in regional areas, were at an age when more fortunate young men like George Emerson had been practicing their profession for several years.

The process of professional advancement without college training was prolonged not simply because it took time for a young man to reach a level of professional awareness in regard to teaching. The occupation itself encouraged a prolongation with its disruptive mobility which teachers of this period felt to be unique to their profession. Communities often did not encourage their teachers to remain more than one winter, unless a teacher was willing to forgo any expectation of a salary increase, for such an ir.crease would have required an additional tax. When teachers did not have their contracts renewed, they were forced to seek employment elsewhere for the following season. Even enlightened communities reinforced this occupational mobility, since they competed with high salaries for teachers whose success had been demonstrated.

Career status for teachers who had little formal education or professional training usually rested upon the variety of schools they had taught and communities they had served. A long tenure at a single school often implied to school committees not a praiseworthy stability, but rather, that an applicant had substituted a sinecure for an apprenticeship. A stable record of employment often gave schoolmen a reputation for indolence rather than for self-improvement. For ambitious young men to profit financially and professionally from school teaching, it behooved them, therefore, to diversify their teaching experience. A few cities like Boston proved the exception to this rule. There a high regard was attached to long service to a particular school. More to the point, however, was the fact that the better schools of the largest towns and cities could usually attract instructors with formal professional qualifications and thus affected the highly mobile career patterns of less educated teachers only as a distant aspiration.

Gideon Thayer experienced these occupational difficulties in his own career, and those experiences in part prompted his effort to change the organization and orientation of the American Institute of Instruction. Moreover, his particular course of advancement in the profession of teaching suggests that if the problems attendant upon entering the teaching profession late and wasting time to prove one's abilities through practice were to be overcome successfully, teachers had to exploit not merely local notoriety but the advantages of cities like Boston and Hartford. Indeed in a sense the career of Gideon Thayer demonstrates at once how much an ill-prepared young man could achieve and how far he could go, if Boston favored him.

Although like Emerson he had been born outside Boston, Thayer's earliest education did not possess the quality or the thoroughness of Emerson's. Thayer's father was a carpenter who had moved from Watertown shortly after his son's birth to take up his trade in Brookline, Massachusetts. There Thayer attended the district schools. Shortly after the move to Brookline, Thayer was orphaned and was subsequently apprenticed, first, to a tallow merchant and then, at the age of fourteen, to a retail shoe merchant for whom he worked six years. In 1814 as George Emerson entered his second year at Harvard, Thayer, four years his senior, began to supplement his job as a merchant's clerk with his first educational work.[52]

Although he was more a disciplinarian than an instructor, Thayer's experience as an usher in Boston's South Writing School provided him with skill in penmanship. At the South Writing School he probably also made his first contacts with influential Boston families, since the school provided writing practice not offered by the neighboring Boston Latin School. Students from that old and prestigious institution frequently attended both schools, though each operated independently. In addition to this work, Thayer conducted an evening school for apprentices like himself. All these endeavors gradually earned him a reputation as a serious and effective teacher, but they served also to tax his health severely. For a year (1818–1819) his career as merchant and part-time teacher was interrupted by a forced interlude in the friendlier climate of the south.[53]

Although he returned from New Orleans in 1819, Thayer's health still would not permit resumption of his former teaching activities with equal vigor. Like Emerson, he took up schoolkeeping on a limited scale while regaining his strength. The next eight years witnessed the gradual emergence of Thayer's reputation as an effective teacher. Until 1828, apart from instruction in district schools, all the education Thayer had received had come from literary associations, reading circles (especially one established by the Reverend William Ellery Channing) and debating societies, all in Boston. In 1828 at age thirty-five Thayer might be said to have "arrived," professionally speaking, for in that year he was entrusted with the establishment of a private school, financed by a stock-holding company of 152 Boston citizens, including individuals of the stature of Appleton, Bowditch, Channing, Frothingham, Holmes, Lawrence, Lowell and Parkman. His suitability for this position was judged less in terms of academic achievements, of which he had almost none, than upon his reputation for effective teaching and his estimable character. The comparable opportunity for Emerson, the principalship of the English Classical School, was offered to him at age twenty-four, soon after he had completed his college education![54]

In spite of his Boston-centered career spanning fifty-five years, Thayer's home during all this time was located outside Boston in the communities of Milton and Quincy, Massachusetts. The geographical division between his professional and social responsibilities dramatized in a sense the kind of detachment from Boston society which his humble origins, his lack of professional advantages and the extensive period of time spent in advancing as a teacher ensured almost as a matter of course. Unlike Emerson, whose benevolent and scientific activities accompanied his professional work in teaching, Thayer labored more prosaically in a host of local efforts outside Boston immediately related to education.

During the 1830s Thayer concentrated attention outside the classroom on the enlightenment of public interest in education through the establishment of a local lyceum, for which he served as president. His familiarity with the state of public education in other local communities broadened with his travels throughout New England as an agent of the Boston Sunday School Union. In addition to work on behalf of public education—arguing the advantages of a public high school, delivering a series of lectures and in Quincy editing for a time the weekly newspaper—Thayer joined with his colleagues in an effort to extend professional teachers' associations at the local level. He played a significant part in the establishment of the Norfolk County Teachers' association (1830) and the Massachusetts Teachers' Association (1845). In 1848 he served as editor of the *Massachusetts Teacher*.

Only in the late 1840s and 1850s did Thayer receive invitations to serve on prestigious Boston committees for social and benevolent purposes, such as the founding of the Boston Public Library, Boston Dispensary, the Washingtonian Total Abstinence Society and the Boston Lunatic Society. The hiatus between his professional success and the solicitation of his services as a leading citizen was most likely as much a function of Thayer's early preference for communal activity outside Boston as it was the delayed recognition of Thayer's stature by the Boston professional establishment. All doubt about his right to the highest professional standing and recognition as an outstanding citizen was fully removed when Brown University conferred upon Thayer an honorary degree in 1854 and Harvard followed suit in 1855.[55]

Emerson's and Thayer's professional patterns and occupational advantages had ramifications in their actual classroom work. Throughout the course of his teaching in the English Classical School, Emerson's intention was to extend the mode of education and branches of knowledge "to fit him [a youth] for active life, and shall serve as a foundation for eminence in his profession, whether Mercantile or Mechanical." [56] Since in his first venture the students were not preparing for college, the three-year course of systematic study stressed geometry, geography, history, and English Literature. While the force of a teacher's personality was considered important, the Boston School Committee demanded (and Emerson concurred) that the most important prerequisite for the school's teachers was the "necessary qualification, that they shall have been regularly educated at some university." [57]

When Emerson took up the instruction of young women, he attempted to provide them with the foundation which would fit them for the duties of a wife and mother. His prescription for the school was thorough study of Latin, on the assumption that the discipline of mind and precision that this study conferred was the limit of benefit a parent could expect from the school.[58] Finally, in 1837 and 1838 as author of the American Institute of Instruction's two memorials to the state legislature, Emerson made explicit the prerequisites for all occupations whether in the established or aspiring professions. Among the important characteristics of the professional teacher which normal schools presumed to cultivate Emerson stressed "a *thorough knowledge* of whatever he undertakes to teach," "to be able to introduce system, and keep it constantly in force," "an acquaintance with the minds of children," and "a knowledge of the human mind and character." [59] While the teacher's role in this process was crucial, Emerson unmistakably placed the burden of success upon the thoroughness of academic accomplishment and a systematic development of studies.

Thayer's experience in actual instruction had to be somewhat different owing to the very nature of the Chauncey Hall School where he taught and served as principal for some twenty-eight years. Unlike Emerson's schools which were first wholly public, then wholly private, Thayer's school maintained a composite character throughout its history. It accepted students like Francis Parkman who from his matriculation there in 1836 was preparing for college by the study of Latin and Greek. At the same time Thayer received young men whose ambitions from the outset were to undertake business and mercantile pursuits. Personally Thayer took great pleasure in the success of this second curriculum, quite possibly because it institutionalized an educational opportunity which he himself had never had.

In addition, Thayer was willing to hire a teacher whose educational qualifications left something to be desired. Rather than preferring only university-educated young men, Thayer advertised in the newspaper for a teacher who was "perfect master of any one thing." [60] By mastery Thayer did not mean necessarily academic accomplishment. One of his most successful teachers had been Clement Durgin, whose natural skills in many subjects had not been developed for formal training or college study. Nevertheless, Durgin's instruction at Chauncey Hall proved Thayer's belief that the manner and courteous demeanor of a teacher's style "alone, unaided by any instruction, will affect tenfold more than all the instruction we can furnish without it." [61] Thayer's encouragement of both academic and nonacademic aspects of teaching extended Emerson's more explicit reliance upon the primary role of intellectual labor in effecting the work of genuine instruction. Thayer developed in his school not only the importance of the classics and science, both taught at Chauncey Hall by William Russell, but fashioned also devices for the direct communication of proper social manners and character.

In addition to the lessons he expected students at Chauncey Hall to acquire, Thayer attempted to impart to all young men who sought his instruction the moral lesson that he felt had confirmed his own success. The quality of one's manners, he advised, gave whatever intellectual accomplishments one possessed greater force and value. There was, one of Thayer's colleagues at Chauncey Hall explained apropos of his students, "a certain respectfulness and sometimes polish in their manners, that recommended them especially to older persons and ladies. . . . So much was this the case," he continued, "that merchants gave them the preference for positions in their counting rooms and applied for them when they needed apprentices." [62] While Thayer no doubt approved of the work for establishing normal schools carried on by Mann and Barnard, his message to teachers contained in the

important address, "On Courtesy and Its Connexion with School Instruction," delivered before the American Institute of Instruction in 1840, carried
an unmistakable implication to large numbers of young teachers: it behooved
young men with professional aspirations but without formalized professional credentials to cultivate good manners as a compensation.[63] After his
retirement from Chauncey Hall in 1855 Thayer reiterated this stress
throughout his manual, *Letters to a Young Teacher*.[64]

The election of Thayer to the presidency of the American Institute of
Instruction at the very moment when regional teachers began to join the
association in relatively large numbers suggests more than a coincidence of
circumstance. Together with the other organizational developments which
the Institute experienced, Thayer's tenure marked the recognition by the
teaching profession that upright moral character as reflected in a young
man's cultivated manner had to be considered a professional qualification
alongside the fruits of formal training.

The development of more precise professional qualifications, which began
by stressing learning and ended by adding to that the role of tone, style and
manner, encompassed the contribution of the first generation of professional
teachers in America. By 1857 with the election of John D. Philbrick, the
superintendent of Boston public schools, to the presidency of the American
Institute of Instruction a whole new generation of teachers took charge of this
important association and of the teaching profession in general.[65] Unlike
their predecessors, this second generation did not have a similar opportunity
to develop and improve still further the occupation of teaching. Instead of
sustained activity spanning almost three decades, men like Philbrick and his
colleague in Connecticut, David N. Camp, had less than one. The work of
guiding the professional teacher had barely passed to the second generation
within the American Institute of Instruction when the Civil War not only
interrupted the trends set in motion by the first generation of the Institute,
but in a sense produced a fundamentally different set of circumstances for
the 1860s and 1870s. American educators after the Civil War faced problems
as fundamental as those of the Institute's founders in the 1830s and so
formidable that they threatened to nullify the gains achieved by 1860.

The changes, however, were not all a direct consequence of the war but in
fact had their genesis during the tenures of Emerson and Thayer themselves.
In 1849 George Emerson published his *History and Design of the American
Institute of Instruction* for the information of the many new members who had
no knowledge of the association's origins, early purposes or founders.[66] The
shift in personnel which this history implied began the process of accommodation to younger men with younger points of view. The Civil War's
effect upon the Institute's membership was, nonetheless, even beyond the
expectation or anticipation of this second generation itself. The immediate
effect of the war was to drain off many of the young men who had entered the

profession in the 1850s. Their teaching positions were filled by women who were paid half the salary of male teachers. After the conflict, competition with lower-paid female instructors compelled many young men to turn their energies to other occupations entirely. The Institute's membership, beginning with the admission of the first female teacher in 1867, experienced a rush of women teachers by the mid-1870s.[67] Many older teachers, especially superintendents and principals who had been adequately trained for their profession, accepted college professorships or transferred their supervisory talents to new business opportunities as administrators of insurance companies or executives of publishing companies.[68]

The membership changes in the American Institute of Instruction were not caused solely by the war's effect on the teaching profession in general. By the early 1870s the Institute itself was suffering its severest financial crisis. The association could no longer resort to wealthy philanthropists as it had done in the early years or in the later decades to teachers themselves who were achieving substantial increases in salary. When William Ticknor, a cousin of George Ticknor, died in 1864, the American Institute of Instruction lost its foremost financial benefactor. Ticknor had served for thirty years as the Institute's treasurer. During all that time he was also the publisher of the Institute's annual volume of lectures and proceedings, which constituted the association's major expense. This crisis passed in the 1870s when a soaring membership rate enabled the Institute to gather ample funds from the dues and donations of members alone. In the previous decade, from 1864 to 1874, new membership in the American Institute of Instruction averaged a respectable fifty-six persons annually. In 1875 new members totaled 227, in 1876 they were 230, in 1877 they numbered 457 and in 1878 there were 2,100 new members.[69] While this membership growth overcame the financial crisis of the 1870s, it caused a fundamental and lasting alteration in the Institute after 1880 and represented one of the major shifts in the history of the organization and of the teaching profession as well.

The phenomenal increase in the membership of the American Institute of Instruction after the war differed markedly in quality from the increases of previous decades, during which membership had never been solicited. Although Thayer had considered public participation a necessary element at the Institute's annual meetings, even he never advocated the admission of every person in attendance to the Institute's official membership. Beginning in 1875 with the presidency of Merrick Lyon, followed by that of Thomas Bicknell, the American Institute of Instruction developed numerous strategies to increase its membership to include as many persons as possible. Many who joined had no direct relation to the educational profession itself, a number being merely wives, husbands or parents of active teachers. To maintain and cultivate this increase in membership the directors of the Institute turned the annual meetings into a composite social affair and professional gathering. Amusements and recreation transformed Thayer's concern for manners as reflections of moral fiber into a less serious and more genteel observation of social amenities.

The seriousness of purpose and evangelical zeal which marked the work of professional teachers during the 1830s and 1840s had been eclipsed entirely by the 1870s when Thomas Bicknell established the custom of holding the annual meetings at resort towns like Saratoga Springs in New York, Fabyan House in the White Mountains and St. Albans in Vermont. This atmosphere set a lighter tone for the actual proceedings of the Institute. Popular recreations, like boat rides, humorous readings, quartet singing, picnics, mountain walks and band concerts replaced visitations to libraries, atheneums, colleges, schools—all activities which were common at the earlier meetings of the Institute. Paid lecturers and large money prizes from the Bicknell Fund—a tribute to that educator's ability to raise money—guaranteed popular curiosity, though not necessarily professional interest, in the Institute's lectures. If national notoriety was desired, Bicknell's strategies seemed to have been successful. In 1881 President Garfield accepted for himself, his Cabinet and their wives an invitation to attend the Institute's annual meeting that year.[70]

All these changes rapidly nullified the strategies, norms and purposes for which the American Institute of Instruction had been founded, and caused George Emerson to remark that the association should dissolve itself, since the organization, as originally conceived, had served its purpose.[71] Thayer had died in 1864, but in spite of his differences with Emerson, one suspects he would have agreed.

William A. Alcott

Rev. T. H. Gallaudet

Horace Mann

Rev. Samuel R. Hall

Cyrus Peirce

Henry Barnard

David N. Camp

George B. Emerson

Gideon F. Thayer

Nicholas Tillinghast

Marshall Conant

Albert G. Boyden

Arthur C. Boyden

First State Normal School, Bridgewater, Mass., 1846

Bridgewater State Normal School, 1871

CHAPTER VI

The Guarantees of Voluntary Associations

The Harmony of Choice and Duty

There were three phases to the work of the first-generation schoolman. In the first (1825–1838) the Friends of Education found means of encouraging less privileged young men into public schoolrooms and legitimized arguments in behalf of a profession of teachers. This first phase was dominated by young men in their thirties whose careers were already or were about to be established by their own educational and social advantages. Their educational thinking favored the extension of scientific and philosophical instruction to wider publics. However, their educational contribution usually fell short of actual instruction in public schools. Thus in the second stage (1830–1850) those first attracted to the actual work of instruction in its new professional trappings carried on through the economic crisis of 1837–1838 and into the 1840s. By the end of that decade a new accommodation had been made to a third and more rural grouping and to a new professional style. That new pedagogy appropriated the evangelical techniques of gospel missionaries and sought out still wider publics. In the final stage (1850–1860) the center of the profession was still an association, the American Institute of Instruction, but the workhorse agency of professional recruitment and training was the teachers' institute. In different ways the profession had been carried to midcentury by successive combinations of professional teachers, in the name of training moral character, through some form of voluntary association.

By 1860 one can detect mounting reservations over the nature and service of voluntary associations, especially in the association at the heart of the profession, the American Institute of Instruction. In its earliest assistance to the teacher, the voluntary association was a town organization, the lyceum. By the 1830s it had acquired a more partisan purpose and for maximum effectiveness had attached itself to a permanent institution, in one important case to the Teacher's Seminary at Andover, Massachusetts. In the wake of the economic crisis and the slow start of the normal school at the end of the 1830s, the teachers' institute became a revitalized and still more specialized extension of the lyceum's lineage. It also separated off from any permanent institution and claimed its own particular autonomy. In addition, the American Institute of Instruction gravitated toward the more didactic teachers' institute and away from the learned society as a model of professional association. Within such associations the earliest efforts of the first generation saw scientific exchange and philosophical disquisition to be the essence of professional practicality; the later efforts of this generation stressed simplified technique and immediate application, whatever the underlying theory, as the higher practicality of their profession. Through the 1850s schoolmen had relied on the voluntary association to transmit both versions of practical pedagogy.

Throughout these institutional changes the voluntary association was deemed the preferred social agency for developing the professional teacher's moral potential, that is, his character. In the process of training character the profession sought to harmonize the potentially conflicting demands of personal choice and professional duty.[1] In the best of times but particularly in the profession's nascent stages, moral character could not be inculcated simply or finally from one person to a group. A flexible organization, sensitive to the different views of its members, permitted the force of one group, morally united, to shape character without undue coercion. That was the essential service of the voluntary association in the minds of professional schoolmen. In this period no one even considered the adjective "voluntary" to imply a grant of license. Similarly no one assumed at any given moment that all choices within an association's aegis were equal in significance or priority. The very fact of association recognized these implicit limits.

In the professional literature there were ambiguities about the nature of voluntary associations which were analogous to the ambiguities about the personal choices of professional schoolmen. Those personal choices Chapter III of this study explored by focusing on the career choice of Horace Mann. Now I propose to examine the other side of the professional ideology, the intellectual patterns which ritualized thought about the nature of its institutions. In those discussions about institutional forms one can grasp their sense of professional necessity, the values and activities which had to endure apart from any single individual's discretion. From the vantage points of Chapters

III and V the analysis should provide some understanding of the unity which nineteenth-century teachers sought to forge between individual choice and professional responsibility. Since both considerations were regularly muted, I have centered attention here on a historical moment when a distinguished schoolman, William Russell, chose interests other than those of his associated fellows. His justification of the maneuver offered paradoxically the weakest yet clearest rationale of the voluntary association. Just before the Civil War his defense emerged as the final contribution of the first-generation schoolmen to their professional literature. Behind that contribution one should see not only the limitations of their institutional insight but also the awkward beginnings of a counter-preference toward bureaucratization which would characterize their second-generation successors.

Internal dissent, overt criticism from members in good standing, always tested the strength of any voluntary association. Although few teachers' organizations ever made their internal problems public, there were ways for members to register professional dissatisfaction. Serious reservations appeared as "suggestions" and the gravest "suggestions" were published. One of the most significant instances of such critical comment was William Russell's essay which he delivered to the American Institute of Instruction in 1856 and which he was allowed to insert in the appendix of the Institute's annual volume. "Has our courage," Russell asked, "been one of *uniform* and *obvious* progress in the advancement of the theory of education? Have our aims been sufficiently *definite?* Have our measures been duly *systematic?* Have they been sufficiently *practical?* Have we not been too much inclined to be contented with the *social* enjoyment of our annual meetings, as a professional festivity?" [2] The questions sound mild to the ears of a more contentious century, but just before the Civil War they struck at the heart of the profession, for the American Institute of Instruction then was incontestably the most prominent voluntary association of teachers and the central organization of professional schoolmen in America.

Implicitly Russell's inquiry challenged the association at its most sensitive point: could it do its duty practically and yet remain as voluntary as it had been? Generally speaking, such a public call for an examination of conscience was singular in the 1850s. Traditionally differences of opinion had been neither aired nor directly confronted, since professionals thought dissention spawned other voluntary associations. The previous pattern followed a different course from that implied by Russell's remarks. When Horace Mann persevered over his critics, the Boston schoolmasters, in 1844–1845, his triumph was a pyrrhic one, since the dissidents immediately reorganized in 1848 into the Massachusetts State Teachers Assocation.[3] In addition, a large number of active public grammar school teachers, most of them from Boston, withdrew from the American Institute of Instruction—a serious blow, since their numbers had assured the Institute a marked degree of professional influence. And again, shortly thereafter, some of the remaining Institute members responded to another call (in 1849), which proposed to organize in Philadelphia another national association similar in intent to the Institute's founding principles of 1830. The Philadelphia convention founded the American Association for the Advancement of Education and elected Horace Mann its first president.[4] Although many of those gathered in Philadelphia retained membership in the Institute, such occurrences were bound to weaken further the older association. The Philadelphia organization did not survive a decade, but while it lasted and after, calls to national conventions continued. The institutional patterns of this period seem to have witnessed more exercise of volition among professional schoolmen than dutiful deference to the needs of teachers as a professional body.

William Russell played important roles in several of these ventures and in 1856 tried once again to reinvigorate the American Institute of Instruction with his extraordinary appeal for open self-criticism. His commanding role in the founding of the Institute in 1830 and his national reputation in the profession of teaching made him one of the few persons who could offer these "suggestions" without risking damage to his own reputation. Still, his commanding role was insufficient to redirect the Institute to its 1830 viewpoint. Russell then initiated another call for a national convention of teachers, once again in Philadelphia. After modest beginnings, this additional organization became the National Teachers Association, one of three groups eventually to form the National Education Assocation.[5] In 1857, however, Russell's concern was, as always, over the moral impact, not the survival or membership rolls, of the organization. Before exploring the import of this pattern of founding voluntary associations, it may be enlightening to consider how Russell came to raise these objections and why his solution established another national association so similar in structure and aim to the American Institute of Instruction.

In 1856 Russell's suggestions to the American Institute of Instruction were threefold: "more definiteness, more system, and more direct efficiency." However, his commentary did not call for more exclusiveness in professional ranks nor did his remedy include the abandonment of the voluntary association as a professional form. He wanted a *more* definite, systematic and efficient organization in order to ensure that the association maintain its professional yet voluntary harmony of goals, needs and procedures. He assured the Institute that all these aims could be achieved by the adoption of one measure, namely, "the appointment by the President, by the vote of the Directors, or by that of the members generally, of committees to furnish annual reports on subjects assigned." [6] These reports, he continued, "would have as much systematic form as lectures, and at the same time, the practical and familiar character of discussions, and would avoid the vagueness of the former and the evanescent impression of the latter." This newer and more refined mode of education sharpened the professional nature of the voluntary association: "The diffusion of the principles inculcated in the lectures and reports, and the practical suggestions accompanying them," Russell was confident, "would have a most happy effect in aiding unity of views and harmony of methods, in the work of teaching." [7]

For schoolmen concerned with practical efficiency Russell here and elsewhere seemed remarkably indifferent to the means for achieving his ends. Explicitly he says that the committee is the essential means; the appointment of committee members is an immaterial procedure. Similarly throughout Russell's long career he worked with three very different types of professional institutions, all of which bore the designation "institute." After his first school teaching in Georgia, he moved during the 1820s to and through the eastern seaboard towns of New Haven, Philadelphia and Boston. By 1830 he had taught the range of positions from private tutor and classical academy instructor to the female seminary principal.[8] In 1830 he helped launch the first national association of professional schoolmen, the American Institute of Instruction. In the 1840s he was instrumental in the promotion of the revival-like teachers' institutes. And intermittently from the 1840s to the end of his career in 1873 he conducted private normal schools, first in Reed's Ferry, New Hampshire and later at Lancaster, Massachusetts. His normal schools were described as seminaries and known first as the Merrimack Normal Institute and later as the New England Normal Institute.[9] In retrospect it is clear that these three brands of professional institutions—the national association, the revival-like meeting and the professional training school—had different purposes, arrangements and clienteles. However, the important point here is that in the nineteenth century schoolmen spent little time dwelling upon and refining such institutional differences. For the most part they accepted an overall professional harmony among many, quite varied operations to improve teaching, a harmony which neither admitted nor denied the differences between given institutions. Only when the harmony itself was threatened did suggestions like Russell's surface and call attention to the professional assumptions which underlay the institutional promotion of professional character training.

Russell's comments dramatize how intense was the schoolman's concern for professional harmony. Neither he nor his fellow teachers were anti-institutional, as so many historians of this period have claimed. They labored for a manifest and not a transcendental unity and knew that it was somehow contingent upon the organizations they designed. One has only to look at the extraordinary number of manuals for school governance, for techniques of instructions, for building and architectural design to be aware of their overweening respect for the formalities of education.[10] What makes their institutional sensibilities seem so misshapen and queer is their apparent ignorance or at least their silence about institutional consequences. Like Russell, they do *not* assume that the more different the views within a committee the less likely that their reports will be harmonious. In fact, the pattern of their thinking is exactly the reverse. The more diverse the views in a committee, an association, a meeting, a seminary, an institute of any kind—the more likely the product would be a healthy, practical and harmonious point of view. Russell's desire for practical efficiency was not a call for a greater technical precision and less personal discretion in institutional functions. In a real sense, his argument for national unity among teachers at the American Institute of Instruction and later at the National Teachers Association assumed that the proper professional harmony was a result of *more* voluntary activity rather than less.

The opposite of professional volition in the nineteenth century was seldom if ever coercion or involuntary prodding. The very role of the teacher, whatever the professional institution, implied a process in which the teacher exercised discretion to develop students in certain ways. Turning students toward the principles of learning resulted, they believed, in the habituation of the mind to the right methods of self-instruction. It was no paradox for them to see that education made a student more self-possessed. Instead of making the student an imitator of his teacher, proper pedagogy produced a person more independent and free to choose for himself. The art of teaching, Russell claimed, enumerating the educational advantages of teachers' associations, included "the most successful methods of imparting knowledge or rather of constituting the mind, as far as possible, its own instructor." The "faithful teacher" possessed a command of subject as well as "the means of operating on conscience and bringing the young mind under an early feeling of the principle of duty, that it may possess the power of self-direction and self-government. . . . In one word," he concluded, "the teacher must acquire skill in managing the mind: his must be 'the gentle hand that can lead the elephant with a hair.' " [11] Resorting to the rod became the practical teacher's admission of incompetence. The gentle hand of the teacher may take a student where he would not have gone on his own accord, yet the rerouting of pupils, done gently, was no infringement or impediment to the proper training of character.

The institutions which best inculcated character and a habit of moral choice were thought to be those with the widest and most diverse sphere of influence. Not surprisingly, the first generation of professional schoolmen, Russell among them, looked to associations like the American Institute of Instruction as the central organization of their work.[12] The national association was as essential to the teaching profession as education itself was to all other attainments.[13] Russell could well assert for educational associations what he claimed for professional teachers: "Their knowledge ought to be the fruit of professional research and extensive reading. They lay the foundation of all attainments. They first put in motion the secret springs of thought. The great living fabric of mental character generally owes much of its strength and symmetry to the patient labors of those who watch over and guide the first stages of its advancement." [14] The voluntary association embodied in purest institutional form the genteel and patient style which so conditioned other institutional norms of the early schoolmen. Professional teachers were concerned with the initial habits of thought rather than their further consequences, with their earliest rather than their later functions. As with the "choice" of a career, starting out was always a more pressing concern than actual or ultimate achievement.[15] Indeed the willingness to be trained for right choice itself became the most discernible and incontestably "worthy" option among professional schoolmen and students in general by mid-century.[16]

At no point did Russell's suggestions to the American Institute of Instruction demand a shift of course. What he required was more effort and exertion along paths established earlier. He called attention to the great enemy within professional ranks, the degeneration of the association's activities to the level of a festivity. The Institute required not new aims and plans but an enlarged purpose. Although the Institute had never before employed committees the way Russell proposed, Russell implied that he endorsed the underlying purpose rather even than the committee form itself. Without the sense of initiation and renewal, indeed with its opposite, self-satisfaction and contentment, the very success of the Institute's twenty-seven-year accomplishments would undermine the worth of its service. Although perhaps more academic and scholarly in his assumption than many of his fellow professionals, Russell had earlier clarified the essential spirit of professional work when he asserted: "Teachers ... must be men of study—of hard-earned acquirement. They must not be content with superficial knowledge; they must exhaust subjects—not merely enter on them." [17] The practical remedy for the ills of self-indulgence and contentment was an institution with "Extended usefulness, ... one coextensive with our national interests and relations." [18] Professional efficiency and practicality implied to Russell's mind tangible and pressing demands which required the assent of different yet cooperative professionals. Institutions at their best were energizers more than yardsticks of achievement.

Behind these notions of professional choice and voluntary institutions lay Russell's notions of rational training. A profession emerged not merely from a scientific body of literature, nor from organizations where ideas were exchanged and exhausted; it came into being with a collective habit or structure of thought. Grounded in the Scottish philosophy of George Jardine with whom he studied at the University of Glasgow, Russell developed his philosophy of "human culture." [19] Largely derivative of John Locke, Russell's philosophy nevertheless denied the malleability of the mind suggested by Locke's metaphor, tabula rasa. Senses conditioned the mind, Russell con-

ceded, but they were not the sole causes of its development. The susceptibil-
ity of all minds to sense knowledge suggested to Russell a larger principle,
a universal law of learning. Any given mind became an individualized variation on the general law of knowing rather than a phenomenon which sense
experience uniquely shaped. Professional training precluded a mental fix
upon either these principles or upon the particular experiences; instead, it
implied a mental culture, a continuing associative exercise of the mind, one
which dwelt on the relations between both. The product was scientific,
meaning for Russell a refusal to acknowledge the authority of principles over
particulars or vice versa.

The all-important committees of a national teachers' association addressed
themselves to the essential interrelations of higher laws and particular
methods. Once discovered—here Russell developed his theory beyond
Jardine[20]—these interrelations formed a distinct science of the mind tailored
to a particular form of work, in this case, teaching. There was thus a different
but analogous science of the mind for every work, a claim which considerably advanced the notions of teaching as a profession, equal to but distinct
from the established professions. Best of all, these newer sciences were easily
transmitted even to untutored minds. Although without full understanding
of the "upper spheres of science," young men pursuing the newer professions "would not be unwilling to be ranked but as among the 'lesser lights,'
and . . . have no ambition beyond that of contributing their silent personal
endeavor to the advancement of knowledge and to the instruction of youth,
yet have minds fraught with untold wealth of acquirement, which they would
readily lend for the profit and pleasure of others less amply furnished." [21] In
his effort to fashion a scientific and harmonious profession Russell pressed
himself to the unusual admission that some members would become more
proficient in scientific inquiry and would endorse the desired harmony more
strenuously and practically than others. The inequities of choice and the
barely muted class distinctions here were not further discussed. Like their
corollaries, diversity and controversy, uneven choices and unequal opportunity comprised the human condition. It was never completely clear to
schoolmen how much these limitations could be controlled or shaped to their
advantage.

By 1856 the American Institute of Instruction no longer sympathized with
several of Russell's notions. In particular, the Institute members ended their
tolerance of three facets of Russell's style which they had originally con-
doned with apparent ease. Russell's willingness to notice class distinctions
within the profession, his emphasis upon intellectual discipline in "human
culture," and his aggressive manner of inquiry reflected his own foreign
origins and training. The cosmopolitan founders of the American Institute of
Instruction were less preoccupied with the implications of these characteristics than were the "lesser lights" who came into control of the association just

before the Civil War. The men of George Ticknor's circle such as Russell himself, George B. Emerson, William C. Woodbridge and others had strongly endorsed such ideas when they publicized the teachings of Johann Pestalozzi.[22] In fact, Pestalozzi became known early in America first through the *American Journal of Education* (Boston, 1827–1839) which William Russell began and edited for three years and, second, through the published lectures of the Institute itself.[23] Russell's own sentiments shaped by his fellow Scotsman, George Jardine, shared many points with the Swiss instructor Pestalozzi, particularly an emphasis on oral and object teaching over bookish and rote instruction.[24] However, the educational biases prevalent among the university men who interpreted Pestalozzi to America favored primarily the Swiss educator's ideas of mental discipline. Only in a few cases before the Civil War did Pestalozzi's American followers apply his teachings as Pestalozzi intended, adapting educational methods to the poor in populated areas and using them to erode class barriers.[25] Generally, like William Russell, the founders of the American Institute of Instruction employed Pestalozzi to criticize and reject a mechanized pedagogy and to create a new role for schoolroom textbooks.[26] By the 1850s Pestalozzi and Russell had lost their credit with a new brand of professional schoolmen who, lacking university advantages yet coveting professional work, trained their attention away from the poor, from service to populated areas and from any sense of the social values within their work.

Russell's educational purposes were always more grand than the operations and achievements of his institutions. The American Institute of Instruction must have demonstrated quickly its intransigence to his suggestions; it failed apparently to energize its collective will, to cultivate "all invigorating and purifying influences in human development," to enlarge and fertilize "the whole field of mental and moral culture," [27] for, one year later Russell participated in the founding of the National Teachers Association. Perhaps appropriately Russell's grand vision caused him more difficulty than it did the American Institute of Instruction. In an address to the National Teachers Association at its first meeting in 1857 Russell assumed an uncharacteristically defensive posture. There he explained how this new venture was neither competitive nor exclusive nor selfish with regard to other educational associations. Whatever its other merits his defense demonstrated how difficult it was on a professional plane to realize one's own version of choice, if it varied from the collective priorities of an organization. Russell's address showed that it was no easy matter, organizational problems aside, to found other associations more conducive to his interests. His earlier commitment to the American Institute of Instruction continued to inform much of his activity in the 1850s, for he always seemed to appreciate the merits of earlier norms rather than the possibilities of the newer purposes of the National Teachers Association. Within the professional association of the nineteenth century there operated a particular set of controls which screened and preferred one type of voluntary activity over another, however voluntary each organization professed to be. Their breadth of moral purpose and the unspecified limits upon professional activity often obscured rather than enhanced the process of changing institutional directions. Russell clearly sensed an aberration from older professional values but perceived no clear procedures within the profession to guide his discontent. In the face of this dilemma how could imbalances be redressed, when did professional schoolmen counsel patience in preference to either internal reform or the extreme measure of founding a new association?

Genteel Competition

The importance of Russell's address to the National Teachers Association lay in its novel recognition of competitive diversity as a professional problem. Within teaching and most professions before midcentury men accepted diversity as a local fact of life. Competition among institutions, of course, existed earlier but local exigencies were invoked convincingly to argue the peculiar merits of any new institution.[28] The potential problem of this tactic became explicit when competing organizations emerged on the national level. There the argument which exploited local exigencies and different clienteles no longer applied, since the contextual locale was not local. The peculiar service of a new national organization, similar to existing associations, became extremely difficult to establish. The membership of the American Institute of Instruction and the National Teachers Association overlapped, and the organizational features of structure and policy were not different enough to make plausible distinctions between them. When Russell defended the new organization in Philadelphia, he had anticipated more than accusations of exclusiveness, competitiveness and selfishness. He had embarked upon a defense of the crucial assumption, so dear to the first generation, that a professional teacher trained to the goal of moral character would not thwart the harmony of professional aims in favor of other motives.

Implicitly Russell had accepted a distinction between local and professional diversity. Schoolmen seldom became overly preoccupied with any justifications of one method of instruction and organization over another. Even the much criticized use of the rod was occasionally acknowledged as a necessity in certain situations. Professional disagreements carefully maintained a polite, hypothetical tone. The exigencies of any practical situation were always left to determine the ultimate refinements of every plan of governance. All plans of governance, whether for national associations or local schools, took for granted their cooperative spirit because of the harmony which supposedly infused each particular educational arrangement.

However, Russell's comments began to suggest that the national association had a peculiar responsibility in clarifying the area of professional consensus. Its duties seemed to precede in importance the operations of any particular school. Moreover, the founding of another national association of teachers raised practical questions about the nature of this professional forum. If the vaunted harmony of the profession informed more than one national association, where might the most fundamental professional differences be aired with candor yet without controversy? Could the teaching profession condone as much diversity within its corporate structure as educational practices did in their accommodations of local conditions? On the other hand, could teachers demand a more explicit harmony, if education were essentially a voluntary activity?

Russell did not cast the problem that specifically or that boldly. Indeed he took great pains to avoid any implicit or explicit suggestion that the smooth surface of the profession was beginning to crack. The appearance of the new association represented, in Russell's terms, the most normal development of the professional schoolman's work. "We feel," he explained, "that, as a professional body, we are distinctly called on to form a national organization, that we may be the better enabled to meet the continually enlarging demands of our vocation for higher personal attainments to the individual, and for more ample qualification adequately to fill the daily widening sphere of professional action." [29] He could have said as much about any "institute" in his career. In the context of his recent efforts to reawaken the American Institute of Instruction to its original purposes Russell's speech was anything but normal.

In spite of his effort to make the founding of another national association appear to be one stage in a process of growth and maturation, Russell had begun with his 1857 address the reformulation of his generation's basic assumptions about professional institutions. The familiar acknowledgment of older professional values in his introductory remarks became an effort to discuss a new and difficult problem with the long-standing conceptions concerning education as character formation. For him differences of institutional structure and arrangements reflected the various formative experience of a given schoolman. He could apply the term "institute" to a national association, to an established training school and to a temporary meeting for reviving teachers' professional élan without feeling any obligation to account for the varied policies and programs of these distinct institutions. The key conditioning factors of any formal process of instruction, professional or otherwise, were the local context and moral character of the principle schoolman. When he faced the potential criticism of fostering competition, selfishness and exclusiveness, Russell carried his assumptions about the relations between institutions and the inculcation of character to their furthest limits. His appeal to peculiar, moral dimensions of his work only repeated old assertions. It did not meet the actual issue, namely, how the new agency was peculiarly moral, what the nature of the institution was. He tried to meet an institutional problem with the rhetoric of moral character which had always effectively been used analogously to mute local crises.

Russell's dilemma suggested not only how seldom his generation had confronted the possibility of fundamental yet legitimate differences of opinion within the profession; it indicated as well how little the rhetoric of moral choice and voluntary discretion actually prepared professional schoolmen for serious divergences from professional ideas. Only infrequently were the brief histories of so many educational institutions in the nineteenth century a cause for alarm among professional schoolmen or, for that matter, the public at large.[30] Like other voluntary associations, colleges and schools of this century expanded quickly and died more often than they survived. Equally commonplace was it for institutions to close operations in one locale and to open again elsewhere with the same faculty, students and official purposes.[31] Just as often as they died or moved, they stayed in the same place and became in a sense a different institution with each change of president or principal. An enormous diversity flourished and yet the underlying assumptions about this complex and tenuous brand of institutional life (can one call it institutional development?) had little to do with any appreciation of how much diversity a profession or a democratic society could sustain. Midnineteenth-century notions about the emergence of unique, individual characters fashioned a professional harmony which at best tolerated rather than understood institutional diversity. In guaranteeing these notions the educational institutions of the period strove to become more voluntary. The very imprecision of these guarantees made institutional operations functionally (though not explicitly) more powerful and less susceptible to change and reform than the more impersonal and bureaucratized institutions which ultimately succeeded them at the end of the century.

Russell made no effort in his appeal to professional harmony to reconcile the consequences of his action with any theory or philosophy of social or professional functions. Instead, he satisfied himself with claims for the peculiarity of the new association: ". . . we have at length recognized our peculiar duty to come forward and take our own appropriate place as the immediate agents and appointed organs of whatever measures are best adopted to promote the highest interest of society, by the wider diffusion of whatever benefits are included in the whole range of human culture."[32] He never explained who determined the "appropriate place" or the mitigating factors which made this duty peculiar. Close upon these claims, nevertheless, he insisted: "In stepping forward to take the professional position now universally accorded us, we do so in no exclusive or selfish spirit. . . . We are, in fact," he continued, "only complying with the virtual invitation given us, by all who feel an interest in the advancement of education, to assume, in regular form, the acknowledged responsibilities of our office, as guardians of the mental welfare of the youth of our country, responsible to the whole community for the fidelity and efficiency with which we discharge our trust." [33] Russell wriggled in the grasp of his dilemma: if he argued that the National Teachers Association was a better means than other national agencies, his effort would be patently competitive and self-interested; if the new organization was not performing an exclusive role with a special service, its sponsors were merely duplicating an effort performed elsewhere. Most of all, the failure to explain the nature of the institution, how it could be peculiar but not exclusive skirted the key question, Why was the new national association necessary in 1857?

Russell's own generation had designed several conditions, consonant with their goal of character formation, to preclude burdensome competition and controversy such as Russell's own 1857 venture. In his explanation to the National Teachers Association Russell used them all deftly. The new national association had admitted forty-three schoolmen from thirteen states and Washington, D.C. and welcomed further professionals from those states and others not represented.[34] New associations appeared to arise spontaneously, to draw no pejorative distinctions among other groups of schoolmen and to endorse a professional harmony. Not only was their welcome open, the new group met a popular call, which underscored a self-evident need and ostensibly muted any possibility of self-interestedness. The founders of the National Teachers Association had not sought this duty themselves but had merely responded to a want among the country's schoolmen. The diversity of the membership and a collective call intimated that the new group reflected a widespread movement rather than a scheme of self-seeking schoolmen.

The important argument for a new institution was always more explicitly moral than those conditions of wide support and popular request. Any laxity in the professional fiber boded ill for the health and future of teachers. The festive airs of the American Institute of Instruction had suggested an overconfidence and lack of seriousness which slackened their resolve to educate properly. "The whole ground of education," Russell exhorted, "needs a thorough survey and revision, with a view to much more extensive changes and reforms than have yet been attempted." This renovation, however, did not imply "the indiscriminate subversion of existing modes of culture or . . . institutions. . . ." [35] Russell focused upon the loftier motives by separating them from the crasser concerns with immediate institutional forms of inculcating character. This deft shift immediately raised questions about the motives of any critic of the newer association. Russell quickly exploited his advantage: "It belongs to others than teachers," he asserted with loaded innocence, "to propose those rash and headlong changes unsanctioned by true philosophy or stable theory, which have demolished without reconstructing, and where toppling fabrics have served the sole purpose of forming the sepulchral monuments of 'zeal without knowledge.' " [36] Any critic of the National Teachers Association had to assume more than an intellectual burden. In assuming any critical stance, he marked himself as unprofessional and questionably moral. If division occurred, the accused party was not responsible. Their intentions and initiatives were more benevolent and sublime. Without ever defining the new basis of the National Teachers Association, Russell created with his "moral" argument a foundation distinct from the basis of the American Institute of Instruction.

Each sally toward a sharp institutional distinction quickly turned and became an additional endorsement of the cooperative spirit among professional organizations. Thus this "broader" and "more extensive" scope of the National Teachers Association, Russell felt, was the opposite of a "withdrawal from the ground which we have hitherto occupied." This effort implied no "exclusive organization, to cut ourselves off from all communication beyond the limited sphere of a close corporation." [37] "In no such spirit," he emphasized, "would we act." Nevertheless, the organization of this other national body was "distinctly called"—taking no responsibility for competitive initiatives—by a professional commitment. The intimation he left unspoken remained, of course, that the National Teachers Association's version of "profession" was simultaneously undated and more encompassing than that of other institutions also "nobly engaged in promoting the interests of education." [38] The major difference, Russell explained, lay with the National Teachers Association's clearer notion of how to guarantee the advancement of individual and professional qualifications.

In earlier years the guarantees of professional improvement had been left to the spontaneous and natural force of moral character, or so the professional rhetoric insisted. Russell's appeal to this notion of character in the American Institute of Instruction, however, dramatized the limitations of this form of improvement. Some versions of character development did lead to unharmonious consequences which words had no power to reform. Russell seemed to know something more was required, but he took much on himself to explain how means other than character could ensure character development. Further, he had to discuss how these guarantees would work without creating an "exclusive" and "close corporation," how he could keep any new institution as professional and voluntary as the earlier ones were thought to have been. In a sense, he met these objections by helping found the National Teachers Association. In the process he altered his older notions, or at least he altered an older professional style which never required him to define explicitly the assumptions behind moral character as a professional ideal. The result·was a new set of assumptions about the key institution of professional teachers, the expansive, voluntary association with a national sweep.

The scope of the voluntary association as an institutional type, schoolmen began to concede, affected its peculiar service to the profession of teachers. The wider the scope the greater the usefulness, their argument ran, and yet with ever enlarged membership came the necessity to manage professional differences *within* the association. Formal, internal divisions shaped procedures for preventing unprofessional contentiousness at the center of the profession. On a national level, where the problem of professional diversity became explicit, the harmony of the profession demanded functionally and symbolically a single organization. "A national association of teachers," Russell explained, "will necessarily give rise to an appropriate organ of communication between its members themselves, and the community in general." [39] "By this means," he argued, "the fruits of the maturest minds in the ranks of our profession, in the ample discussion of the great primary questions of education, may be daily reaped by the youngest of our corps, while the zeal and enthusiasm, and the ardent aspirations of the youngest, may communicate life and fire to all." [40] Through the committees of the association and the participation of nationally recognized schoolmen like Louis Agassiz and Arnold Guyot, the "lesser lights" (Russell's designation) could be guaranteed competent guidance.[41] The nature of this guidance as well as the nature of the voluntary association had begun to rest upon something other than the inculcation of character. The class divisions and social arrangements preceding instruction were raised (though were not explored) in Russell's 1857 speech. The teachers' association, now an "organ of communication," had gone beyond its earlier duties of mutual instruction of professionals, whether their lights were greater or lesser. Whether or not they had ever been otherwise, Russell's allegiances and those of his fellow founders shifted to maturer minds and "those who have made a life-time's business of education." [42]

The newer national association would guarantee a new professional style formulated by the most philosophical and maturest minds of the profession. Widening the range of action provided not only "fellowship and sympathy in common labors and common interests, but [a scene] . . . of peculiar and elevated intellectual advancement and gratification." [43] The new qualities were imperative if teachers and their profession were even to be properly voluntary, self-governing. Russell developed this point by discussing appreciatively an analogy with "scientific associations, with their strict classification of subjects, their brief practical papers, and special committees." The merits of this analogy illuminated the etymological meaning of "profession." His explanation of "profession" began with its "university origins and applications" and ended with a confident assertion of the "new relations" implied by the "liberal profession." "In other vocations persons of any class might enter at will, but for admission to the ranks of the liberal callings a previous profession of qualifications, and correspondent examination and license, were indispensable." [44] This screening process would also reflect the wisdom of the maturest minds of the profession. He hardly need add that that eventuality would also institutionalize the social and educational norms of those National Teachers Association founders who convinced teachers of the need for such professional choices.

The voluntary character of teachers' associations had seldom remained long voluntary for all members. In most of these organizations, for example, officers were nominated by small committees appointed by the incumbents. Most elections were unanimous, and few—none in the eighty-six-year history of the American Institute of Instruction—were contested.[45] The same held true for most national, state and local associations. Policy matters were dealt with similarly. The debates which Russell had felt were so time-consuming resulted at best in nonbinding resolutions of the members. The nature and tenor of any such voluntary association depended heavily on the unanimity of its members. Russell's effort to create a more harmonious and professional voluntary association followed the familiar pattern and quickly reached the ultimate step of founding a new association. Given a choice, he seemed to prefer a more voluntary to a more harmonious association. However, his pivotal issue for this measure impinged directly upon the nature of a voluntary association and by implication upon the process of founding them. For all his professed faith in the existing institutional structure of education, he could not preserve his older preference for a voluntary association at the center of his profession and at the same time establish another national association. Ultimately preferring the latter option, he made his newer institution become much more than "an organ of communication." If it actually fell short of becoming a certification center, the National Teachers Association did at least try to guarantee a "scientific" rather than a voluntary consensus of the best educational ideas and practices.

This new professional purpose formalized a distinction between scientific and voluntary notions of education, which earlier schoolmen thought to be compatible and informally related. Russell's version of science connoted a thorough understanding of the empirical *and* theoretical aspects of education. Science brought no moral assurance to professional choice but it did indicate a deliberation and care that Russell found lacking in the untutored. His science was not experimental but synthetic and, though empirical, his assumptions did not coincide with positivistic modes of inquiry which were becoming increasingly popular in the intellectual circles of the nineteenth century.[46] By the 1850s Russell stressed science as a means of curbing precipitous choices among schoolmen. It antedated professional preparation as preparation itself antedated professional teaching. The process seemed regressive rather than progressive. Poor teaching required not supervised practice but previous preparation; poor preparation required not greater natural talent but meticulous study earlier. Once the principles were learned, then one could become prepared, then one could practice teaching, then one could engage fully in the work of the professional schoolman. The new formalities enlarged and defined a greater and greater distance between the first aspiration of a young man to teach and his ultimate successful governance of a school.

Similarly a starker and more formal separation evolved between the work of the professional teacher on the local and on the national scenes. Professional associations on the national level, Russell now proposed, would adopt a new brand of inquiry, would refine the art and science of education and would generate a reasonable agreement upon their basic principles. This role also established an important distinction between such "scientific" inquiry and the actual practice of instruction in local "institutes." Educational institutions on both local and national levels became more aware of their significant structural differences. Consequently the term "institute" itself became more narrowly applied and new terms—kindergarten, high school, university—developed to reflect the special purposes of particular institutions within school systems. The general effort to keep education decently voluntary, for teachers and students alike, gradually began to disappear. By the end of the 1860s and thereafter Russell's successors did not take up his torch and make the national association the scientific body he envisioned. Rather, they turned enthusiastically to the local level of practical instruction where they hoped to do something more fundamental and scientific than the formulation of general scientific principles. Instead, they planned to organize the evidence upon which those scientific principles would be based. In their hands the center of the profession shifted from the national associations to the normal schools.

The national association continued to play a visible, if no longer a pivotal, role in the teachers' work. Both the American Institute of Instruction and other latecomers to the national scene failed to realize the full significance of the practicing teachers in their membership until the mid-1880s. Between 1860 and 1890 the membership of the National Teachers Association and the American Institute of Instruction reflected the interests of the forty-three members who had gathered in Philadelphia in 1857. The majority of the schoolmen who listened to Russell but who did not heed his directives were second-generation schoolmen, men like James P. Wickersham, Daniel Hagar, Thomas W. Valentine and J. W. Bulkley.[47] Many of these men were connected, like Russell, to normal school teaching, but, unlike Russell's experience, their schools were public, accountable to state or city governments. These schools were integers in school systems, not self-sufficient entities able to concentrate their primary attention upon moral development. The younger men did not discount Russell's particular viewpoint and yet their duties made it almost a foregone conclusion that Russell would become as disenchanted with the National Teachers Association as he had been with the American Institute of Instruction. For the last sixteen years of his life, from 1857 to 1873, there is no evidence that Russell ever again participated in a national convention of teachers.

CHAPTER VII

From Inspiration to Domestication: The Operational Centers of the Schoolman's Profession, 1840–1890

The Normal School Principal: Two Generations

Between 1830 and 1890 schoolmen had created at least two institutional models of their professional work. One accommodated the outwardly loose, voluntary forms and evangelical ideas of ante-bellum America; the other, directed by faithful lieutenants in the second generation, attempted to routinize the best aspects of their mentors' views into professional custom. In the ante-bellum period schoolmen centered their attention and activities in the large association with national pretensions, the American Institute of Instruction. From the initiatives in that body schoolmen sent forth through a network of teachers' institutes the most current, creative ideas about education. Their meetings, their facilities, their public and philanthropic support, their leadership and their explicit policies were as effective yet impermanent as any specific teaching position in their careers. By the late 1850s the larger and more central voluntary association, like the American Institute of Instruction, and the smaller, ubiquitous teachers' institutes, formed a single paradigm. However, this network had already begun to erode in the face of professional problems which it could not meet or settle. Even before the upheavals of the Civil War accentuated these problems and confirmed the various institutes, large and small, into more peripheral professional roles, the normal school had begun to assume a new function and place in the work of professional teachers. The second-generation schoolmen who engineered the significant shift of priorities and structure in the work of education between 1860 and 1890, nevertheless, continued to be hampered by the earlier evangelical roots of their profession.

In a sense, the nineteenth-century normal school always determined as its first priority the creation of a common, moral purpose out of the diverse needs and interests of school teachers. Even among those schoolmen who began to stabilize and focus the evangelical nature of professional teaching, one finds repeated educational sentiments of a quasi-religious or explicitly religious content. Albert G. Boyden whose forty-six-year principalship of the Bridgewater (Massachusetts) State Normal School did much to ensure the development of his institution as a professional type, insisted always that "the first normal school of which we have any record was opened in Palestine; its sessions were held upon the hills and plains of Galilee, Samaria and Judea." [1] In this context the school's first principal stressed "the inspiration of its students with the spirit of the true teacher, who has the spirit of service, and comes to his pupils as the Great Teacher comes to men, that they may have life and have it abundantly." [2] Such images ensured a common set of notions throughout the century for dealing with professional problems. However, professional reactions and refinements of such rhetoric were always more varied than the rhetoric itself. If their first-generation predecessors understood the normal school as a "standing teachers' institute," Boyden and his second-generation colleagues maintained at least the evangelical values of that formulation. Their subsequent contribution simply made other more prosaic and practical problems equally significant with those earlier ones of moral inspiration.

Professional problems assumed a more practical and formal cast after the Civil War because of the altered relationships within the educational profession as a whole. Throughout the 1830s and 1840s professional schoolmen who called for improved teaching possessed clearer ideas of professional behavior than their successors after the war. In many instances their own social origins and educational advantages in academies and colleges established a functional though unofficial professional style. At the head of key organizations and schools these men took for granted many assumptions which their less fortunate disciples had to defend and strive for outright. First-generation schoolmen like George Emerson and Cyrus Peirce, Thomas Gallaudet and William Russell all assumed that professional training began after maximum levels of scholarship had been achieved. Their focus fixed upon problems of moral inspiration and the governing tone of schools rather than problems of status, social class and opportunity which determined financial resources and study time in preparation for professional work. Indeed the educational goal of moral character had succeeded before the Civil War because the habits of thought it spawned skirted those mundane yet formidable considerations in all open, professional discussions. Moreover, the first generation could rely on voluntary associations to carry on their work efficiently, precisely because they assumed a manifest variety and inequality of talent. Distinctions within a profession went unobserved publicly, because such recognition divided fellow members against each other. They took for granted inherent and conditional differences and took for granted that a proper professional élan would prod forward the improvable and enable the unfit to opt for employments more suitable to their abilities. Even by the 1850s when the weaknesses of these assumptions began to appear, the first generation would call only for invigorated resolution and more voluntary associations.

Actually, however, the very success of the evangelical impetus of educational reform was the most powerful factor in changing this viewpoint. The early schoolmen and their organizations drew into the work of teaching young men whose social status and origins were collectively less diverse than their own. The first generation contained a large number of men, moderately affluent and college trained; it also welcomed a second echelon of talent whose aspirations and prospects once made them hope for work in the established professions of medicine, law and the ministry; finally, a third echelon comprised young men distinguished for their personal drive and willingness to serve in a worthy social enterprise. By contrast, the second generation could boast fewer leaders with college degrees or affluence.[3] If ever they had the opportunity to attend college and pursue an obvious professional calling, these aspirations were frustrated, more and more, before college study had ever begun. The second generation drew its members largely from self-sufficient but not affluent farming regions (Table 5) and from the moderately fixed mechanical trades (Table 8).[4] During the 1850s the teachers' institutes plied regions farther and farther from the populated towns, searching for professional talent. For those years where information is available, normal schools like Bridgewater in Massachusetts drew in the 1850s some 64 percent of its students from the farms and mechanical trades of its own county, Plymouth, and nearby Bristol County (Tables 5 and 6).[5] The second generation had, in effect, expanded the third and lowest echelon of the first generation and reduced in later ranks the upper college-oriented groupings. These realignments explain much about the new professional needs and institutional paradigms of the postwar nineteenth century.

With more reason than their mentors, the second generation could take for granted a professional harmony of outlooks and values among their co-workers. The postwar normal schools housed faculties and students who together had experienced remarkably similar sets of educational and occupational experiences before entering upon teaching as a life career. The same had not been so for schoolmen one generation earlier in the 1830s and 1840s. Take for example, Cyrus Peirce's circuitous route to the principalship of the first normal school in America. Peirce had been ordained a minister

Table 5

Bridgewater Normal School Students: Origins by Massachusetts County, 1840–1876

Plymouth	702	Barnstable	132	Hampden	5
Bristol	381	Suffolk	99	Franklin	4
Norfolk	250	Essex	71	Hampshire	2
Worcester	170	Nantucket	37	Berkshire	2
Middlesex	162	Dukes	14		

Table 6

Bridgewater Normal School Students: U.S. and Foreign Origins, 1840–1876

Massachusetts	2,031	Kentucky	1
New Hampshire	100	Minnesota	2
Jaine	85	Michigan	1
Rhode Island	40	Colorado	1
Vermont	15	South Carolina	1
Connecticut	10	Alabama	1
New York	11	Texas	1
Pennsylvania	44	California	1
New Jersey	1	Canada	1
District of Columbia	2	Nova Scotia	3
Maryland	3	Burma	2
Ohio	3	Japan	1
West Virginia	1		
Illinois	2	*Total*	2,324

after graduating from Harvard and after three years' further preparatory study. He had been the youngest of a large farming family whose resources permitted him to study first at the Framingham Academy and then under the tutorship of a Reverend Dr. Stearns of Lincoln. His social views, especially his espousal of temperance, had clashed with his several congregations and culminated in a personal crisis over the ministerial role. After a decade in the ministry he turned to private schooling and to Nantucket where his efforts were finally both popular and lucrative. In 1837 he accepted a request to reform the Nantucket school system and on the merits of that work two years later Horace Mann solicited his talent for the principalship of the first normal school in America. In 1839 Peirce took up his third career, which in no small way drew upon his earlier pursuits, one professional, the other profitable.[6]

The early normal school principals had all experienced several important features reflected in Peirce's career. Before the late 1850s they had all achieved reputations of successful teaching in colleges, private academies or in well-established, select schools. Like Peirce, the principals of the other early Massachusetts normal schools came from strong academic traditions. At Barre (later Westfield) the first principal, the Reverend Samuel Phillips Newman, came to the training of teachers from Bowdoin College's faculty where he had taught first Greek, then Latin, then political economy.[7] His successor, the Reverend Emerson Davis, had graduated from Williams College before designing a career as a minister and academy principal.[8] His tenure of office was succeeded by David S. Rowe, also a Bowdoin graduate.[9] At the Bridgewater Normal School the first principal, Nicholas Tillinghast, though not a minister, had been trained at West Point in scientific and engineering skills and used that learning in a successful military career, portions of which involved service on the West Point faculty.[10] Peirce's own successor at Lexington (later Framingham) Normal School, the Reverend Samuel J. May, was, like himself, a Harvard-trained minister with a reputation of enlightened educational service.[11] The traditions which they all established at their respective schools continued on in qualified form even into the next generation of schoolmen. However, if they did not wholly discard the academic temper of professional training, the second-generation normal schoolman spoke as much for his second-generation fellows as he did for himself when he remarked about his predecessor: "He was more skillful in communicating knowledge to others than in leading them to investigate for themselves." [12] These differences of norms and experience between the first and second generation ultimately turned the moral purpose of the normal school to very different ends.

The contrasts of career patterns between the pre- and post-war normal school leadership sets the context for the very different institutional types each group created. The first eight normal school principals in America had reached an average age of forty-four upon assuming control of their respective normal schools. Their immediate successors in the next generation—men like John D. Philbrick and David N. Camp in Connecticut,[14] John W. Dickinson at Westfield, Massachusetts,[15] George Bigelow at Framingham, Massachusetts,[16] Dana P. Colburn in Rhode Island,[17] Richard Edwards at Salem,[18] William F. Phelps in New Jersey [19] and Albert G. Boyden at Bridgewater [20]—averaged age thirty-three when they became normal school principals. This younger age reflected other significant differences in the careers of these later principals before they assumed the work of training teachers. Invariably reduced finances had obstructed their educational plans. John Dickinson, whose collegiate study at Williams was uncommon for the second group, nevertheless had forfeited his professional plans to study law because of pressing debts. Most later principals like Boyden and Camp had terminated any realistic professional training not after college but, rather, earlier when collegiate study became a clear impossibility. Moreover, the necessity to work on the family farm or in a trade until one's early twenties, to finance education, also drastically qualified later schoolmen's familiarity with older or advanced notions associated with academic instruction. At the same time, this very experience of manual labor, along with the age factor, placed the later normal school principals into the same social and economic class—and for a time into the same generational groupings—as their students.

Still, these differences did not lead to immediate and drastic transformations. Both generations of schoolmen professed to share, and did share, a number of social and educational values. Throughout the century most normal school instructors claimed that education was a moral work; that the normal school and the national associations must cooperate in the formation and dissemination of scientific principles of education; that the focal concern of the teacher sought the inculcation of character; that the parent and the community were necessary agents in the creation of practical pedagogy; that controversy and partisan teaching, especially where politics and religion were involved, must be finessed;[21] that conciliation rather than imposition maintained a proper professional style in any effort of educational reform; and that a genteel if not a loving demeanor improved techniques of instruction and avoided the use of the rod in governing a schoolroom. Within these cliches of nineteenth-century educational literature, however, differences of emphasis were both tolerated and expected. While the first generation bridled at all forms of contentiousness and called continuously for greater solidarity and harmony in professional councils, the second generation took that harmony for granted. The later group set itself the task of refining individual modes of professional instruction. Both stresses, however pronounced, were viewed as perfectly compatible within their common evangelical tradition.

The Normal School as a Revival Agency

By contrast with their official rhetoric, the record of the early normal school principals reflected the plight of teachers who could not bridge the differences between themselves and their students. "Alas! Alas!" Cyrus Peirce mourned privately, "on the principle that one must first learn to be a good scholar in order to become a good teacher, what sort of Teachers will such pupils [as those he faced] make?" [22] The longer he continued teaching in the Lexington Normal School, the more difficult Peirce found the instruction of such students. His assessments were not wholly without cause. He had compromised, time and again, his primary concern with the "Art of Teaching," turning his classes to drills and recitations on district school subjects. The failures of the "normalites" previous educations made the pretense of professional training doubly difficult.

Unlike his own training in the ministry which continued for three years uninterrupted and which followed a four-year collegiate course of study, normal school students in the 1840s came to their professional work directly from the district schools. In some cases they had studied in academies but these schools were so varied in quality that such "academy" preparation often differed from common school study only in minor ways. Faced first with remedial work, Peirce drilled, then despaired. "We have been," he objected in his journal, "day after day and week after week, hammering upon this matter [verb inflections in grammar], and I think it is provokingly ridiculous and absurd. Why do they not set about the business—learn it, and [have] done with the matter?—!" [23]

Peirce's ventures into more advanced studies again and again confronted, he felt, something more than reasonable confusion and average ability. "Heard one [of] my pupils, this day talking about Combe's Physiology being 'dry', 'so dry'. Dry! Combe's Physiology 'dry'! If it were as dry as the seared leaf I am sure there is *sap* enough in her soft head to moisten it." [24] His journal entries become increasingly cynical in his early terms in the school. He remarked over and over at his exhausted alternatives in the face of poorly prepared students and the necessity to maintain the school with unprofessional talents. At no point did he comment as sharply or as resentfully upon other facts of his case, particularly upon the social conditions from which his students were drawn or else upon the general conditions for educating females. (Unlike many normal schools, Peirce's school at Lexington and its successor at Framingham, Massachusetts, never admitted males to professional preparation.) Without the foundations of scholarship little wonder that Peirce found lacking the refined discussions and informal conversations so essential in his eyes to professional training.

The central cause of Peirce's discontent, however, was not simply the lack of scholarly preparation. This deficiency must have been a predictable characteristic of "the new experiment" which the normal school represented. From other comments in his journal Peirce clearly anticipated that the normalites would at least bear comparison with his high school students at Nantucket. Early terms at Lexington seemed to confirm this estimate. The real turning point in his attitude toward this work stemmed from two unanticipated aspects of the school which undermined his inchoate assumptions about training professional teachers. The first was a shift in the students' manners, not only significant enough to merit a journal citation but ultimately, as it spread among the other normalites, to warrant Peirce's resignation. "For one thing," he recorded in his third term at Lexington, "the day is remarkable. It is the *first time* that the Teacher has had the unhappiness to receive a short abrupt answer from any of the Pupils of the Normal School, or to witness any unhandsome manifestations from them. Today I have to record the first exception to this uniform propriety, in the *manner* and *intonation* of one of the Young Ladies." And later, reacting to similar incidents, he never ceased to be surprised at their unprofessional pertness. "Very unexpectedly to me, one of my pupils expressed an unwillingness to go into the Model School. This was wholly unexpected to me. I think she should have merged her own preferences in the interest and usages of the school." [25] His inability to understand or accommodate his students' attitudes illuminates the gap between teacher and student at the early normal school.

Second, more formidable to professional training than his students' educational and class disadvantages was his own loss of control within the classroom. For Peirce, a teacher's governance determined all success or failure. Unless a teacher could secure adeptly the cooperation of his charges, no mastery of subject, previous experience or other circumstances mattered. The "Secret of Keeping good Order lies in your own breast," he told his normalites, "and you must bring it [the Order] out. It will appear in your *looks* and *gestures* and every *movement* as well as in your *words*. If it cannot be found here it can be found nowhere." [26] On other occasions he put it more concisely: "Indeed a man may nullify all his precepts and Counsels by an unhappy manner." [27] His greatest cause of alarm, heightened by student peevishness and an accelerating rate of absenteeism, remained his inability to reshape their attitudes as well as their minds. In Peirce's own eyes he could not blame himself for this disorder, or he satisfied himself that he had done all he could. His own classroom efforts had not succeeded in establishing that spirit of harmony which was more essential to instruction than any other factor. This failure of governance prompted his resignation, not for lack of professional resolution but, rather, he claimed, for the illness his increased resolution conveniently engendered.[28]

Though this central problem extended in its origin and further consequences beyond the classroom, Peirce restricted his own authority almost entirely to schoolroom matters. In actual classroom activity he concentrated all his efforts upon the enlightment and improvement of his students' characters. The normal school was a class, and the principal had no connection with his students outside that context on a regular, official or compulsory basis. Although at times he made suggestions about extracurricular affairs and unofficially took his entire school to several county teachers' meetings and institutes, the students were of sufficient age to go unsupervised and follow the principal's suggestions as they saw fit. Daily class attendance was not compulsory. Peirce limited his formal powers to the admission process and the granting of certificates for satisfactory teaching ability. These minimal formal restrictions increased rather than diminished the authority of the principal. Peirce always considered his "suggestive" power more conclusive and irrepressible than any impersonally delegated authority. The voluntary obedience which his recommendations commanded established the real success of any school, particularly a professional one.[29]

The grave importance attached to the informal areas relating teachers and students made successful teaching a relatively imprecise artful activity. Perhaps most important, professional instruction ultimately had more to do with behavior and attitude than with stages of intellectual development, at least in the face of Peirce's remedial problems. Accordingly Peirce's banner day at the normal school came in his second year there, and it burst upon him as unexpectedly and surprisingly as the first instance of student recalcitrance. One of his pupils before class "came to me this morning and bursting into tears, asked me to forgive her" for a supposed wrong of the previous day. Peirce forgave her and commented in his journal: "She is a dear girl and good Scholar, and, I think, will make a good teacher. I think this is the right spirit to cherish; and where this spirit reigns in school, all things will go well. . . . The above is one of the most interesting [events] that have occurred since the opening of the Normal School." [30] The opposite of this obedient deportment undermined the all-important "moral atmosphere of the school." Near the end of his tenure at Lexington, Peirce candidly described the implications of the school's diametrically different ambiance: "There is less unity of spirit —kind sympathetic feeling: less of the feeling of Responsibility, less of a spirit of Accommodation—less disposition to fall in with and carry out the views of the Principal." [31]

This very spirit of responsibility and unity, embodied in the leading teacher of the school, would not be improved with an elaborate educational system. While the character of the principal was the soul of any school, his role could not be formalized without interfering with the character development of his students. The transformation of a school into a harmonious moral entity implied forceful yet informal limits upon a teacher's power. "A little observation," Peirce had asserted, "would show the visitor that we have no block or mold by which all are cast, so that there may be uniformity of character in the 'Prepared Teacher.' " "I would have a way," he continued, "a mode, a system; but still I would not have it so unyielding and restrictive as to *preclude* rather than aid individual developments." [32] These imperatives not only fixed his professional attention upon classroom teaching but prevented such gestures as soliciting students for his school, seeking advantageous positions for favored pupils, arranging tacit ties with feeder schools, or extending in any way the larger control over his school's products. Restricted thus, Peirce faced the work of the normal school with a single formula: "prospective teachers must give over their minds, hearts, and time to the Business—they must make school the great object of their attention and of their affection. It must be uppermost in their souls. If they are not willing to do this, they have not yet counted the cost . . . and need to be regenerated spiritually and intellectually." Like their predecessors, the teachers' institutes, the first normal schools had become revival agencies.[33]

Collegiate Influences on the Normal School

The successors of Cyrus Peirce viewed his central problem, not as he had, namely, as a problem of governance, but rather, as an impractical stress upon an academic mode of study. The two views define a spectrum for understanding the social and educational values embodied in their different brands of normal school training.[34] Both groups of schoolmen permitted college study as an educational and social ideal to affect the training of teachers. As the century progressed, college attendance became less and less a concrete possibility for most prominent schoolmen. Yet the college as a model arrangement for thorough learning and teaching continued to play through definitions of the normal school's goals. Neither generation dared claim the normal school was a competitor of the college, or before 1890 that the normal school was a college in its own right.The first generation did not because the allegation would have been so obviously hostile and false, even though in terms of evangelical traditions, student size, buildings, books and public support, there were areas which supported comparisons.[35] The claim was false, because from the outset the successful normal schools received state support and supervision and never attracted students in any numbers from the wealthy and professional classes. Moreover, most "normalites" were women in a period where no major effort had been made to educate the opposite sex beyond the intermediate levels of female institutes or seminaries. In the ante-bellum period these contingencies checked most specific analogies between the college and the normal school.

After the war the second generation characterized academic instruction as impractical, they said, because it left students generally passive. Academic lectures and disciplined courses of study had always presumed a profound inequality between teacher and student. The burden of the inequality had to be borne by the student. His or her preacademic education determined the relative degree of passivity and interest experienced in the lectures and recitations of advanced training. Here were parallel impracticalities for the teachers who, like Peirce, saw their best efforts falling on barren ground. Significantly these frustrations of the teacher, so prevalent in Peirce's journal, seldom found spokesmen among his younger successors. Instead the second generation assumed control of the normal schools in the late 1850s and early 1860s with attitudes either identical to or sympathetic to students unready for regular academic work. The greater affinity between such teachers and their students undoubtedly caused the rapid disappearance of "the problem of governance." In its stead there appeared equally severe problems more familiar to ambitions which had been frequently dislocated.

The regenerative work Peirce assigned to normal school instruction continued on in the later professional schools for teachers but did not remain the distinct prerogative of the principal. The new affinities of age and origin

144 THE CLASSLESS PROFESSION

among the school's personnel altered the principal's role and the revivalistic
notions about the school itself. Normal schools became institutions which
housed a qualitatively distinct educational ambiance. The new institutional
form and its special educational orientation were in large part the product of
the second generation of normal schoolmen. The context for these changes
are set in the career patterns of men like Albert G. Boyden, the third principal
of the Bridgewater (Massachusetts) State Normal School. This office was
tendered to Boyden, not only because he was himself an alumnus of the
school—the first alumnus to become principal—but undoubtedly because he
had served the previous two principals as an assistant faculty member. This
training and his youthful age, as practical credentials, differed sharply with
the college study, teaching experience and age of his precedessors. Among
the earlier incumbents of such offices, only Bridgewater's first principal,
Nicholas Tillinghast, had any familiarity with a normal school before directing such an institution.[36] Instead of the few months Tillinghast spent
observing the Barre (Massachusetts) State Normal School, Boyden had
served a genuine apprenticeship in the work over a period of thirteen terms,
or more than six years. Also, before attending Bridgewater,Boyden had
studied and then taught seasonally in the winter schools of his native district
of South Walpole, Massachusetts. His most rigorous and systematic education at Bridgewater began when he was twenty-one, only twelve years before
he became the school's principal.[37] By contrast, Cyrus Peirce had received
thorough, academic instruction before college, and his other teaching positions had taken him beyond the bounds of his native place. In his case the
comparable time between his first year at Harvard (1806) and his first normal
school office spanned thirty-three years.

Behind the contours of such careers there lay two disparate attitudes
toward unprepared young men and women, and these two viewpoints
worked themselves out in discussions over instruction in technique and
methods. Like Boyden, the second generation had chosen teaching after
relatively long labor in manual work. While they clearly had rejected certain
extreme features of physical toil, their experience in farming and trades left
them with an appreciation of orderly physical work. Indeed their willingness
to submit to such labor, as well as their proficiency and success in it, had
become a major factor recommending them to teaching in the first place. The
second generation did not, as did the first, premise the application of
professional techniques upon academic study. Their appreciation for methodical skills became a dominant feature of their work, and among the
prominent clichés of the late nineteenth century the authority of environ-
mental and empirical evidence over bookish precedent in pedagogical issues
came more easily to the second-generation schoolman than to the first.

For all the differences between the first and the second generations they
tended together to explore new uses and notions about instruction in

pedagogical methods. This new direction, which grated against collegiate and academic models of instruction, grounded itself in the careers of professional schoolmen. There were particular reasons why Bridgewater Normal School in Massachusetts developed such lines of thought earlier than other normal schools. At Bridgewater even the earliest principals—Nicholas Tillinghast and Marshall Conant—had to account for the experiences of young men like Albert G. Boyden. Boyden had begun teaching at age eighteen, but this new work was not a clean and permanent break from the earlier and more familiar routines upon the farm or in the blacksmith's shop, his father's trade.[38] His work in both farming and mechancial trades not only conditioned the realities of his formative years but shaped his professional prospects. These features did not clash with academic values as sharply at Bridgewater as they might have elsewhere, largely owing to the school's location in southeastern Massachusetts where clothing and shoe manufacturers increasingly dominated the society and economy of that section of the state.[39] It is likely that such conditions led Bridgewater trustees to appoint principals as familiar with practical as with academic affairs.

Before 1840 West Point where Tillinghast had gone for his education was the leading institution in the country in mathematical, geological and mineralogical studies. His applications of his learning at West Point bore analogies to the experience of his successor, Marshall Conant, who had gone to Illinois to seek his fortune. When Conant became principal of Bridgewater in 1853, he resigned his duties with a local Bridgewater factory, the Eagle Cotton Gin Co. There, as in his earlier experience constructing the Boston Water Works and railroad-building in New Hampshire, he had developed something of a reputation for solutions to technical engineering problems.[40] Like Tillinghast, Conant had usually combined his practical employment with academic teaching. By the time Boyden succeeded Conant in 1860, Bridgewater's curriculum reflected a basically new tradition, which in content and method met the backgrounds and felt needs of students accustomed to the order and rigor of manual labor more than it met the demands for classical instruction prior to collegiate study.

This more practical, curricular emphasis set the direction of most normal schools in America. However, classical study, so rooted in preprofessional education, continued to pull like a magnet on the normal school's compass.[41] The Board of Visitors for Bridgewater, a special committee composed of three members of the Massachusetts Board of Education, showed more than a little of the older literary bias, when they criticized Conant's course of study in 1857. They commented that "the study of language and literature and practical teaching exercises may be observed as made too far subordinate to the higher mathematics." [42] Under Tillinghast and Conant Bridgewater arranged its students into five sections: (1) Didactics; (2) Literary Studies; (3) Mathematics; (4) Natural Science; (5) Miscellaneous Studies, such as music, drawing and the Latin language.[43] Uncommitted funds as well as money for the purpose went primarily to the purchase of scientific and technical apparatus, cabinets of geological and mineralogical collections, maps and physiological plates and other collections of scientific specimens.[44] The order of priorities preferred the nonliterary studies in the prewar period at Bridgewater. More than the other two normal schools in Massachusetts, schools dominated by men like Peirce, Newman, Davis and May (all college-bred and ordained ministers), Bridgewater's practical orientation drew from the outset one of the largest bodies of students and one of the largest male contingents of any normal school in nineteenth-century America.[45]

In spite of these curricular and institutional differences between prewar Bridgewater and its sister schools in the state, the focus on particular subjects, the age and experience gap between teacher and student and the pivotal role of the principal as the single force in generating a new spiritual commitment to teaching bound all three schools into a single genre. The comment of Tillinghast's biographer could have referred as well to the more obvious religious and academic inclinations of the other principals: "The true secret of this power of his over his pupils, which enabled him to fill them in a great measure with his own spirit, as well as of the remarkable affection which they entertained towards him,—the secret of all that lay in his personal character, in that quiet but unflinching devotion to principle, that heroic and real abnegation of self, which to those who knew him intimately, appeared as a ruling trait of his moral nature." Even his admirers asserted no originality to the man but, higher praise they insisted, he was for the institution "a soul,—the animating principle that moves this otherwise dead machinery." [46] For Tillinghast and for the less scientific Peirce the evangelical impetus of all proper schooling made moral character the central fact of the teacher's work. The tone, manners and demeanor of a schoolman made his most important and lasting influence a matter of direct and "unconscious tuition." [47]

In the hands of men like Boyden this principle began to take on a new meaning. "The want of apparatus and of assistants," Boyden explained later, "must be supplied by increased skill and effort on the part of the Principal; he must be the factotum of the school." [48] In one generation the metaphoric image of the teacher had shifted from a ministerial to a tradesman's referent. Still more important, the ubiquitous presence of the principal had become not the fundamental essence of instruction so much as a compensation for the missing technical aids of early normal school training. The principal for both was the source of school policy. However, with the second generation unconscious tuition, still very much a part of professional education, no longer rested wholly upon the personal qualities of the principal's character. The silent impress of moral character had to account for the role played by other members of his faculty as well as those portions of instruction which were technical, systematic and the opposite of indirect and unconscious.

Boyden's first years at Bridgewater witnessed the transformation of both the faculty's role and the nature of professional instruction. During Tillinghast's thirteen-year tenure and the seven-year administration of Conant a total of twenty-eight assistants served two men. The turnover was quite rapid owing largely to the reduced salary appropriation—first $300, then $400 in the 1850s, by contrast with the principal's recompense which ranged between $1,200 and $1,500.[49] The assistants of the first twenty years taught for an average of three terms under the first principal and for four under the second. Of the twenty-eight, seventeen stayed a year or less.[50] At least for the male assistants higher-paying teaching positions siphoned off the younger faculty into public high school principalships in cities or else into creating new institutions—colleges and normal schools alike—in the West.[51] Boyden himself had not served the first two principals sequentially. He served Tillinghast for a time, left Bridgewater for Salem and the principalship of the English and Classical High School for three years, then to a submastership in Boston's Chapman School. In 1857 he returned to Bridgewater to serve Conant as first assistant. (His experience seems to argue that professional opportunities descended in rank as one approached positions in city systems.)

However this intraprofessional mobility benefited individual and institutional prospects in the long run, this rapid turnover rendered unstable a given normal school's study and curricular arrangements. Academic notions of thorough training, whether in literary or in nonliterary subjects, compounded the problem. The early faculties openly conceded that the required three terms, varying in the early 1840s from eleven to twenty weeks, could not rely upon an applicant's mastery even of district school subjects, much less the professional techniques to teach them. Consequently the early normal schoolmen viewed study time as largely spent in remedial work, evening out the basic knowledge from which professional training might begin.[52] Even though most of the faculty members of a normal school were graduates of the institution they served, few could aver that their training had been distinctly professional. Some, like Boyden, who had remained at their alma maters for postgraduate terms, never boasted a preparation so complete that afterward private study alone sufficed to maintain competency. In the teaching profession throughout the century no clean break ever developed between professional preparation and practice. Professional schoolmen continued to attend even short-term institutes, like summer schools, to maintain the claim, if not the achievement, of professional proficiency. Their careers were endless shuttles back and forth from institutions for teaching to institutions for learning. The most satisfactory professional institution, the teachers' institute, embodied both processes, and in the hands of the second-generation normal schoolmen the normal school gave up the pretense of trying to distinguish the two phases of education. The essential differences between the teachers' institute and the normal school were not normative, at least not until the 1890s.

In 1860 Boyden's major obstacle, professionally speaking, appeared to be an impermanent faculty. Like Peirce, he desired that "merging of interests" between teacher and students, a harmony which for both men represented the epitome of professional training. Even were the faculty permanent, the professional tone would not be clearly established on the merits of previous normal school training. In an understandable move to meet the problems of unstable and unprepared faculty members, Boyden introduced to the normal school well-known lecturers whose impact would affect the present faculty as well as current student body. Beginning in 1864 a troop of lecturers, led by the well-known and aging schoolman William Russell, came once a week to Bridgewater. Significantly until 1870 this strategem introduced literary —Elocution, Music, English Literature, Civil Polity—rather than techno- logical subjects into a traditional normal school curriculum. There were some nonliterary subjects like geology and anatomy, taught by established scientists like Sanborn Tenney and Lewis G. Lowe, but collegiate studies prevailed.[53] This content and these lectureships served as an important attraction for Bridgewater, yet the policy of the normal school by its very success seemed to belie the normal schoolman's claim that their training was distinctly professional. These special measures to upgrade professional teaching merely favored traditionally academic notions of professional preparation.

During the latter half of the nineteenth century the normal schools dis- tinguished themselves in particular by their effort to integrate their evan- gelical origins with an academic tradition. They refused to establish the distinctiveness of the teaching profession upon a separation of teacher and student roles. They could not, however, merely fuse the two. In 1870 Albert G. Boyden, perhaps the most ambitious and effective figure in the design of this new type of school, terminated the program of distinctive scholar-lec- turers and declared that the normal school required a new kind of teacher.[54] In particular, he enjoined the normal school itself to create its own cohort of teachers. He proceeded also to assign the art and science of teaching a special place in the curriculum. The soul of the normal school was no longer exclu- sively the principal nor even his new personally trained faculty. It was now more formally the course of study and particularly the most professionally useful study, psychology, where the process of mind meeting mind was examined. Quickly a literature and a special set of inquiry procedures—ob- ject methods—surrounded this study, not to mention its special name, psychology.[55] These demarcations from past teacher-training practices in- dicated how pressing was the need to make teaching a work separate from that of other professions. Implicit too was the need to make professional education an essentially separate brand of instruction and not simply the modified form of a single academic model.

In the name of distinct and innovative techniques normal schools competed for students with other educational institutions. Only in the cities had graded systems and bureaucracies of education emerged. There normal schools quickly became both vocational and exclusively female, forecasting the future of such schools after 1890. The city training schools, of which Oswego Normal School was the most prominent, usually employed a single-tract two-year program which supplied teachers to the city which financed its operations. It was distinctly nonacademic and catered to a class of young women whose origins precluded all professional and academic aspirations. For a generation Bridgewater resisted this paradigm of professional training—urban, vocational, female—and as a model of the normal school type competed with its only effective rival, Oswego Normal School, until the 1890s, when Nicholas Murray Butler effectively introduced into the New York Teachers College a third and novel norm for teacher training in America.[56] The city quickly solved the dual problem of the early normal school—the expenses and the distractions of life away from home. Yet these solutions forfeited any pretense of developing character in any traditional manner. The urban school ultimately directed its attention to a lower-class student body, and admitted greater numbers of rural and immigrant youth.[57] Such students might readily master regulated methods, however rudimentary their elementary instruction. The integration of physical, intellectual and moral facets of character development became little more than a matter of ingenious devices and mechanical skills.[58] So long as Bridgewater resisted this erosion of its evangelical roots the normal school could still hope to draw from the middle and upper classes for its professional talent.

The state normal school particularly followed Bridgewater's lead of an integrated practical-classical curriculum which informed a distinctly professional and moral style.[59] Its location, thirty miles southeast of Boston, ensured the school's control over those urban trends which transferred other normal schools into different institutional types. Bridgewater's lines were sufficiently lubricated to the city to send its most successful graduates there to teach,[60] but sufficiently far, until the 1890s, to prevent substantial numbers to come from the coastal towns of Bristol and Plymouth counties. In the pre-1890 period few students, even those of Irish extraction, were born outside Massachusetts and the majority of their parents were native Americans. Between 1840 and 1876 only 293 students at Bridgewater came from outside the state; from inside Bristol and Plymouth counties, scholars (381 and 702 respectively) numbered more than from all the other Massachusetts counties combined (948).[61] The normal school served a sharply defined region of the state, whose largest towns, Fall River and New Bedford, did *not* supply the majority of students. Only when it began to dilute its academic offering in the 1870s did Bridgewater begin to send its graduates primarily back to the urban classes which had begun to supply the school with increasing numbers of students. These two developments—the decreasing portions of academic study and an increasing lower- and lower-middle-class student body [62]—accompanied and likely caused the virtual elimination of Bridgewater's minority of male students. By the 1890s normal schools became almost exclusively female institutions.

Twenty years before these important changes began, Albert G. Boyden designed an institutional structure which avoided any specification as to the social and economic classes his school served. Boyden did, however, keep reasonably careful records of students' origins, fathers' occupations and subsequent teaching positions. These data never became the basis for any public remarks about teachers' status and class. This information helps explain the peculiar meaning that normal schoolmen gave to the role of academic study. The two major developments of Boyden's first years as principal of Bridgewater Normal School were efforts to accommodate academic teaching in a peculiar and distinctive way. The first was the arrangement of lectures delivered by established academics; the second was the elimination of remedial connotations associated with the daily work of the school. For second-generation schoolmen staffing the normal schools in the 1860s, distinctive professional methods could never be taught apart from the subject to which it referred, and each subject in some sense had a method all its own. Neither the method nor the subject alone, but both together, comprised the work of the normal school. Boyden summarized his generation's attitude toward academic study without any mention of its social consequences. As the author of the National Education Association's report on normal schools, he offered the wisdom of a career: "The academic studies should not be taken in the normal course for academic study, but the time will never come when we can safely dispose with the educational study of these subjects in the normal schools. The normal school is to be made professional, not by the exclusion of these studies from the course, but by the inclusion of the educational study of them. The one function of the normal school is the education of teachers." [63]

However obliquely, Boyden had spoken to a particular class of budding professionals when he preferred "objective" teaching to an orthodox academic curriculum. He had obviously conceded that the normal school could not attract college-bound youth in numbers; he had, however, not closed his mind to the possibility of attracting them eventually. He did create more quickly than other normal schools, first a three-year and then a four-year program, long before such terms of study were officially sanctioned by the state.[64] In addition, he initiated and promoted an early connection between Bridgewater and Harvard's Lawrence Scientific School. (Unlike Harvard College, the Lawrence Scientific School also taught students from a lower social class and was, like the normal school students, subject to adverse prejudices which linked academic study and advantageous social arrangements.[65]) This formal tie permitted normal school graduates—only male—entrance to the university without the usual examination; it granted credit to some courses taken in the normal school.[66] Massachusetts put its imprimatur on this relationship by granting eight tuition scholarships ($150 each) annually. The allotment equaled the cost of tuition. Even though few normal school graduates outside the four-year program took advantage of this arrangement, the normal schoolmen promoted it and eventually broadened the number of participating colleges to Radcliffe, then Boston University.[67] In spite of their rejection of a traditional academic program the introduction of a four-year course in 1869 welcomed, they claimed, a new era. In 1890 this program was the only male-dominated course of study at Bridgewater. At its fiftieth-anniversary celebration the four-year course, now over thirty years old, was in the principal's eyes "the most important step forward in the history of the school, in the beneficial influence which the advanced pupils exert upon the tone and feeling in the school, in raising the standards of scholarship, in drawing in better-prepared pupils, in sending out better-trained teachers for the high and normal schools, in giving the school character and standing in the community." [68] If he had explicitly denied that "objective" teaching coincided with a collegiate curriculum, Boyden never eschewed the social benefits related to academic study.

By the 1880s Boyden had succeeded in staking out a distinctive and stable area for normal school work. Not only was Bridgewater held up as a model teacher-training institution, but some college men—usually from the midwest rather than the east—admitted that the quality of its instruction compared favorably with university work.[69] They saw little difference between normal schools and colleges. Bridgewater's four-year course was always singled out for special mention, as covering "the ground of the average New England college, literally," and taking "all the studies with special reference to teaching." [70] Boyden never minded such applause but never let such praise push him to make the normal school *more literary* than it already seemed to be.[71] Boyden himself nor any of his fellow principals after 1860 indulged the term "college" when describing the nature of their institution. At the same time that they accommodated academic instruction in their special way, however, they also insisted upon the distinct moral purpose of the institution. Here too, accommodation had been made, and the revival imagery of Cyrus Peirce and an older generation had been abridged. Instead of the lofty spiritual rhetoric which enabled minister-principals to sanction a holy calling in teaching, Boyden merely claimed that in the normal school "the moral element is the leaven hidden in the meal." [72]

This domestic imagery and its implications, far more than analogies to the college, captured the distinct nature and special *locus* of the normal school after the Civil War. The major transformation of the normal school in the 1870s and 1880s involved the enlargement of educational and professional responsibilities beyond the classroom itself. Where Peirce had limited his "unconscious" influence to the classroom, Boyden, then other normal schoolmen, addressed themselves officially to the outside influences which once made "governance" the normal school's preeminent bane. Behind the lack of will and professional resolution Peirce had witnessed at Lexington lay the poor preparation of district grammar schools, short attendance, interrupted lessons, and the professional immaturity of age sixteen. "Some of them seem to me," Peirce had puzzled, "to be more interested in *home*, (in going home and hearing from home) than in anything else." [73] Once the vehicle of moral instruction became less strictly academic and more objective, as it did in the 1860s, such extra-institutional problems became less important. The connotations of deficient backgrounds were softened by the mere arrangement of studies into topical discussions. The elimination of both the model school and inspirational homilies argued against the divorce of practice and principles. In familiar conversation with fellow students and teachers who shared common origins, the domestic metaphors made more sense of school life than revival images.

The evangelical currents, nevertheless, continued to flow through the transformed normal school. In the earlier ante-bellum period the revival assumptions had tried to fuse a highly disparate body of young men into a single harmonious moral entity. So long as the harmony was maintained, schoolmen felt they had provided the context for the moral work of professional education. Thus unity of moral purpose suffused the essential nature of all proper schooling. While allowance was made for local variations, on the level of principles education was the same everywhere. The very success of this professional ideology made doubly perplexing and serious the dissension within the profession by the end of the 1850s. Neither generation could acknowledge explicitly the enlarged disharmonies of social class within their fellowship without abrogating their long-sanctioned defense of character as asocial and apolitical, that is, morally neutral. The first generation sought their solutions in the counsels of voluntary associations, while their erstwhile protégés sought more concrete and permanent professional establishments. The sociological division within the schoolman's work quickly turned their voluntary associations, both local and national, into forums of empty, moral rhetoric. The more prosaic alternative of the second generation did not meet the problem at its source but, till the end of the century, sustained the hope that professional levels could be attained more by professional training and practice than by agreement upon unpracticed principles. In a sense, both options sustained different aspects of their evangelical tradition: one continued to endorse rhetorically a collective will through a chain of voluntary associations, the other indulged a professional will which maintained the chain of voluntary associations but made the normal school its most permanent link. The "subtle play of daily life" [74] entered the institutional and professional structure of teaching and gave high-blown principles a domesticized and customary dimension which voluntary associations alone could not give.

Domesticated Professionals

Within two decades, the eighteen-fifties and sixties, this domestication of professional norms was complete. The rhetorical change from a collective harmony to a distinct, "self-made" man as the embodiment of professional character paced the transformation of the social class of educational policy-makers. Where collegiate values had spurred benevolent support and middle- if not upper-middle-class individuals to work for and in the teaching profession, after the Civil War only the "shells of custom" remained. Thoroughness and discipline still remained dominant ideals, yet in practice manual training rather than classical and literary study became the means of realizing them. (Manual training, of course, never rejected classical and literary "culture," any more than it allowed itself to be made synonymous with "vocational" training.[75]) The rise of manual training, especially the design and construction of special shops and laboratories for its practical instruction, signaled the normal schoolman's acquiescence in a noncollegiate mode of instruction. The attractions of the college proved too strong for the normal school to compete on equal levels for the best-prepared and most affluent students. In the contest for normal schoolmen the reliance on older goals of collective harmony ensured a secondary stature for professional teachers.

Instead of sheer resignation to such stature, the normal schoolmen exploited their weakness as an asset. In the postwar years, they indulged all manner of comparisons between teachers and other professionals, between normal schools and other institutions, concluding that teaching *at present* held an inferior and disadvantaged place. Such concessions, wholly new to professional discussions, enshrined humility as the teacher's preeminent virtue and dutiful (read unobtrusive) service as its characteristic practice. The candid admission lent a novel candor to their councils, and even to their greatest competitors—the colleges and their affiliates, the academies—they appeared to offer cooperation rather than hostility. In some cases no doubt these tendencies were only genuine, and there the evangelical tradition, which made deference to truth a liberating and powerful motivation, lived on intact. At the same time deference served other purposes. It provided a context for exploring distinctions and comparisons which otherwise would have disrupted their own neutralized and harmonious professional style. Schoolmen developed a stylized deference which itself recognized the exist-

Table 7

Matriculation Ages of Bridgewater Normal School Students, 1854–1904

	15	16	17	18	19	20	21	22
1854–1862 [a]	0	67	90	59	63	35	31	39
Male	0	2	44	25	34	17	17	24
Female	0	65	46	34	29	18	14	15
1878–1886 [a]	14	100	139	95	54	30	22	21
Male	0	8	29	18	11	12	6	7
Female	14	92	110	77	43	18	16	14
1887–1895	5	111	177	163	112	52	28	19
Male	0	9	38	26	22	12	8	3
Female	5	102	139	137	90	40	20	16
1896–1904	6	67	193	218	147	58	39	23
Male	0	4	21	16	14	7	10	7
Female	6	63	172	202	133	51	29	16
Male Subtotal	0	23	132	85	81	48	41	41
Female Subtotal	25	322	467	450	295	127	79	61
Total	25	345	599	535	376	175	120	102

[a] The eight-year sequence here permitted comparable figures given the incomplete nature of the evidence. The first year of the first two sequences represents one class, or the equivalent of one-half year enrollment. Until 1895 each year contains the sum of two classes. After 1895 the school's register has one class each year. There are no comparable data for the years 1862–1878.

ence of operational rankings both within and without the profession of teaching. Without appearing arrogant or hostile they could feed intra-professional competition. In this context, too, they examined the inequities between teaching and older professions without appearing to engage in open defiance of those occupations. If inferior social status became a commonly accepted feature of teaching, schoolmen themselves unintentionally had much to do with the creation of that stigma.

By the end of the 1860s schoolmen observed coteries within their ranks as distinctly fertile areas of cultivation. Those years between the late 1860s and the late 1880s witnessed the spawning of numerous regional organizations which specified the institutional realities of American education. More than explicitly local or statewide yet less than national, new sectional organizations mushroomed. In the cities numerous schoolmasters' clubs not only identified the prominent and influential schoolmen but created a highly genteel and enriched domicile for such men to fraternize with the wealthy and literary men of the moment. Outside the city, associations, like the New

Table 7—Continued

Matriculation Ages of Bridgewater Normal School Students

23	24	25	26	27	28	29	30 [b]	Known Ages [c]	23 and Older [d] Number	Percent
19	6	11	8	7	1	3	5	444	60	13.28
10	3	7	4	3	0	1	2	193		
9	3	4	4	4	1	2	3	251		
12	10	5	2	1	0	2	6	513	38	7.41
6	3	3	1	1	0	0	0	105		
6	7	2	1	0	0	2	6	408		
20	13	11	9	7	3	3	7	740	63	8.51
6	5	3	4	1	0	1	2	140		
14	8	8	5	6	3	2	5	600		
32	21	29	22	15	9	11	34	924	173	18.57
6	6	2	4	6	2	3	0	108		
26	15	27	18	9	7	8	34	816		
28	17	15	13	11	2	5	4	546		
55	33	41	28	19	11	14	48	2,075		
83	50	56	41	30	13	19	52	2,621		

[b] These figures include students older than thirty.

[c] Unknown ages amount to less than 4% of the total.

[d] Twenty-three was the age by which most nineteenth-century college students had *graduated*. The time differential indicates the relative social advantage college became vis-à-vis the state normal school.

England Normal Teachers Association, the New England Association of Colleges and Preparatory Schools, Middle State Schoolmasters Association and ultimately the American Institute of Instruction (once the National Education Association became genuinely national in the 1890s), all became singularly powerful regional forums for creating and maintaining alliances within the schoolman's profession. These institutions thrived in their regional contexts only so long as the distinctions between educational institutions maintained some observance of the older tradition of professional harmony. By the end of the nineties the nature of distinct levels and institutional types, not to mention the classes they served, became relatively set, and a newer grid of explicitly local, state and national interconnections became the dominant rationale and system for arranging the schoolman's work and profession.

For the schoolmen of the seventies and eighties the regional swath of their professional organizations clearly depicted their aspirations and influences. Within these forums the schoolman employed a refined sense of his limitations as a means for attracting and confirming institutional and professional alliances within his ranks. On the part of the normal schoolmen the major energies of this period were devoted to an alliance not with the college but with the emerging city high school.[76] Until the late 1860s the majority of normal school students came in varying proportions from grammar schools, academies and high schools. The periods of study in these schools varied considerably and few stayed in the academies and high schools long enough to graduate from a completed course of study. Through the 1870s neither the normal school nor the college were exceptionally served by the academies whose poor college-preparatory record only barely surpassed that of the high school. By the late seventies, however, prominent normal schools like Bridgewater unofficially but effectively turned to high school students and gradually to high school graduates for their supply of potential professionals.

These shifts preceded official directives or acknowledgments of such changes from the state legislatures or Boards of Education until the 1890s, after which these official agencies began to assume unprecedented initiatory and regulatory powers over instruction. Not only did normal school principals offer special concessions (different graduate certificates, different oral and written exams for admissions, etc.) to high school graduates, they also created advanced courses and individually arranged programs for graduates of other normal schools and colleges who wanted professional training.[78] Perhaps most important, they explicitly favored students older than the official age minimum of sixteen for female and seventeen for males. The Bridgewater catalogue for a number of years carried the suggestive observation: "A greater age than is here prescribed, with some experience in teaching, will make the course of instruction in the School much more valuable to the pupil." [79] During this period females' ages actually ranged in class averages between eighteen and twenty (Table 7) while average ages for males fluctuated between nineteen and twenty-two. Significant minorities of older students attended—and in many cases experienced rapid professional rises after normal school study—whose ages upon entering ranged in the late twenties. The oldest entering student of the period was forty-three.[80]

Under Boyden Bridgewater not only initiated and led many such unofficial developments but gradually realigned the total nature and structure of the normal school within the contours of an unaggressive, genteel style. At the very moment normal schoolmen like Boyden began to seek out older experienced teachers for their schools or else to solicit interested high school graduates, they also began to arrogate formal responsibility for the whole life of the professional trainee. In the name of prudent economics Bridgewater consolidated the student eating clubs and student-dominated boarding-houses in the town. The construction of a dorm in 1869 and its extension in 1873 assured the students an immediate saving of $1.25 per week over older measures of room and board. The new feature of this facility was, however, not the financial saving but the quarters of the principal and his family in the dorm itself. Housing a majority of the school's students brought their lives outside the classroom into direct, sensible contact with the principal at numerous points of every daily routine. "No pains are spared," the Bridgewater catalogue pledged, "to make the Hall in every respect a home for the pupils." [81]

This promise of domesticity accompanied an abnormal imposition of normal school regulations. With the opening of the Boarding Hall in November, 1869, Boyden put aside the cautions and hesitancies which men like Peirce manifested toward the student's extracurricular activities and accommodations. Pupils were now expected to attend Sunday worship at any church of their choice; at least one hour of exercise in the open air became a daily requirement, weather and health permitting; all study hours, at home and at school, the catalogue insisted after 1869, "are to be spent quietly, and *without* communication." Moreover, the hour "for retiring is *not later* than *ten o'clock*, at all seasons of the year." Pupils must devote, the circular warned, a proper amount of time to sleep, and "seven hours of undisturbed repose is the minimum. Unseasonable rising and study will be regarded as a violation of the rules of the Institution." Two final regulations made Boyden's role particularly clear: "No absence or tardiness is allowed except in extreme cases" and "Absence from town must be on leave previously obtained from the Principal." [82]

The student eating clubs and boardinghouses had always met more than physical needs. When the school brought onto its own grounds the means of room and board, Bridgewater also adopted the social dimension of the earlier facilities. In addition, it combined these casual places of entertainment and conversation with the unofficial debating societies. By the early seventies a self-consciously "educational" association, the Normal Lyceum, gathered together the last remaining facets of student life under the aegis of the school itself. After the turn of the century in the wake of dramatically different social and professional forces the Normal Lyceum specialized its many functions into separate associations: alumni clubs, fraternities, sororities, religious and athletic organizations. Before that, all these activities operated as arms of the Normal Lyceum which almost always designated its officers (as did the Alumni Association since 1842) from the male minority and which maintained close ties with the principal and faculty of the school.[83]

A convenient corollary to this organizational realignment in the student life of professional trainees was the arrangement for discovering jobs and placing students in teaching positions. The constant traffic between graduates and students *at Bridgewater* eliminated the need for formal control over placement. Until 1897 the informal arrangements were sufficient to guarantee Bridgewater a dramatic record of achievement in filling the policy-making positions of professional schoolmen. In 1891 Boyden could justly boast 113 classes of students filtering into all levels of education. Most important, one third of Massachusetts' teachers were normal school students. No other state commanded so high a percentage of comparably trained teachers. Boyden's most enthusiastic praise went, however, to the city of Boston where the superintendent of schools, Edwin Seaver, two of the supervisors, fifteen of the masters and seventeen of the submasters had graduated from his school. Even more important, until 1906 the agents of the State Board of Education on whose shoulders rested the work of visiting and advising all the schools of the state had been dominated for more than three decades by Bridgewater graduates. After 1906 the Bridgewater influence could still be felt through the chief office of the state, if not the country, the secretaryship of the Board of Education, held by George H. Martin. The most influential educational journal in the nation, the weekly *Journal of Education*, had been edited since 1886 by still another graduate, Albert E. Winship, who served in that capacity until his death in 1933.[84] Boyden himself maintained his presence over this entire record until 1906. His lifetime career at Bridgewater spanned fifty-five years and was surpassed only by the fifty-six-year tenure of his successor and son, Arthur C. Boyden.[85]

The ubiquitous presence of a Boyden at Bridgewater from 1860 to 1933 exaggerated the lengthened tenures of both principal and faculty, typical of the second- and third-generation normal schoolmen. Edward Sheldon of Oswego served as principal from 1860 to 1897; John Dickinson at Westfield discharged his duties at the normal school there for twenty-five years, serving as principal from 1856 to 1877, then expanding his concern for all the state normal schools into his work as secretary of the State Board of Education from 1877 to 1893.[86] Richard Edwards, a Bridgewater graduate, served as normal school teacher and principal for twenty-eight years, ending his career with a thirteen-year presidency at the State Normal University at Normal, Illinois. Following another typical pattern, Edwards passed that office—as had Boyden to his son, Sheldon to I. B. Poucher, Dickinson to Joseph Scott—to a hand-picked and carefully trained amanuensis. Though such successors usually graduated from the institution which they ultimately directed, in Edwards' case the choice went to a fellow Bridgewater graduate whom he had brought to Illinois. This man, Edwin C. Hewitt, turned a long teaching career at the Normal University into a presidential tenure, a service which lasted thirty-two years in all.[87] With variations the pattern holds for the Salem Normal School, the Boston Normal School and the other state institutions founded before 1860.[88] Normal schoolmen of the second generation generally graduated from normal schools or colleges, held remarkably long tenures and passed their offices on to hand-picked lieutenants whose work would not likely depart from the self-contained policies established by their predecessors. At Bridgewater after Boyden assumed the principalship, the average length of faculty tenure extended two years beyond that of earlier faculties.

In the last half of the nineteenth century it was not uncommon to have normal school faculty serving extensive periods. Most normal schools contained faculty members comparable to Bridgewater's Eliza Woodward (1857-1887), Frank H. Kirmayer (1870-1919), George H. Martin (1864-1882), William D. Jackson (1883-1926), Fannie Comstock (1888-1913) and Isabelle S. Horne (1875-1906).[89] After the 1880s it was also uncommon not to have alumni forming a large percentage of the normal school faculty.

The new postwar normal school gave rise to a professional standard which made loyal attachment to the alma mater the gauge of moral and professional character. The schoolman's commitment fixed on a single institution which in turn specified the overriding principles of educational work. Graduates became proselytizers not simply for educational principles but for principles as filtered to them through their school. Normal training had clarified procedurally the process of awakening and inculcating character at the heart of this essentially evangelical work. The mechanics of their work paradoxically, they still believed, would lead to a moral and professional rather than a mechanical and uniform mode of instruction. In their mind the formalities and schedules of training became starting points which, once understood and domesticated into a trainee's routines, would guarantee superior levels of performance, however much the idiosyncrasies of his personality modified them. No matter how regimented and methodical the product of the normal school, the professional evaluation of every successful teacher rested finally on the degree to which his achievement was self-made and fashioned according to his own choices.[90] As is the teacher, their cliché ran, so is the school. Well before Charles Eliot damned uniformity as he created an elective system for collegiate study, the normal schools systematized their training in order to ensure that professional choice was both voluntary and efficient. Ultimately they never dreamed that their procedures would become so powerfully efficient that professional choice would become altogether powerless.

Their creation of an enclosure for professional training intended no myopic insularity. The normal schools prided themselves on the features of their expanding campuses. Unlike the colleges, they raised no walls to make distinctions explicit between school and society. The normal school principal, in the realignment of his powers, became the school's representative at conventions and public festivities. More and more his own role shed the responsibility of classroom teaching for the more delicate task of spreading the message and spirit which made his normal school distinct.[91] The work of conventions became no less evangelical but only less inspirational, since the integrated work of a single normal school society was transmitted both to his own and to other schools through the eyes of a given principal. The contact with the sponsoring state representatives, the Board of Visitors, became perfunctory. By the 1880s the visitors' positions implied not visits and inspections at irregular times of the year, nor were they any longer rotated among the Board of Education members from all over the state. Instead, public appearances at commencement exercises became the occasion of "visits," and visitors from the school's own or neighboring county served that school alone for longer and longer tenures.[92] The rotations of ante-bellum days became after the war permanent appointments. Visitors were no longer representatives of the public; they became, rather, defenders of the school. Not only had the institutional structure of the normal school changed drastically, its place in the scale of professional values had transformed the significance and nature of preparatory training.

The major professional innovation of the second-generation schoolman was his effort to place his profession and its institutions within a practical social context. This effort stopped short of cultivating a peculiar sensitivity to institutional power as distinct from the force of a teacher's character. His early normal classes took over meeting houses, town halls and hotels with no sense that these forms affected his work. When he built special structures for normal training, a professional schoolman fashioned a structure which looked like nothing so much as a steepleless church. The enlargement of normal facilities after 1860 somewhat derivatively followed the colleges' earlier solutions to the problem of teaching groups beyond adolescence. At the moment they developed something of a professional leverage—salary increases, a literature, a historical sense of their work and increasing public support—at that moment in the late 1860s and early 1870s two patterns emerged which dramatically affected the personnel of the normal school: they failed to attract the same kind of personnel as the other professions and they began to admit a still poorer and even less talented trainee than ever before.[93] Unlike the first, however, the second generation strained to use their assumptions of harmony to explain the social alignments which disrupted their work and their aspirations. Well before immigration exacerbated these tendencies, as they did after the turn of the century, the problem of social class divisions within the professional schoolman's ranks forced an abridgment of older ways of understanding the nature of the teacher's work. More than the earlier generation's problem of governance was the later generation's need to determine whether schooling held any place at all in the professional spectrum.

The whole question of whether teaching could be a profession endangered the meager self-sufficiency that schoolmen had actually achieved during the 1870s and 1880s. Their key institution, the normal school, became less and less the domicile of professional norms and a symbol of equilibrium. No longer did they indulge the boasts of earlier schoolmen that education was the balance-wheel of the social machinery. Perhaps more apt than he intended, Boyden in 1890 drew an analogy from fictional literature and called the normal school a "reservoir" which, in some indistinct fashion, ensured the practical self-sufficiency of its society some distance away.[94] The price of self-sufficiency for professional schoolmen became insularity. The traditional reticence which once well served the interests of harmony worked against them by the end of the century. Habituated against direct measures and political initiatives, schoolmen could not believe that extraordinary collective action against specific problems would help rather than hinder their general principles.

The "Classless" Profession

In the nineteenth century considerations of social class and actual career advantage seldom intruded into the open discussion of professional schoolmen. When they were entertained, such considerations were employed to defend the normal school from accusations of rigidity and competitiveness with existing educational institutions. Such ideas were never marshaled to specify the distinct advantages and services of the normal school. The evangelical roots of their thought and special institutions enabled schoolmen to boast a peculiar moral dimension to the work of education. The connection between instruction and moral development was sufficient achievement for the first generation. Professional schoolmen then and later maintained that equation between moral instruction and public education.

They did convince their public that indirect moral control was an ideal for both individual and society. The actual mechanics of this control, indirect and gradual as it was, made specific problems of governance particularly poignant and difficult (witness the plight of Cyrus Peirce at the Lexington Normal School, to take but one example). Schoolmen could not refine distinctions between an individual and his society or between a teacher and his students, except to acknowledge that divorces between the two disrupted a desirable moral harmony. Analysis of governance problems in terms of social class became, as it were, too impersonal and too detached from the moral spheres of life which they earnestly sought. This moralized process of schoolmen's thought continually demanded that their professional aims and achievement be distinguished from all activities connoting social privilege and private advantage. One searches the educational literature of the nineteenth century in vain, trying to find institutional definitions or institutional records which might translate their ubiquitous assertions of moral worth into patterns of practical achievement.

In 1859 Professor Alpheus Crosby, once a classicist on the faculty of Dartmouth College, then a principal of the Salem Normal School, tendered one of the boldest ante-bellum definitions of the American normal school.[95] By contrast to the general instruction of common school, high school, and academy and college, the normal school was, he said, a professional school like those which serve theology, law, medicine, the military, agriculture, commerce, mechanics, mining, the fine arts, etc. He looked to the teachers' seminaries in Europe to elaborate this broad distinction. Americans avoided the objectionable European practice of taking "young men or boys of the lower classes and of very moderate previous attainments, and by a course of appropriate exercises, to drill them into a preparation for conducting, according to prescribed routines, schools for the limited education of these lower classes. . . . In this station they are generally expected, without essential change or hope of change, to continue, repeating the beaten round, through life. Were the fixed and mechanical processes not objectionable enough, still more offensive was the corollary to such practice: appointment to particular places usually emanates from the same authority that sustains the Normal Schools." [96]

The American example differed dramatically, Crosby asserted, and, speaking to an audience of normal schoolmen, he met only agreement in the pursuit of a counter-Euorpean model of professional training. In America, he stated, the pupils are from no particular grades in society, and are least of all from those families which would be accounted lowest in social position.[97] Not only were they better prepared now than ever before, but teachers experienced in their professional schools much less uniformity in respect to their plans for life. Normal schools prepared one for all general instruction. Study at these institutions also did not soften the need for thorough study, since school committees examined normal school graduates no less rigorously than they did (or did not) other candidates for positions.[98] Normal schoolmen were proud that normal school training offered no privileges to potential teachers in the face of such examinations. Study at such an institution in no way lessened the obligation, in school and after, for teachers "to make places for themselves." [99] As a consequence and also as an ideal, patterns of professional placement were not easily predictable, nor should they be in the eyes of normal school faculties. "He who can teach," Crosby generalized, "scientifically and adroitly a primary school, may be trusted, if his literary attainments are sufficient, in any department of instruction up to the university." Though his remarks betrayed the college-slanted norms of the first generation, Crosby correctly stated the general expectations of both the first- and second-generation schoolmen about the professional consequences of the work.

The well-trained teacher should have access to all grades of teaching positions. College teaching, which demanded the highest "literary attainments," posed the only sphere restricted to normal school trainees. Even here the exact relationship was ambiguous since the early normal schoolmen had been themselves college-trained. This traffic from college to normal school, which normal schoolmen encouraged with their scholarship programs and four-year academic courses, suggested the possibility that soon the traffic would become comfortably bilateral. In spite of several notable exceptions, however, especially after the 1890s, normal school graduates never provided colleges with faculty members. Serious efforts were made by first-generation schoolmen to avoid a sharp institutional division. Through the 1850s Henry Barnard had approached several colleges to establish scholarships and professional chairs devoted to educational subjects. Barnard seemed to have been quite anxious about colleges refusing to train teachers.[100] His applications to all sorts of institutions of higher education suggest that his aim was to register the teaching of teachers as a legitimate collegiate enterprise. Had his efforts succeeded, the collegiate prejudices against normal schools would likely have never sharpened into the social class divisions of the early twentieth century. Likely too, men like Alpheus Crosby would have worried less about American normal schools aping the errors of Europe.

Still, social class divisions did emerge as the work of the second-generation schoolmen drew to a close in the 1890s. Gradually these divisions became apparent, first as divisions within normal schools, then as divisions between colleges and normal schools as competing institutions. Even at normal schools like Bridgewater, which schoolmen accepted as a model of its kind and which perhaps resisted open class divisions more effectively than did its sister schools, the peculiar structure of the student body placed the normal school in a subordinate class position by the end of the nineteenth century. In

Table 8

The Occupations of the Fathers

of Bridgewater Normal School Students, 1854–1904 [a]

Occupation	1854–1862	1878–1886	1887–1895	1896–1904	Total
Farmer	183—39% [b]	103—19%	125—17%	150—16%	561—21%
Unskilled Laborer	4—0.9%	49— 9%	59— 8%	108—11%	220— 8%
Mechanic and Craftsman	126—27%	191—33%	283—38%	311—33%	911—34%
Merchant	40— 9%	90—17%	119—16%	188—20%	437—16%
Manufacturer	17— 4%	27— 5%	28— 4%	19— 2%	91— 3%
Professional	23— 5%	24— 5%	26— 3%	36— 4%	109— 4%
Teachers	5— 1%	9— 2%	14— 2%	14— 1%	42— 2%
Unknown	68—15%	51— 9%	89—12%	127—13%	335—12%
Total	466	544	743	953	2,706

[a] The sources for these figures are the manuscript admission records, in the Archives of Bridgewater State College, Bridgewater, Massachusetts. See #101, page 217 for a complete description of the categories of occupations.

[b] The percentage figure represents the fraction of the total for that eight-year sequence. For example, for the period 1854–1862, 39 percent of the students had fathers who were farmers.

the ante-bellum period the normal school was not a clear competitor for college-bound youth (though the leadership of both generations seemed to draw upon that category of youth), but equally clearly these schools had good reason to hope that they would eventually attract young men with genuine professional prospects. They kept these options open, at least until the 1890s. Before that date they resisted class demarcations as avidly as they professed to keep education clear of political and partisan biases. To avoid becoming a school which served any special class, age or sex exclusively, normal schools had to seek college-bound males and experienced teachers older than the majority of young women who sought teaching as a profession in the period of reconstruction just after the Civil War.

In spite of many effort to achieve other results, normal schools attracted youth from the upper social strata only in small numbers. In fact, such youth can be found less and less among normal school trainees as such schools neared 1900. Equally significant the middling social class of self-sufficient farmers and mechanics, who came in large numbers to the normal schools before the war, did not continue after the conflict to supply the same percentages of trainees. The index of these changes can be found in the pattern of occupations pursued by the fathers of normal school students at Bridgewater, where such information is available.[101]

The most important feature of Table 8 is the percentage of students whose fathers were physicians, lawyers and clergymen, showing how little professionals (and teachers) supported the normal school by entrusting their children to them. The percentage of these students remains stable at relatively 4 percent throughout the fifty-year period, while the student body increased more than threefold, from eighty-six students in 1862 to 257 in 1904. While the actual members more than tripled, students from farming families dropped by half over the same period. From the mechanical trades, especially that of shoemaking, students increased from more than one-quarter in the ante-bellum period to more than one-third of the student body by the turn of the century. Most important, by the late 1870s and early 1880s, transportation made Bridgewater Normal School accessible to Boston Irish. After those decades the normal school's student body began to draw from dependent classes rather than from merely the less affluent and poorer classes of rural New England. If the admissions of sons and daughters of hostlers, teamsters, sailors and gate-tenders made normal schools more democratic and classless than colleges, these alignments ensured firm distinctions between normal schools and most liberal arts colleges by 1900.

Few normal schools had Bridgewater's advantages in slowing these realignments. Throughout the nineteenth century the school consistently taught and graduated more male students than any other in the United States. Table 9 shows that Bridgewater's student body always had a large male minority, ranging between forty-two to twenty-one percent until the 1890s.

Table 9

The Sexes of Bridgewater Normal School Students, Admitted and Graduated, 1840–1909

Years	1840s	1850s	1860s	1870s	1880s	1890s	1900s	Total
Graduated	390	487	345	409	678	968	1,049	4,326 [a]
Male	167-42.9%	184-37.7%	107-31.0%	106-25.9%	148-21.8%	152-15.7%	93- 8.9%	957
Female	223-57.3%	303-62.2%	238-69.0%	303-74.0%	530-78.1%	816-84.2%	956-90.1%	3,369
Admitted	578	624	566	556	—	—	—	[6,875 [c]]
Male	264	234	184	122	—	—	—	—
Female	314	390	382	434	—	—	—	—
% Admitted Who								
Actually Graduated	67.3%	78.2%	60.9%	39.3% [b]	—	—	—	[66.7% [d]]
Male	63.2%	78.6%	58.1%	39.3%	—	—	—	—
Female	71.0%	77.6%	62.3%	39.4%	—	—	—	—

[a] I have used the *History and Alumni Record: Bridgewater State Normal School* (1876), until 1876 the most authoritative account of student attendance. From 1876 to 1909 I used the *Register of Graduates: Bridgewater Normal School, 1840–1913* (1913).

[b] The figures in this column represent only the years 1870–1876: Total-219; Male-48; Female-171.

[c] This figure represents the years 1840–1913 and is given in *Register of Graduates* (1913), p. 178.

[d] This percentage is based on figures given in *Register of Graduates* (1913), p. 178. There the total number of graduates for the years 1840–1913 is 4,586.

The actual number of men studying at Bridgewater Normal School remained relatively stable. However, the number did drop, expectedly, during the Civil War and the unstable economic period which followed into the 1870s. Still, even during this period from 1860 to 1890 male students represented from one-third to one-fifth the whole student body. More significant than these comparisons was the sharp decline in students who were admitted but failed to graduate. This change seems to have been felt more severely after the war than during the actual war years themselves. Subsequent records did indicate that later student attendance eventually redressed this percentage decline. In 1913 the school announced that 66.7 percent of all students since 1840 had actually graduated. To achieve that percentage, competitive with Bridgewater's accomplishment in the 1850s, the normal school had to en-courage substantial increases in females during the 1890s and 1900s. By the end of the first decade of the twentieth century, teacher training had become an educational alternative for women. The favored treatment of male students suggests that this was not entirely a welcome outcome. During the 1880s and 1890s the male minority continued to outnumber women in the four-year professional course, and they maintained their hold on the pivotal student associations. The small minority of males and the four-year course of professional studies had been eliminated from almost all other normal schools by 1900.

At the turn of the century normal schools had been overtaken by women and by vocational training for specific skills. The curriculum had quickly lost its pretense of academic training and had gained methods which collegiate minds deemed unprofessionally mechanical. The large majority of graduates now staffed almost exclusively elementary grades in city systems.[102] During the nineties schoolmen initiated one last effort to salvage their older notions of a normal school as a bastion and a reservoir safeguarding society in intricate, genteel and complex ways. The State Board of Education mandated higher admission requirements (a high school diploma), higher teacher salaries, more rigid tests for graduation and more concerted action among the schools.[103] In addition, they founded three more normal schools committed exclusively to staffing the systems of their host cities. With the reorganiza-tion of the Board of Education in 1909 the new processes of increased rationalization, namely, departmentalization, began, resulting in a state sys-tem with each normal school responsible for a particular professional specialty:[104] kindergarten instruction for Worcester Normal School; commercial subjects for Salem; household arts for Framingham; practical arts for Fitchburg; music for Lowell; correspondence courses for North Adams; summer schools for Hyannis; standard elementary grades for Westfield; and, as its history might have suggested, upper-grade teaching (ultimately junior high school training) for Bridgewater. In 1913 Bridgewater made one last appeal to save its college-slanted academic course, which kept it from shedding totally all its earlier aspirations.[105] However, even as selected normal schools like Bridgewater became teachers' colleges, teacher-training institutions never transcended those professional traditions which appeared disparaging to educators with academic assumptions about professional instruction.

In 1913 Arthur C. Boyden tried to defend Bridgewater against the worst effects of the new specialized normal school. In a remarkably candid and illuminating letter to David Snedden, the newly appointed commissioner of education of Massachusetts, he tried to create as Bridgewater's special field of teaching an older notion of normal school training. He argued to Snedden that Bridgewater should conduct exclusively for the Massachusetts normal school network a four-year course of professional study.[106] In defense of his proposal he offered Bridgewater's unique record in such a program. The four-year course had begun in 1869 and to date [1913] had graduated 386 individuals. Almost all were men. This program had achieved the highest aspirations of normal school training: (1) a course of study with easy access to colleges which credited many of the normal school courses and (2) its impartial service to all schools and grades of school systems. The four-year course had in a few cases done what few normal schools had done, namely, placed normal school graduates on college faculties. Seventy-five of the 386 had gone to college. Of these, five were still attending and two had died; fourteen had taught in normal schools and twenty-five in high schools; seven became city grammar masters, five superintendents, nine departmental teachers, two college instructors, two book publishers and four ultimately entered other professions. Considering the 386 as a whole, thirty-two had taught in normal schools, fify-five in high schools, 113 in grammar schools; 116 became grammar masters, fifteen superintendents, thirty-six departmental teachers; and seven developed into primary teachers or supervisors.

Boyden's rationale stressed the equation between the academic and cultural studies, on the one hand, and on the other, educational leadership. Such training restated the promises Alpheus Crosby had made more than a half-century before to the American Normal School Association. Properly trained, a teacher could instruct any group, whatever its social class, whatever its educational level, whatever the subject. The instructor's talent rested partly on skill and preparation, predominantly on his or her character. Bridgewater had succeeded in filling many of the major directorates of education, especially the superintendencies, the principalships, and the offices of the Board of Education, between 1850 and 1890, operating on these assumptions and the programs deriving from them. Had Boyden addressed these arguments to Snedden's predecessor, he likely would have received a more receptive hearing and have probably won his point. Snedden's prodecessor had been Boyden's own colleague on the Bridgewater staff during the elder Boyden's tenure, namely George H. Martin. Martin represented perhaps the most concrete illustration of Bridgewater's professional achievement. He had been a student at Bridgewater in 1862, a faculty member there from 1864 to 1883, agent of the Massachusetts Board of Education from 1883 to 1892, a member of the Boston Board of Supervisors from 1893 to 1905, and climactically he succeeded to Horace Mann's office, the secretary of the Board of Education of Massachusetts in 1906.[107] By contrast Snedden was not only not a Bridgewater graduate, he had not even attended a normal school. Moreover, not only was he not a Massachusetts schoolman, he had not even been born in New England. Snedden had improved upon his studies at Stanford with graduate work at Teachers College, Columbia University, where he had refined in several books notions of education conditioned by organized social grouping.[108]

Snedden offered neither understanding to Boyden's appeal nor continuity to Martin's work and disrupted a deep-rooted but informal educational tradition of professional efficiency. The norms and careers of Bridgewater's graduates rested upon the pivotal role of the normal school. Boyden and Martin had derived their professional views from a special educational environment and from a distinct moral frame of reference. Their genteel style, as a consequence, domesticated but did not transform the evangelical habit of thought characteristic of the earliest professional schoolmen of the antebellum period. Both Boydens, father and son, like Cyrus Peirce, relied heavily on the intangible educative force of moral character. In spite of the numerous differences among these generations of schoolmen in the nineteenth century, their moral vision sought a harmonious fellowship as a professional and social ideal. In the face of exceptions to such an order, they habitually restated the ideal rather than analyzed the problem. Professional schoolmen as a whole never conceived in the nineteenth century that their moral harmony was ultimately anything other than a matter of voluntary cooperation among different individuals. When political machination abruptly intruded, as it did with the forced reorganization of the Massachusetts Board of Education in 1909, George Martin was compelled to resign his office. Although the victim of a rude power play, Martin continued to serve as adviser to his successor, David Snedden. In many respects Bridgewater graduates who knew he had been "demoted" were nevertheless more proud that Martin deported himself as a gentleman than they were of his once eminent position. His example could serve well as a cameo for normal schoolmen as a nineteenth-century educational and professional type.

CHAPTER VIII

The Passing of the American Institute
of Instruction

New Alignments in the Nineties

In 1891 the American Institute of Instruction experienced one of its final surges of membership. Since the spectacular success of the association under Thomas Bicknell in the mid-1870s, no meeting boasted increases of a hundred members or more. In fact, during the whole preceding decade of the 1880s, the Institute languished. For the first time in its history it kept no record of its members. Between 1877 and 1891 only 269 educators had been admitted.[1] The large new membership, however, was not the most significant feature of the 1891 meeting.

The profession's journal of record, the *Journal of Education*, founded by the energetic Bicknell and in policy changed only slightly since the 1870s, reported that the Bethlehem (New Hampshire) meeting was "one of the every way best in the history of the American Institute of Instruction."[2] Though the ties between the association and the journal were very close—both Bicknell and the later editor, Albert E. Winship, had been or would become presidents of the Institute—the special report of the 1891 convention was not mere self-congratulation. The special merits of the meeting were enumerated. More than its strong program and large attendance, Winship explained, it "was the only meeting of the kind that we ever attended in which we heard no word of complaint from any source. . . . The officers," he continued, "did not growl because the teachers went on excursions, as they did in 'ye olden times', the weather was not a cause of complaint; there were excursions of all

Table 10

Third-Generation [a] Presidents of the American Institute
of Instruction, 1887–1918

Name	Life Dates	College	A.I.I. Dates	Professional Position While President
J. Milton Hall	1836– ?	(Bridgewater N.S.)	1887–1888	Grammar (pub.) Sch. Prin.
George A. Littlefield	1851–1906	Harvard	1889–1890	Supt. of Schools
Ray Greene Huling	1847–1915	Brown	1891–1892	High School Prin.
George H. Martin	1841–1917	(Bridgewater N.S.)	1894	School [Asst Supt] Spvsr.
W. W. Stetson	1849–1910	(xMonmouth College)	1895	Supt of Schools
Charles W. Parmenter	1852– ?	Tufts	1896	High School Prin.
Albert E. Winship	1845–1933	(Bridgewater N.S.)	1897	Ed, *Journal of Education*
George E. Church	1846–1913	Amherst	1898	Grammar School Prin (pub.)
Orasmus B. Bruce	1840–1903	None	1899	Supt of Schools
Mason S. Stone	1859– ?	U Vermont	1900	Supt of Schools
William F. Bradbury	1829–1914	Amherst	1901–1902	High School Principal
Charles H. Keyes	1858–1925	St. John's	1904–1905	[Supt] Dist. Principal
Walter E. Ranger	1855–1941	Bates	1906–1907	School Commissioner
Henry C. Morrison	1871– ?	Dartmouth	1908–1909	Supt of Schools
Payson Smith	1873– ?	None	1910–1911	Supt of Schools
Charles T. C. Whitcomb	1861–1931	Amherst	1912–1913	High Sch. Principal
Franklin B. Dyer	1858– ?	Ohio Wesleyan	1914	Supt of Schools
William T. Orr	1860– ?	Amherst	1915	Agent [Asst Supt] Bd of Ed
Carlos B. Ellis	1860– ?	(Unknown)	1917	High School Principal
Wallace E. Mason	1861–1944	Bowdoin	1918	Normal School Principal

[a] The last seven presidents do not belong, strictly speaking, to the third generation, which describes those schoolmen born twenty-five years after the second generation, or around the year 1845. Since the majority have not yet established a clear fourth generation I have grouped them all under the designation "third generation."

kinds; there was no electioneering for office; there was no discussion that caused hot blood; indeed everything seemed to go as if by magic." [3] Most remarkable of all perhaps was the sharp divergent attitude between Winship's report and olden-times views of the Institute as a harmonious professional agency. Still more, his remarks help illuminate those features and those forces which altered the schoolmen's profession at the turn of the century and shortly after caused the demise of the Institute itself.

The public admission of growling, complaint and bad blood emerging from professional discussions in its way announced the passing of the rhetoric of professional harmony. The consensus of earlier meetings, at least the appearance of consensus in all official and informal accounts of their proceedings, no longer captured the priorities of the profession. The second generation had fragmented that harmony by making the center of their work the numerous self-contained professional and preparatory schools. After the Civil War schoolmen maintained the ante-bellum conceptions and language of their teachers but applied those terms with different institutions and meanings. Where first-generation schoolmen had employed voluntary associations and their successors distinct, practical training schools, the third generation, coming to power at the turn of the century, turned more and more to administrative values for educational success. In 1891 the absence of dissension "as if by magic" from the meetings of the American Institute of Instruction stemmed from the "tact and modesty" of its officers. Earlier such success might as easily have been attributed to the communality of the membership or the exercises with suggestive pedagogical styles.

After 1889 the third generation of professional schoolmen filled the presidency of the Institute, just as they were then filling elsewhere the policy-making positions of their profession. In Table 10 one can see that not only were these positions generally being filled by another generation of schoolmen, but the positions they sought were also changing. In post-bellum America schoolmen frequently moved from superintendencies to principalships of normal schools, headmasterships of preparatory academies and large city high schools or even in some cases to college faculties.[4] At the turn of the century upward mobility within the profession ended with the superintendent. If a young man abandoned a supervisory position, usually his motion was lateral to another superintendency in a more urbanized context. It was hardly surprising that eight of the last thirteen presidents of the American Institute of Instruction were drawn from the supervisory sector of the profession.[5] By 1908 more presidents had been drawn from that position than elsewhere in the ranks of schoolmen. Indeed Table 11 dramatizes that after the turn of the century the superintendent category experienced the most dramatic increase in the Institute's membership. In the last decade of its history superintendents exceeded by double every other group of profes-

Table 11

The Presidents of the American Institute of Instruction: Professional Grouping, 1830–1918

Professional Position	1830s	1840s	1850s	1860s	1870s	1880s	1890s	1900s	1910s [a]	Total
Superintendent			1	3	1	3	3	4	3	18
Grammar School		1			1	1	1			4
Academy		1	1		1					3
High School			1	3	1	1	2	1	2	11
Normal School					1				1	2
College/University Professor	1				1					2
Friend of Education	1	1								2
Education Editor						1		1		2
Total	2	3	3	6	6	6	6	6	6	44

[a] This column accounts for only the years 1910–1918.

Table 12

The Presidents of the American Institute of Instruction: College Affiliation, 1830–1918

College	1830s	1840s	1850s	1860s	1870s	1880s	1890s	1900s	1910s	Total
(Bridgewater State Normal)						1	1	1	2	5
Dartmouth						2	2	1		5
Amherst			1		2		1		1	5
Brown					3	1	1			5
Union			1	1						2
Harvard	1	2		1						4
Yale	1		1	1						3
Bowdoin									1	1
Tufts							1			1
Other				3			1			4
(College Unfinished)						2			3	5
No College		1			1				1	3
Unknown									1	1
Total	2	3	3	6	6	6	7	2	9	44

sional schoolman.[6] A contrast of Table 11 and Table 1 presents the historical discrepancies between leadership and membership in one significant voluntary association. Such a match documents the increasing stratifications and undemocratic representations which the schoolmen's ideology produced in the course of the nineteenth century.

The forces which made supervision newly attractive at the end of the century rasied the fortunes of many schoolmen who were not explicitly superintendents. Such men did reach important professional positions like the presidency of the Institute. The president of the very successful 1891 meeting was Ray Greene Huling whose long tenures in the high schools of Fitchburg, New Bedford and Cambridge, Massachusetts bore witness to his management abilities.[7] More revealing, Huling with several fellow graduates of Brown University had been instrumental in founding the New England Association of Colleges and Preparatory Schools in 1885. That organization had been responsible for engaging the interests of Harvard's Charles Eliot and selected college leaders in the work of public education. The New England Association also had laid the groundwork for the famous Committee of Ten of the National Education Association, which in turn had formalized the curricular relationship between high schools and colleges.[8] Unlike many of his predecessors in the American Institute of Instruction, Huling moved easily between the practical and the collegiate spheres of education, not the least tribute to the "tact and modesty" which Winship had so admired. More and more this kind of talent figured centrally in the work of the professional superintendent.

Accordingly one of the special features of the Institute's successful meeting was the presence of several prominent college presidents and professors.[9] Huling's many contacts and affiliations with academic men undoubtedly played an important role in this participation. There were, however, other pressures which awakened college men to the work of the American Institute of Instruction. In the early nineteenth century teaching had attracted about one-twentieth of the graduates of American colleges; by the end of the century it had absorbed about one-quarter of them, about 5 percent more than any other profession. After 1880, on a graph of the professions followed by collegians, the line for teaching crossed that of the ministry, and after 1890 that of law. At the close of the century teaching had become numerically the dominant profession for American college graduates, with business its closest competitor.[10] The leadership of American colleges entered the proceedings of the American Institute of Instruction and its sister institutions in the 1890s partially to respond to the changes in the aspirations of their students. Among this leadership at the 1891 meeting of the Institute were Merrill E. Gates, president of Amherst College, the Reverend William DeWitt Hyde, president of Bowdoin College, Harvard's philosopher Josiah Royce (lecturing on "Tendencies in the Development of the American University"), Edmund

Table 13

College Graduates in the American Institute of Instruction, 1830–1908

College	1830s	1840s	1850s	1860s	1870s	1880s	1890s	1900s [a]	Totals
Dartmouth	8	6	13	12	12	6	9	7	73—17%
Harvard	23	1	6	7	3	6	7	8	61—14%
Yale	17	—	6	7	7	4	4	6	51—12%
Brown	6	4	11	4	3	2	4	4	38— 9%
Amherst	1	3	4	5	11	4	2	4	34— 8%
Bowdoin	3	4	3	3	3	4	1	3	24— 6%
Williams	3	2	2	2	3	1	1	2	16— 4%
Colby	—	—	—	2	3	3	4	3	15— 4%
Wesleyan	—	1	1	2	3	2	2	2	13— 3%
Bates	—	—	—	—	2	—	6	3	11— 3%
Middlebury	—	7	2	—	1	—	—	—	10— 2%
Union	1	—	1	—	2	1	—	—	5— 1%
Tufts	—	—	—	1	—	—	3	1	5— 1%
Michigan	—	—	—	1	1	1	1	1	5— 1%
Assorted [b] (3 or less)	5	2	4	6	4	7	16	9	53—13%
Unknown	2	—	2	—	1	1	1	—	7— 2%
Totals	69	30	55	52	59	42	61	53	421

[a] Available data for the 1900s include only new members for the years 1900–1908.

[b] The "Assorted" category includes: Oberlin (1); Columbia (1); Chicago (3); Syracuse (2); University of Georgia (1); South Carolina College (1); West Point (1); Transylvania (1); New York University (2); Allegheny College (2); Trinity College (1); Princeton (3); Vassar (1); Germany (3) (many of the above held German degrees; here listed are those with *only* German degrees); University of Glasgow (1); Hamilton College (3); University of Vermont (3); University of North Pennsylvania (1); Ohio Wesleyan (2); Smith College (1); Cornell (2); Stanford (1); Denison (1); Hobart (1); Rochester (1); Antioch (1); Queens College, Belfast (1); Michigan State (1); Wellesley (1); Cleveland University (1); Monmouth College (2); City College of New York (1); Franklin College (1); Boston University (1); University of California (1); Kenyon College (1); Wittemberg College (1).

J. James of the University of Pennsylvania and then president of the American Society for the Extension of University Training, and Paul Hanus, the first professor of education at Harvard and personally brought by Charles Eliot to that position from the Colorado Normal School in Denver that same year, 1891.[11]

The participation of college leaders was not totally a novelty to the Institute. The novelty in 1891 and for the remaining years of the Institute's history rested upon the significant number of institutions and viewpoints not indigenous to New England. In fact, Hanus before going to Colorado had been raised and educated in Wisconsin and Michigan; Royce originated from California; James from Illinois and even Hyde had come to the presidency of

Bowdoin from his New Jersey congregation.[12] These college and university men seemed to share in common the view that higher education required some accommodation between the traditional notion of academic discipline and the newer practical values represented by professional schoolmen. Their appearance at the Institute in the early 1890s represented one effort to work out that accommodation with the leaders of the teaching profession.

Before 1890 there had been only two other surges of college leaders into the ranks of schoolmen. The first had been in the 1830s when graduates especially of Harvard and Yale created the Institute. The first president, the Reverend Francis Wayland of Brown, was the only college president ever to head the Institute. The second surge occurred during the second generation's sway (1860–1890) when the graduates of Brown together with the back-country colleges of Amherst, Dartmouth, Bowdoin, Williams, Waterville (Colby), Wesleyan, Bates and Middlebury provided the college men who joined the Institute.[13] Table 13 shows that only Dartmouth consistently provided professional schoolmen with their prominent men, though the alumni of four schools dominated the presidency of the Institute. In the scale of known college men who joined the Institute Dartmouth provided almost 20 percent.[14] If these earlier academic cohorts in the Institute had been more successful in their particular aims, the third surge of the nineties might have signaled a less dramatic and novel reorientation of the Institute.

Equally significant with the presence of college men with new purposes, Winship reported, was the return in 1891 of Boston schoolmasters to the Institute's meetings.[15] In the late 1840s and 1850s Boston schoolmasters, bristling at their inability to modify the reforms of Horace Mann and the course of the Institute, had turned their energies toward the state associations, of which the Massachusetts State Teachers Association, founded in 1847 by "practical schoolmen," had been the first. Between the ante-bellum period and the nineties, Boston's schoolmen had never returned enthusiastically to the Institute's meetings. Over the history of the Institute, grammar schoolmen had composed 25 percent of the entire membership, but that category of schoolmen, perhaps lacking the support of the Boston group, never assumed a real leadership in the organization.[16] In fact, only two public grammar schoolmasters—J. Milton Hall (1887–1888) and George E. Church (1898)—ever served the Institute as presidents. Both men made their careers in the school system of Providence, Rhode Island and presided late in the Institute's history.[17]

Of the twelve Boston schoolmasters Winship counted in 1891 only ten appear on the official roster of the meeting, but this small group (the overall attendance had been 887) [18] indicated some of the career features affecting the future of the Institute and the profession at large. Boston offered the most prestigious and lucrative educational positions in the state which consistently offered the highest or near-highest average salaries in the country for public

Table 14
Geographical Distribution of the American Institute
of Instruction Membership, 1891

1891 Residence	Number	Percent
Maine	47	5.3%
New Hampshire	97	10.9%
Vermont	27	3.2%
Massachusetts	536	60.4%
Rhode Island	56	6.4%
Connecticut	65	7.3%
Elsewhere	59	6.5%
Total	887	100%

SOURCE: *Lectures and Proceedings of the American Institute of Instruction*, 62 (Boston, 1891): xxxvi-xxxvii.

instruction. These attractions had drawn men from all parts of New England and the country,[19] a fact which changes the meaning of Table 14 and keeps the Institute at least a regional association even in its final years. At times it seemed as if Massachusetts men were a minority in the teaching personnel of that state. Though they had generally taught for long periods in their particular school, Boston schoolmasters were seldom natives of the city. Like the first public grammar schoolman who served the Institute as president in 1888, four of the ten in Winship's group had taken professional courses in the Bridgewater Normal School and, unlike many of the remaining six, had found places in the Boston school system as soon as their professional training ended.[20] Of the known members of this group only Augustus D. Small was a college graduate (Colby), though several had been prepared for college or had attended once for a short period. In the 1840s and 1850s when Boston schoolmasters took their leave of the Institute, those departing were largely college graduates and ministers and likely had not been raised and educated far from Boston itself. By contrast their successors, the then old-line grammar schoolmen of the second generation, facing a mounting number of immigrant children in their classes, found themselves in the early nineties in common cause with the younger superintendents and academic men, eager to give an academically biased curriculum a more practical bent. This objective also implied a rejuvenation of older professional associations like the American Institute of Instruction.

Perhaps as important as the new influences upon the Institute were the decreases in certain categories of professional teaching, particularly the orthodox academic sectors which had played prominent roles in the Institute until the end of the century. Winship's report of the 1891 meeting omitted mention of the role of academy teachers. While new academies continued to

Table 15
Normal Schools in the United States, 1876

Years	Number	Region	Number
1835–1839	2	New England	17
1840–1844	2	Middle Atlantic	27
1845–1849	3	South	35
1850–1854	6	Middle West	55
1855–1859	6	West	3
1860–1864	9		
1865–1869	43		
1870–1875	61		
Unknown	7		
Total	139		137

SOURCE: Thomas Hunter, "Normal Schools in the United States," *The Cyclopedia of Education: Dictionary of Information,* ed. by Henry Kiddle and Alexander J. Schem (New York, 1883 [1st ed., 1876], p. 810.

Table 16
Bridgewater Normal School Graduates in the American Institute of Instruction:
Professional Positions, 1840–1908

Professional Position [a]	1840s	1850s	1860s	1870s	1880s	1890s	1900s	Total
Superintendent	1	—	4	1	1	2	—	9— 5.6%
Grammar School	15	16	16	13	7	5	—	72—44.7%
High School	2	3	1	1	4	1	—	12— 7.4%
Academy/Private High School	2	2	—	—	—	—	—	4— 2.4%
Normal School	6	3	4	4	1	5	—	23—14.2%
College/University	—	—	—	1	—	—	—	1— .6%
Other	1	—	1	—	2	—	—	4— 2.4%
Unknown	2	8	5	7	7	5	2	36—22.7%
Total	29	32	31	27	22	18	2	161—100%

[a] "Professional Position" indicates the generic educational role held in the year the person (there are 45 women in this computation) joined the Institute. That year determined the placement.

Table 17
Bridgewater Normal School Graduates in the American Institute
of Instruction: Male and Female, 1840–1908

Sex	1840s	1850s	1860s	1870s	1880s	1890s	1900s	Total
Male	28	24	23	15	16	10	0	116
Female	1	8	9	12	7	8	2	45
Total	29	32	32	27	23	18	2	161

be founded to the end of the century, these increases were not reflected in the ranks of the Institute's members. By the 1900s the representation of the academy had declined to half the high levels of the 1870s.[21] Similarly Winship made no mention of the decline of normal school graduates, which, like the history of the academy, contrasted with the marked increase (Table 15) in that genre of schooling in the latter half of the nineteenth century.[22] Both the academy and the normal school had been very much in evidence through the 1870s, but afterward their effect came through members who had attended such schools but who represented other kinds of institutions in the Institute and the profession. The record of Winship's own school, the Bridgewater Normal School, illuminates this pattern (Table 16). While nineteen Bridgewater alumni and alumnae had joined the Institute in the 1880s and fifteen in the 1890s—half the numbers which joined in the 1850s and 1860s—only two new members from Bridgewater, both female (Table 17) entered the Institute in the 1900s.[23] Given the dramatic increases in normal schools generally, normal training affected the professional associations by directing their trainees away from national councils and forums. For different reasons the academy and the normal school had too effectively provided their students with a self-contained educational experience. Whatever its other benefits these institutions tended to drain professional talent out of the national assemblies of professional schoolmen.

As dramatic as the rise of the superintendent in the Institute was the increase of the high school principal in its membership. In this respect too the 1891 president of the association, Ray Greene Huling, indicated the new alignments in the professional structure. The representation of high school principals and teachers had waned in the 1880s but had improved remarkably by the turn of the century. Over the entire history of the association this sector of the profession formed the third largest group and contributed 15 percent of the entire membership.[24] At the same time the academy contributed half or less than half the number of the high school. Though their pattern paralleled the high school between 1840 and 1880, after that period the high school representation nearly doubled. After the 1880s the distinctions between the academy and the high school spokesman widened sharply. As with the colleges, some academies pressed themselves to accommodate the more practical concerns of the new century. However, the majority of both the academy and the college representatives experienced a joint decline of 50 percent by 1908 as compared with their levels in the Institute during the 1870s. Over the Institute's entire history academy men contributed about 14 percent of the Institute's membership while colleges sent 11 percent.[25]

The third stage of the Institute's history, begun in 1891, turned not on the withdrawal of academic schoolmen but on the influx of superintendents. More and more the superintendents' professional interests joined those of the public grammar schoolmen and schoolmen of the high schools. Their rapprochement with academic schoolmen from colleges, academies and normal schools like Bridgewater, however tenuous it was, gave the American Institute of Instruction life for two decades more. The most important service of these alliances was the formalization of the superintendency as a professional agent. The widening gap between the high school and the grammar school, or in a word, between public education and the academy and the college (or private education), gave the superintendent's office a new professional responsibility and function. In particular, superintendents in the Institute as in their practical work labored energetically during the last years of the nineteenth century to maintain a general forum where different ideologies could communicate with and accommodate each other. Their achievements and failures can be understood best in the context of the evangelical traditions which they drew upon. Ultimately they were not able to preserve the Institute and its values of professional harmony. But their failure was not total and and many of their nineteenth-century norms and institutions grafted themselves easily onto twentieth-century professional practice. The transformation of the superintendent's role in professional education thus explains more than the central norms and behavior of schoolmen at the end of the nineteenth century; it also illuminates the last essential features of the American Institute of Instruction and how that long-lived association could not survive whole in the twentieth century.

The Discovery of the Superintendent

During the 1870s the American Institute of Instruction and professional schoolmen nationally experienced sharp and rapid turns of fortune. After disinterest nearly ended the association in the early 1870s, the reforms of Thomas Bicknell and his Rhode Island supporters produced the largest meetings in the Institute's history, culminating with the convention in 1877 in Montpelier, Vermont.[26] By the end of the decade, however, the membership and leadership had lapsed once again. Younger, more precisely national, organizations like the National Education Association fared no better.[27] Apart from other causes, perhaps the most telling had been the pressure of renewed criticism of public education in the 1870s.[28] Against a profession committed to moral character and a collective harmony of divergent professional styles, criticism itself had always presented a terribly troublesome challenge. But the criticism of the 1870s, launched from outside the reaches of the profession, focused on the most vulnerable feature of nineteenth-century education, its overweening confidence in the moral power of the teacher. The Institute had itself been instrumental in defending that ideal. In particular, at virtually every meeting, some lecturer or commentator had distinguished the relative merits of the physical, intellectual and moral dimensions of instruction. These aspects were considered compatible but nevertheless possessed unique properties. The moral sphere always escaped easy and detailed rationalization. Hence the teacher had to be given the leeway and responsibility of vitalizing any classroom lesson. Any detailed program or specification of duties endangered the moral charge of education. Hence routines were aids, were morally neutral, and provided only minimal levels of competency. True education rested with the character of the individual teacher. The ability to avoid sheer routine and mechanized procedures became a given of the teacher's work. Often the dangers of routine were graphically depicted to awaken teachers to their duties to attend and participate in the meetings of the Institute and other professional organizations. Sanctioned and controlled by such organizations and the character of their leadership, criticism then became and was a force of destruction to these professional norms.

In the 1870s, schoolmen did not answer the charges of mechanization and routine immediately. Sheer denial, they seemed to feel, would only lend credibility to the critics; examples of good teaching would be dismissed as exceptions; failure to respond effectively would be tantamount to a concession of the critics' claims. Schoolmen's hesitancy to counter their critics emanated fundamentally from their realization that their most cherished norms were at stake. They could not specify and rationalize the procedures within or outside the classroom without undercutting many of the highly individualized assumptions which proceeded from their focus on moral character. When called to the court of reason alone, schoolmen described a process which appeared extraordinarily cumbersome and inefficient. In point of fact, as they also bore witness later, the numerous enclaves and loyalties which each schoolman had created to make his "character" effective—former Boston superintendent, John D. Philbrick, approvingly noted that a grammar school master should rule his domain like a king [29]—proved to be very efficient in turning back the reforms which followed from the criticism. In Boston, where dissension became uncommonly pointed, schoolmen and critics alike conceded that city schools of all grades had become lordships and baronies. Each side, of course, attached wholly different meanings to the metaphors.

Professional credit deteriorated precipitously in the 1880s. The American Institute of Instruction registered its smallest membership gains in its history. (Until the National Education Association attracted the talents of Thomas Bicknell from the American Institute, it too languished, and though it experienced a few dramatic meetings like Bicknell's 1884 meeting in Madison, Wisconsin, its fortunes on a larger scale fluctuated like the Institute's.[30]) In the mid-seventies the sharp increases in the Institute had been superficial in many ways. As teachers and wives of teachers, women enrolled in the Institute in droves. Few schoolmen, however, seriously acknowledged this shift in policy as anything more than a temporary expedient to keep the Institute peopled and solvent. In fact, the overt solicitation of women by holding meetings in recreational locales measured how dire the Institute's leadership thought their straits were. This incursion of females reflected their increase in teaching in general, and similarly these years also witnessed the elimination of males almost completely from elementary grades and from the rolls of normal school training. New barriers and levels became firmly fixed, and for the first time clear tracts of professional preparation and success were designed.

The admission of women was precipitated by the realignment among (male) practical schoolmen in public education and academic spokesmen, especially from colleges and universities. By the 1880s this latter group included not merely a younger generation of college leadership but, somewhat surprisingly, men like Charles Francis Adams who in the 1870s had levied some of the most trenchant criticism against the schoolmen.[31] Practical schoolmen, too, drawing upon their long-standing reflex in behalf of professional harmony, began cautiously yet publicly to concede that education harbored some deficient educational sectors.[32] In part, these academic-oriented individuals were college men like those whose presence caused such remark at the 1891 meeting of the Institute. They were young men speaking to young men, for the Institute at the end of the century had virtually eliminated the wide range of ages in their newer membership (Table 18) and attracted after 1890 primarily schoolmen in their thirties, with few exceptions no older than forty-five.[33] Their age, their appreciation of both the virtues and the vices of orthodox academic instruction and their

Table 18

Joining Age of the American Institute of Instruction Membership, 1830–1908

Ages	1830s	1840s	1850s	1860s	1870s	1880s	1890s	1900s	Total
Pre-21	2	—	2	—	1	—	—	—	5— 1%
21-25	9	3	4	4	4	1	5	2	32— 6%
26-30	15	5	9	12	4	1	3	3	52—10%
31-35	24	6	18	14	7	4	18	7	98—20%
36-40	16	5	16	17	14	6	10	9	93—19%
41-45	22	6	3	12	12	3	5	10	73—15%
46-50	7	3	5	9	7	12	9	6	58—12%
51-55	1	3	1	11	10	2	9	3	40— 8%
56-60	2	—	3	4	5	3	2	3	22— 4%
61-65	—	2	1	4	1	4	1	2	15— 3%
66-70	—	2	—	—	2	1	—	1	6— 1%
71-75	—	—	—	—	3	1	—	—	4— 1%
Over 75	1	—	2	1	—	—	—	—	4— 1%
Total	99	35	64	88	70	38	62	46	502

anxiousness for education to accommodate new social obligations provided a formidable area of agreement. The further sanction in professional circles of men like Charles Francis Adams provided in the 1880s an endorsement analogous to the stimulus of George Ticknor and the Friends of Education at the Institute's inception in 1830. In addition, normal schoolmen with an appreciation or at least an aspiration for a greater academic prestige in the work of public instruction began to study and offer public reports of their own, suggesting improvements in education. These two groups especially —young men with new obligations for higher education and practical schoolmen with academic leanings—created a bridge which permitted the reduction of hostilities spawned in the 1870s. This bridge centered on the role of the superintendent as a new instrument in the improvement of the profession and education in general.

In 1880 Charles Francis Adams offered a new conception of the superintendent as a professional agent.[34] This notion differed from his previous broadsides against public education. Earlier he had drawn the authority for such criticism from the rather special experience of schools in Quincy, Massachusetts where he lived. Adams' service on Quincy's school committee led to the appointment of Francis W. Parker as superintendent. Parker's orientation in turn had led to procedures later considered among the earliest models of Progressive Education.[35] In 1880 Adams no longer needed to generalize from the tangible success of his town's experience. New evidence, systematically collected and examined by a highly respected schoolman, corroborated much of Adams' earlier criticisms of public education. Importantly the material had been gathered at the authorization of the secretary of the Massachusetts Board of Education and appeared as part of his report for that year. The investigator was George A. Walton, a graduate of the Bridgewater Normal School, long-time grammar schoolman and then agent of the State Board of Education.[36]

Walton's report merited and received Adams' highest accolade, and the commendation revealed essential assumptions of each about proper supervision. The report, Adams declared, was unique in its presentation, not of inferences and conclusions but, rather of a mass of new material, enabling any reader to judge for himself the quality and value of education. The report, he stated, was scientific. Conveniently Walton had examined the schools of Norfolk County (Massachusetts) which included Quincy and thereby gave a perspective for judging Adams' earlier claims and criticisms. The evidence was damning of the public school record, particularly in providing basic literacy and the rudiments of mathematics. Walton had also demonstrated that facilities and money had not been the cause, given the state's and the county's history of allocation. Adams concurred with Walton's central observation, that "more depends upon the supervision of the schools than upon all other causes combined." Adams, however, went further and asked for a definition of good supervision.[37]

Adams' intimation, of course, questioned the nature and practice of the superintendent under its older guises. It was no small irony that the older guise had been developed largely by Horace Mann, the first incumbent of the office which provided Adams with the evidence for his critical commentary. Mann had responded to the numerous political pressures of the moment to argue that his office, the paradigm of the superintendent of his day, possessed no direct or coercive power. Hostile politicians, he claimed, need not fear the authority of an office whose power is purely educational. The power of the office, Mann went on, lay with language, with suggestion, with the ability to convince rather than with any force to impose forms of teaching and educational practice. His office would be neutral and would avoid all obvious current controversies in actual classroom instruction, particularly those involving the partisan disaffections of religious and political life. Mann's nonpolitical office ensured that the superintendent in its enlightened form would represent an advocate rather than an executive. The immediate political advantages of a nonpolitical directorate ultimately ensured—whatever Mann's probable intentions—that the scales of power would tip away from the superintendent.[38]

Adams' effort to transform this office took exception to the advocacy role of the superintendent, but he did not argue that that office should possess either executive or coercive power. Instead that office's power should rest with the impersonal, factual knowledge it collected. The task of collecting information impartially was more difficult than the work of drawing inferences and conclusions. Presumably the application of new information lay with the increasingly different work of classroom instruction. Factual knowledge, like institutional arrangements, were not the problem, and further centralization of power in the superintendent would not improve school systems. Rather than carry the problem into the political arena, Adams tried to draw the superintendent and the educational process into an area which he considered intellectually and morally (nonpolitically) safe. The university and the college should, Adams declared, take up the work of making education a science and of training men to fill the most scientific posts in the profession, the superintendencies.

This set of assertions modified the aspects of his earlier criticisms which schoolmen considered most unfair and uncommonly vituperative. In fact, instead of his wholesale attack upon existing organizational procedures, his comments now revealed a keen appreciation for the necessity of a certain order and reasonable rigidities. The new discussion of the superintendent compelled Adams to deal with schooling in terms other than freedom versus rigidity. He now posed the question in terms of varying alternatives of organization. His remarks still included attacks upon mechanization but, after his approval of Walton's report and his appreciation of the potential of the superintendent, his observations seemed less trenchant and biting. Adams scored the "drill-sergeant stage in education, or the school company front" and embellished that military metaphor elaborately but, even were his remarks translated into the existing educational structure, they would have fallen more on the regimented and feminized city training schools which were coming more and more to be seen as necessary but not professional parts of educational work. Besides, the rejection of mindless routine had become itself a cliché in the schoolman's literature.

For Adams the problem had become the organization whose concerns were unscientific. The remedy must begin, he asserted, not with the applications of principles but at the other end: "The operations of a child's mind—the natural processes of growth and assimilation which go on in it—its inherent methods of development and acquisition, must be long and patiently studied. . . . The superintendent of the future," he predicted, "is thus a Baconian in his filosofy [sic]." [39] His conclusion put the brunt of reform on the universities. There the science of education should be supported and maintained through chairs and departments of pedagogy but, he feared, the ingrained prejudices of eastern colleges especially—Cambridge and New Haven were college towns specifically mentioned—would impede this stratagem. Adams ended his remarks with a qualified appreciation of education, stressing the need for officers "imbued with the science of their calling." [40] Resolutions of these problems remained individual matters, dependent at last on the character of the supervisory officer, imbued now not merely with the moral but with the more tangible, scientific nature of his work.

For both Walton and Adams the creation of a new superintendent became an attractive solution to the educational crisis, precisely because neither spokesman desired a further rationalization of the educational apparatus. In a sense both the peculiar normal school tradition of Walton and the qualified academic norms of Adams [41] sought nothing more than a surer way to produce men of wisdom and moral character. Adams' criticism of Harvard and Yale for their snobbery toward public instruction struck a responsive chord in schoolmen's circles, for it soothed the schoolmen's long-standing ambivalence of purely academic training. This accommodation helped schoolmen see another. In essence Adams had urged them to view the superintendency in a very traditional manner, namely, as the principal spirit of a unified—but not a uniform—system in much the same way that a teacher with character became the central focus in his classroom and school. This emphasis did imply a further centralization of sorts, though not necessarily a bureaucratic one. A man of sound learning and self-discipline would gain through the science of education the authority of enlightened practice. Rightly positioned, such a man could guide his followers, professional and

lay alike, to a reasonable and true educational practice. Perhaps most important, Adams' institutional solution gave a greater academic aura and thus
a more orthodox professional appearance to public instruction without dis-
abusing schoolmen of their deep-set apolitical habits of thought.

The strongest demand of these new views became a greater cooperation
among the self-contained and isolated schools of the profession. On a practical basis, the superintendent represented the degree of coherence or disar-
ray of any educational system. After the 1880s the thrust of reform hinged on
how much the office had become an enlightened arena of exchange.[42] On a
larger scale these tendencies implied new life for professional arenas like the
American Institute of Instruction. Understandably the institute quickly endorsed the views of science and supervision which Walton represented. In
1883 he became the president of the association, the second Bridgewater
graduate to be so honored. In addition, between his tenure and 1897 three
more Bridgewater graduates—J. Milton Hall, George M. Martin and Albert E.
Winship—succeeded to this office and maintained that particular viewpoint
in educational discussion and debate.[43] Unfortunately the increased credit of
this professional ideology posed more and more a challenge to those
academic traditions still steeped in classical training. At the 1891 meeting of
the Institute a minor exchange involving Walton depicted the trends of the
new alignments. In a public discussion Walton openly rejected all military
forms of training. Perhaps mindful of Adams' deft use of military metaphors
against schoolmen, Walton insisted that military drill connoted "the ultimate
settlement of difficulties by force of arms, and it awakened in the minds of
children ideas of warfare not to be awakened in the minds of the young." [44]
His views were warmly opposed by a formidable array of academy principals, heads of some of the most prestigious collegiate preparatory schools
in the country.[45] The younger university and college men who had raised
schoolmen's hopes were themselves hampered by several long-standing alliances of their own, and early in the twentieth century those classics-steeped
traditions effectively drew the attention of higher education away from the
work of professional schoolmen. Though one might point to Columbia's
accommodation of Teachers College in the nineties or the creation of the first
graduate school of education at New York University in 1891,[46] universities
as a genre did not heed Adams' call or Walton's hopes for at least two more
generations.

Retrospectively the alliance represented by Walton and Adams in the
1880s did affect the American Institute of Instruction in profound ways. Most
significantly, it drew into the membership of that association twice as many
superintendents between 1880 and 1908 as had joined in its entire previous
history. Moreover, men holding such offices dominated the presidency of the
Institute. The effect of this shift proved deadly to the structure and existence
of the association. For the Institute as for the profession of teaching as a

whole the rise of the superintendent in these years institutionalized several major confusions which endured through much of the succeeding century. In the first place, the preeminence of the superintendent meant that in the profession of teaching the paradigm was not an instructor. In addition, it meant that the work of training minds distracted itself systematically from the work of reflective inquiry. Instead, the most esteemed professional work consisted of the accommodation of different educational ideologies into some definable structure. Finally, as the superintendent moved from advocate to executive in spite of the profession's best-laid plans, the education of the public—outside the specialized sphere of adult education—became less and less a primary duty of the schoolman's professional life.

The transformation of the superintendency permanently affected the profession and the American Institute of Instruction. The increase in the office's executive authority, the positivistic interpretation given to Adams' scientific prescriptions plus a whole new set of procedures celebrated for their efficiency quickly outran the worst fears of both Adams and Walton. The evangelical traditions which supported their apolitical educational notions clouded their perception of the essential problem. In the face of mounting educational crises after the turn of the century, the American Institute of Instruction responded with a habitual call for professional harmony. In 1908 under the guidance of not only a Bridgewater graduate but the son of Bridgewater's preeminent ideologue, Albert Boyden, the Institute urged the alliance of the proliferating local and regional associations under its aegis.[47] The birth of competitive associations , not the revival of the Institute, followed the call. The energies of the Institute continued to dwindle, repeating the call for professional harmony in eight more annual meetings, until in 1918 the Institute itself was absorbed in a new harmony its directors could not control.[48]

Notes

Introduction

1. For an illuminating analysis of "generation" as a construct for historical inquiry, see Alan B. Spitzer, "The Historical Problem of Generation," *American Historical Review*, v. 78, no. 5 (December 1973): 1353-1385. In this study see the discussion on pp. 193-194.

2. An incisive discussion of this point can be found in Allan S. Horlick, "Radical School Legends," *History of Education Quarterly*, v. 14 (Summer 1974): 251-258.

3. "Ideological" here means a central core of ideas from which individual thinking begins. An ideologist is one of a group contributing to a historically plausible and coherent set of ideas and who senses the limitations of the viewpoint. The notion of character is the keystone of the ideology of nineteenth-century schoolmen; it was the idea which different groups accepted as the irreducible minimum for professional activity. In Karl Mannheim's sense of ideology, character became the idea which schoolmen were most conscious of, and that consciousness bound them into a working social unit in spite of other conceptual or temperamental differences. See Karl Mannheim, *Ideology and Utopia* (New York, 1936), p. 125, but also the pertinent discussions in Chapters II and IV.

The term "ideology" here can be used synonymously with "theory" and is not a term of disparagement. It draws attention to a pattern of thought which helped a certain group of men make sense of their experience. Here the term does not possess its popular American connotations of narrow deference to a particular manifesto or rigid apologia impeding practical action. In my judgment that version of ideology is itself a historical phenomenon and confuses historical issues in a dangerously anti-intellectual manner. I have tried to employ the term without those pragmatic connotations and have assumed that genuinely practical and political action always reflects an ideological structure of thought.

4. "Evangelical" here refers to the schoolman's adaptation of a didactic style, first developed by gospel missionaries. Nineteenth-century schoolmen tried to eliminate the theological content of this instruction while retaining its proselytizing techniques. In the schoolman's eyes their

187

evangelism accommodated many diverse norms and through a graphic and impressionistic pedagogy cultivated the minds and hearts of individuals. Though deeply personal in intent and effect, this style usually implied a heterogeneous audience and indulged few distinctions which might exacerbate existing differences of thought or behavior. Optimally, they thought, it would appear unthreatening yet would inevitably benefit both society and its members in unforeseeable ways.

5. One cannot ignore three significant books which laid groundwork for this recent literature: Lawrence Cremin, *The Transformation of the School* (New York, 1961); Raymond Callahan, *Education and the Cult of Efficiency* (Chicago, 1962); and Richard Hofstadter, *Anti-Intellectualism in American Life* (New York, 1962).

A new focus upon bureaucracy began in the late sixties with the work of Michael B. Katz. His two books—*The Irony of Early School Reform* (Cambridge, Mass., 1968) and *Class, Bureaucracy and the Schools* (Chicago, 1971)—remain the best analyses of the problem in my judgment. Among other contributions to the literature see Marvin Lazerson, *The Origins of the Urban School* (Cambridge, Mass., 1971); Joel Spring, *Education and the Rise of the Corporate State* (Boston, 1972); Colin Greer, *The Great School Legend* (New York, 1972); Carl Kaestle, *The Evolution of an Urban School System* (Cambridge, Mass., 1973); Stanley K. Schultz, *The Culture Factory* (New York, 1973); Joel H. Spring and Edgar B. Gumbert, *The Superschool and the Superstate* (New York, 1974); and the recent book by David Tyack, *The One Best System* (Cambridge, Mass., 1974). There are numerous critical discussions of this literature and related problems in various issues of the *History of Education Quarterly*.

6. These numbers represent the school positions held by American Institute of Instruction members at the time they joined the association. There is no definitive list of the membership. My figures are based on a compilation of several years' research, and at present they include over 4,300 individuals who came to be identified as members and participants at the Institutes eighty-six annual meetings. At several points in the study (see especially p. 205, n. 33, below) I discuss the qualified authority of this and other statistical sets.

Virtually every figure treated in major or minor fashion in this study was an active member of the Institute. The important exceptions are Emma Willard and Charles Francis Adams, who are discussed in chapters IV and VIII respectively.

Chapter I

1. "Review of Essays upon Popular Education, containing a particular Examination of the Schools of Massachusetts, and an Outline of an Institution for the Education of Teachers. By James G. Carter. Boston, 1826," *North American Review*, 24 (January 1827): 169.

2. *Ibid.*, p. 157.

3. Rev. Samuel J. May, *A Brief Account of His Ministry, Given in a Discourse preached to the Church of the Messiah in Syracuse, New York, Sept. 15th, 1867* (Syracuse, N.Y., 1867), p. 48.

4. *Ibid.*, Appendix.

5. See William Russell (ed.), "Advantages to be Expected from the Formation of a Society for the Improvement of Education," *American Journal of Education*, 3 (February 1828): 85.

6. Rev. Samuel J. May, *The Revival of Education* (Syracuse, N.Y., 1855); "American Educational Biography: Rev. Samuel J. May," *American Journal of Education*, 16 (March 1866): 141-145; "Samuel Joseph May," *Dictionary of American Biography*, 12 (1929): 447-448.

7. May, *The Revival of Education*, Appendix 6.

8. Samuel J. May, "Errors in Common Education: An Address delivered at the Lyceum in Brooklyn, Connecticut, October 22, 1828," *American Journal of Education*, 4 (May–June 1829): 214.

9. *Ibid.*

10. *Ibid.*

11. *Ibid.*, p. 215.

12. *Ibid.*, pp. 221-222.

13. *Ibid.*, p. 215.

14. See, for example: [Henry R. Cleveland], "The Profession of a Teacher, and the Conduct and Discipline of a School," in *Remarks on the Classical Education of Boys, by a Teacher* (Boston, 1834), pp. 107-114, and "Professional Education of Teachers," *American Annals of Education*, 3 (October 1833): 455-457.

15. [Rev. William Ellery Channing], "Review of the American Annals of Education and Instruction, 8 vols.," *The Christian Examiner*, 15 (November 1833): 262.

16. William A. Alcott, *A Historical Description of the First Public School in Hartford, Conn., now under the Superintendence of J. Olney, A.M. with a Particular Account of the Methods of Instruction and Discipline Accompanied by General Remarks on Common Schools* (Hartford, 1832), p. 1. The best-known experimental seminary of the 1830s was located at Andover, Massachusetts and was directed by the Reverend Samuel Read Hall. A detailed account of this experiment and its significance in the development of professional teachers can be found on pp. 21-43.

17. The uses of the lyceum were as varied as the interests of its most influential participants. In the early years of the lyceum's history, that is, in the late 1820s, the primary goal of lyceum activity was oriented exclusively toward the community and based almost entirely upon the personal and material resources of a specific locale. Later as teachers began to play more prominent roles in the work of educational improvement, the service of the lyceum became more specialized. In particular, lyceum activity became for a while an essential element in the plans for developing special institutions for the professional preparation of teachers. During the 1830s lyceums corresponded with each other and established larger bases of activity on the county, state and even national level. The American lyceum, for example, was founded in 1830. By the mid-1830s men like Josiah Holbrook who reputedly founded the peculiar association began to centralize and systematize lyceum activities about a particular educational focus. His work with the Reverend Samuel Read Hall and the efforts of lyceum proponents to establish a seminary for teachers in Andover, Massachusetts forms the basis of the discussion in Chapter II of this study.

18. Barnard, *Memoirs of Teachers*, pp. 249-267; William A. Alcott, *Confessions of a Schoolmaster* (Boston, 1839). See also William A. Alcott, "Sacrifices by Teachers," *American Annals of Education*, 8 (February 1838): 67-71.

19. Alcott, *Confessions*, p. 17.

20. *Ibid.*, p. 13.

21. *Ibid.*, p. 84.

22. *Ibid.*, p. 118.

23. *Ibid.*, p. 136.

24. *Ibid.*, p. 138.

25. *Ibid.*, p. 145; Alcott, "Sacrifices by Teachers," pp. 67-71.

26. *Ibid.*, pp. 155-156.

27. *Ibid.*, p. 198.

28. *Ibid.*, p. 235.

29. *Ibid.*

30. *Ibid.*, p. 173; William A. Alcott, *A Word to Teachers: or Two Days in a Primary School* (Boston, 1833), pp. viii-ix. This manual was actually conceived by Alcott as a service to teachers and parents who could not visit schools; it was in Alcott's mind a substitute for a visitation. The very fact of the manual is evidence of the teacher's growing disenchantment with the visitation as an effective professional procedure. Numerous school histories written during this same period, works like those by Alcott, the Reverend Jacob Abbott and the Reverend Joseph Emerson, tried to provide the same service in addition to the customary service of such histories of advertising the school's best features. See Alcott, *A Historical Description of the First Public School in Hartford, Conn.*; Rev. Jacob Abbott, *A Description of the Mount Vernon School in 1832, being a Brief Account of the*

Internal Arrangements and Plans of the Institution, Addressed to a New Scholar (Boston, 1832); Rev. Joseph Emerson, *Prospectus of the Female Seminary at Weathersfield, Comprising a General Prospectus, Course of Instruction, Maxims of Education and Regulations of the Seminary* (n.p., 1826).

31. Much of the educational literature during the 1830s and 1840s concerns the mutual duties of parents and teachers in which visitations always are discussed. To observe the transition referred to here see the two lectures on this subject by two men who reflect the values and ambivalences of their respective generations. Their statements, though delivered four years apart, amount virtually to a debate on the subject. See Rev. Jacob Abbott, "The Duties of Parents," *Lectures and Proceedings of the American Institute of Instruction,* 5 (Boston, 1835): 83-98; David P. Page, "On the Mutual Duties of Parents and Teachers," *Lectures and Proceedings of the American Institute of Instruction,* 8 (Boston, 1838): 143-162.

32. Alcott, *Confessions,* pp. 99-101.

33. See Joseph Kett, "Growing Up in Rural New England, 1800-1840," in Tamara K. Hareven (ed.), *Anonymous Americans* (Englewood Cliffs, N.J., 1971), pp. 1-16.

34. S. C. Phillips, "On the Usefulness of Lyceums," *Lectures and Proceedings of the American Institute of Instruction,* 2 (Boston, 1832): 75-76; see also Henry Ewbank, Jr., "A Preliminary Historical Survey of the American Lyceum from 1826 to 1840," unpublished master's dissertation, University of Wisconsin, 1948; John A. Munroe, "The Lyceum in America Before the Civil War," *Delaware Notes,* 37 (May 1942): 65-75.

35. Edgar Knight and Clifton Hall, *Readings in American Educational History* (New York, 1951), footnote, p. 151. As early as 1835 there were, Knight and Hall wrote, in addition to a national organization, many state, more than one hundred county and more than three thousand town and village organizations throughout the United States.

36. "Review of an Address on Lyceums (presented to the American Lyceum by William C. Woodbridge)," *American Annals of Education,* 5 (May 1835): 197-198. See also Nehemiah Cleaveland, "On Lyceums and Societies for the Diffusion of Useful Knowledge," *Lectures and Proceedings of the American Institute of Instruction,* 1 (Boston, 1831): 149, and "Judge Williams' Address," *American Journal of Education and Monthly Lyceum* N.S. 1 (June 1830): 244-245.

37. Phillips, "On the Usefulness of Lyceums," p. 85.

38. Rev. Samuel J. May, "Address to the parents and guardians of children respecting common schools in Windham County [Connecticut] . . . held in the autumn of 1832," *American Journal of Education,* ed. by Henry Barnard, 5 (June 1858): 147; see also "Lyceums," *American Journal of Education,* ed. by William Russell, N.S. 1 (January 1830): 2-4. For a similar view, see Cornelius C. Felton, "An Address, pronounced on the anniversary of the Concord Lyceum," *American Journal of Education,* N.S. 1 (March 1830): 132-133, in which the author says: "This interest, and not the actual amount of knowledge communicated, I consider the most decidedly important point to be gained by the establishment of Lyceums. It is next to an impossibility to impart, by popular lectures, anything more than a mere outline of literature, or science; but there is the combined force of numbers, the resistless power of sympathy, the spur of noble emulation, the thirsting of excited curiosity, the increasing love of social knowledge, to bear onward the mind, when once awakened, in the glorious career of intellectual improvement."

39. Alcott, *Confessions,* p. 172.

40. This equation between the condition of the schoolhouse and the character of the town amounted to a cliché by the end of the 1830s in the educational literature. One of the most succinct formulations of the sentiment and also one of the earliest came from the pen of William Alcott himself. His *Essay on the Construction of School-Houses to which was awarded the Prize of the American Institute of Instruction, August, 1831* (Boston, 1832), was widely distributed and frequently copied in this period.

41. "Amos Bronson Alcott," *Dictionary of American Biography,* 1: 139-141. See also *The Journals of Bronson Alcott,* edited by Odell Shepard (Boston, 1938); Odell Shepard, *Pedlar's Progress: The Life of Bronson Alcott* (Boston, 1837), especially the entries for September 12, 1828 and December 4,

1828. Up until the arrival of both Alcotts in Boston in 1830 Amos Bronson Alcott's career was so closely and so consciously patterned upon his older cousin's experience that for several winters after they both had traveled the south seeking teaching positions, Bronson Alcott simply taught the school which William had taught the previous winter.

For additional information on Bronson Alcott's work in education, see Amos Bronson Alcott, *Essays on Education: 1830–1862* ed. by Walter Harding (Gainesville, Fla., 1960), and Elizabeth Peabody, *Record of a School* (Boston, 1835).

42. "Rev. Samuel J. May," *American Journal of Education*, p. 144.

43. Barnard, *Memoirs of Teachers*, pp. 249-267.

44. While Amos Bronson Alcott published several accounts of his educational methods and experiments in the 1830s, his cousin entered the work of lecturing and writing as a professional teacher with a frenzy. At his death in 1859 his bibliography numbered 108 volumes, some of them going through over twenty editions. See "Catalogue of Dr. William A. Alcott's Publications," *American Journal of Education*, 4 (March 1858): 655-656.

Chapter II

1. Apart from the literature in educational journals, which only began in 1826, some of the important contributions to this discussion were the following: William Russell, *Suggestions on Education* (New Haven, 1823); Walter R. Johnson, *Observations on the Improvement of Seminaries of Learning in the United States* (Philadelphia, 1825); James G. Carter, *Essays upon Popular Education: containing a particular examination of The Schools of Massachusetts, And an Outline for an Institution for the Education of Teachers* (Boston, 1826); Rev. William Ellery Channing, "Review of American Annals of Education and Instruction, 8 vols.," *Christian Examiner*, 15 (November 1833): 257-276; Rev. Samuel Read Hall, "On the Necessity of Educating Teachers," *Lectures and Proceedings of the American Institute of Instruction*, 4 (1834): 257ff.; Rev. Charles Brooks, "School Reform or Teachers Seminaries," *Lectures and Proceedings of the American Institute of Instruction*, 8 (1838): 161-179; Rev. Calvin Stowe, *Common Schools and Teachers' Seminaries* (Boston, 1839). Stowe's comments were originally published as *Report on Elementary Public Instruction in Europe*, which was made to the General Assembly of Ohio, in December 1837. It was also published in the *American Biblical Repository* (July 1839) and later in the *American Journal of Education*, 15 (December 1865): 688-704. Denison Olmstead, "The State of Education in Connecticut: An Oration at the Commencement of Yale College, 1816," cited in Henry Barnard (ed.), *Memoirs of Teachers, Educators, Promotors of Education, Literature and Science*, (New York, 1861).

2. Rev. Heman Humphrey, *Life and Labors of the Rev. T. H. Gallaudet, L.L.D.* (New York, 1858), pp. 250ff.

3. Rev. Thomas H. Gallaudet, "Remarks on Seminaries for Teachers (January 5, 1825)," in Henry Barnard (ed.), *Normal Schools and Other Institutions, Agencies and Means Designed for the Professional Education of Teachers* (Hartford, 1851), p. 47.

4. *Ibid.*, p. 48.

5. *Ibid.*, p. 52.

6. *Ibid.*, p. 51.

7. *Ibid.*

8. *Ibid.*, p. 47.

9. Bailey B. Burritt, *Professional Distribution of College and University Graduates*, U.S. Bureau of Education, Bulletin No. 12. (Washington, D.C., 1912), p. 65.

10. Chauncey Goodrich (1759–1815), like Gallaudet, graduated from Yale and had been a tutor in the college. By the time Gallaudet entered his office of law in 1805, Goodrich had been a Hartford lawyer for some twenty years. He had married into the Wolcott family and had thereby assumed an important position in the Federalist faction, which had controlled Connecticut

politics for a number of years. In 1807 Goodrich reached the pinnacle of his career with his election to the United States Senate. He should not be confused with the clergyman and educator, Chauncey Allen Goodrich (1790–1860). See Dumas Malone *et al.* (eds.), *Dictionary of American Biography*, 7 (New York, 1929): 397-398.

11. Henry Barnard (ed.), "Thomas Hopkins Gallaudet," in *Memoirs of Teachers, Educators, Promoters and Benefactors of Education, Literature and Science*, pp. 97-118; Dumas Malone *et al.* (eds.), *Dictionary of American Biography*, 7. For additional information, see also Henry Barnard, *Tribute to Gallaudet: A Discourse in Commemoration of the Life, Character and Services of the Rev. Thomas H. Gallaudet, L.L.D., delivered before the Citizens of Hartford, Jan. 7, 1852* (Hartford, 1852); and Edward Miner Gallaudet, *Life of Thomas Hopkins Gallaudet* (New York, 1888).

12. Letter to Dr. Mason G. Cogswell, Edinburgh, Scotland, January 11, 1816, in Humphrey, *Life and Labors of Gallaudet*, p. 49.

13. Gallaudet, *Remarks on Seminaries for Teachers*, p. 47.

14. "Samuel Read Hall," *American Journal of Education*, 16 (March 1866): 146; Ellwood P. Cubberley, *Public Education in the United States* (Cambridge, Mass., 1st ed. 1919), pp. 375-376; Willard S. Elsbree, *The American Teacher: Evolution of a Profession in a Democracy* (New York, 1939), pp. 138-139; Mason S. Stone, "The First Normal School in America," *Teachers College Record*, 24 (May 1923): 263-271.

15. Barnard, *Memoirs of Teachers*, pp. 169-181; Dumas Malone *et al.* (eds.), *Dictionary of American Biography*, 8: 142-143; Ellwood P. Cubberley, *Readings in Public Education in the United States* (Boston, 1934), p. 323.

16. Richard G. Boone, *Education in the United States* (New York, 1890), pp. 209-221. See also Edward Potts Cheyney, *History of the University of Pennsylvania* (Philadelphia, 1940), p. 103. In 1768 ten students of the University of Pennsylvania received the Bachelor of Physic, the first medical degree given in America; Anton-Hermann Chroust, *The Rise of the Legal Profession in America*, 2 (Norman, Okla., 1965): 210.

17. Henry Barnard, "Teacher's Seminary at Andover," *American Journal of Education*, 5 (September 1858): 386-388.

18. See Henry K. Rowe, *History of Andover Theological Seminary* (Newton, Mass., 1933).

19. *Catalogues of the Teacher's Seminary in Phillips Academy, Andover: 1831-1836* (Andover, 1831-1836); Barnard, "Teacher's Seminary at Andover," pp. 386-387. See also Claude Fuess, *An Old New England School: A History of Phillips Academy* (Boston, 1917), pp. 207-209.

20. Barnard, "Teacher's Seminary at Andover," pp. 386-387.

21. *Catalogues of the Teacher's Seminary, Andover, Mass., Oct., 1835* (Andover, 1835).

22. Barnard, "Teacher's Seminary at Andover," pp. 386-387.

23. See the forthcoming book by David F. Allmendinger, Jr., *Paupers and Scholars: The Transformation of Student Life in New England, 1760-1860* (New York, 1975).

24. *Catalogues of the Teacher's Seminary, Andover, Mass.,* 1831-1836.

25. Josiah Holbrook, "Lyceum Seminaries," *Family Lyceum*, 1 (May 18, 1833): 159. See also Charles A. Bennett, *History of Manual and Industrial Education up to 1870* (Peoria, Ill., 1926). The means by which students might meet *all* their expenses are explained in "Seminary for Teachers at Andover," *American Annals of Education*, 1 (July 1831): 329-330.

26. Barnard, "Teacher's Seminary at Andover," pp. 386-387.

27. "The American School Society," *American Journal of Education*, 15 (1869), p. 118; see also Josiah Holbrook, "School Agents' Society," *Family Lyceum*, 1 (July 28, 1832): 3; and "American School Society," *Cyclopedia of Education*, 1 (New York, 1911): 112-113; "School Agents' Society," *American Annals of Education and Instruction*, N.S. 3 (September 1, 1832): 443-445; (October 1833): 463-474; (November 1833): 524-530.

28. Holbrook, "School Agents' Society," p. 3.

29. Josiah Holbrook, *The American Lyceum, or Society for the Improvement of School and Diffusion of Useful Knowledge* (Boston, 1829), in *Old South Leaflets*, v. 6, no. 139, p. 293. See also S. R. Hall,

Lectures on School-Keeping (Boston, 1829). For Hall's description of this massive need, see S. R. Hall, "On the Necessity of Educating Teachers," *Lectures and Proceedings of the American Institute of Instruction*, 4 (1834): 241-259.

30. Dumas Malone *et al.* (eds.), "Josiah Holbrook," *The Dictionary of American Biography*, 9 (New York: 1929): 130-131; see also Carl Bode, *The American Lyceum: Town Meeting of the Mind* (New York, 1956), pp. 7, 10ff.

31. Josiah Holbrook, "Constitution of the American School Agents' Society," *Family Lyceum*, 1 (September 1, 1832): 11.

32. Josiah Holbrook, "Lyceum Seminaries," *Family Lyceum*. 1 (April 27, 1833): 147.

33. Barnard, "American School Society," pp. 118-119.

34. Holbrook, "Lyceum Seminaries," p. 147.

35. Josiah Holbrook, "School Agents' Society," *Family Lyceum*, 1 (October 27, 1832): 43.

36. Josiah Holbrook, "School Agent Society," *Family Lyceum*, 1 (May 4, 1833): 151.

37. Barnard, "American School Society," pp. 121-122; "American School Society," *American Annals of Education*, 4 (September 1834): 432.

38. *Ibid.*, p. 122.

39. Samuel Read Hall, *Lectures on School-Keeping* (4th ed. rev.; Boston, 1832), p. 76.

40. See, for example, Horace Mann's own assertion, delivered in 1838 to prepare the public mind for the experiment of the first state-supported normal school in the United States: "Every mother is ex officio a member of the College of Teachers." Horace Mann, *Lectures on Education* (Boston, 1845).

41. Josiah Holbrook, "Prospectus of the Family Lyceum," *Family Lyceum*, 1 (July 28, 1832): 1.

42. By "itinerant teachers" here reference is made only to those traveling teachers affiliated with the School Agents' Society. During this period many teachers not affiliated with the society traveled the countryside and taught schools in numerous towns. In the educational literature such itinerants were usually of dubious reputation and were regarded as a higher form of peddler. Even when they were proficient in their work, as in the case of Horace Mann's tutor in the classics, rumors of intemperance and undisciplined habits which were associated with such persons precluded communal favor and in a sense ensured their itinerancy. See the description of the itinerant in Louise Hall Tharp, *Until Victory: Horace Mann and Mary Peabody* (Boston, 1953), pp. 30-31.

43. *Catalogue of the English Department in Phillips Academy, Andover, Mass. Established as a Seminary for Teachers. Fall Term, 1831* (Andover, 1831).

44. "Plymouth Teachers' Seminary," *American Annals of Education*, 8 (January 1838): 43; and "Teachers' Seminaries at Plymouth," *American Annals of Education*, 8 (April 1838): 190.

Chapter III

1. The generations designate roughly two cohorts of schoolmen, based largely but not exclusively upon the membership of the American Institute of Instruction (1830-1908). The first cohort consists of those born within five years of 1796, Horace Mann's birthdate. His place in the profession, one of the themes of this essay, argues this use of him, not to mention the important fact that a remarkable number of the prominent schoolmen of the period were of his age. There are several important figures who shared many of the values of one cohort or the other but who do not fall neatly near the key dates 1796 and 1821 to form the twenty-five-year split in generational patterns. Still, the number of pivotal figures who cluster about these dates accounts for the majority of schoolmen instrumental in the shaping of the nineteenth-century profession of teaching. The years of maturity for the first cohort ranges approximately from 1830 to 1860 and the second from 1860 to 1890.

In the first group the prominent figures are Amos Bronson Alcott (1799-1888), William A.

Alcott (1798–1859), Ebenezer Bailey (1795–1839), Charles Brooks (1795–1872), Gould Brown (1791–1857), Warren Burton (1795–1865), William B. Calhoun (1795–1865), James G. Carter (1795–1849), George B. Emerson (1797–1882), Nehemiah Cleaveland (1796–1877), Warren Colburn (1793–1833), Lyman Coleman (1796–1882), Emerson Davis (1798–1866), William B. Fowle (1795–1865), Samuel G. Goodrich ["Peter Parley"] (1793–1860), Samuel Read Hall (1795–1877), Edward Hitchcock (1793–1864), Walter R. Johnson (1794–1852), John E. Lovell (1795–1877), Lowell Mason (1792–1872), Samuel J. May (1797–1871), Samuel P. Newman (1797–1842), Denison Elmstead (1791–1859), Cyrus Peirce (1790–1860), William Russell (1798–1873), Thomas Sherwin (1799–1869), Gideon F. Thayer (1793–1864), D. P. Thompson (1795–1868), George Ticknor (1791–1871), Francis Wayland (1796–1865), William C. Woodbridge (1794–1845), Alva Woods (1794–1887).

In the second cohort the prominent figures are: William T. Adams ["Oliver Optic"] (1822–1897), Lorin Andrews (1819–1861), John Newton Bartlett (1823–1895), Samuel W. Bates (1822–1882), James F. Blackinton (1819–1891), Isaac F. Cady (1818–1884) Albert G Boyden (1824–1915), Norman A. Calkins (1822–1895), David N. Camp (1820–1916), Paul Chadbourne (1823–1883), Dana Colburn (1823–1859), John W. Dickinson (1825–1901), John H. French (1824–1888), Benjamin V. Gallup (1821–1878), John M. Gregory (1822–1898), Daniel B. Hagar (1820–1896), John Hancock (1825–1891), Albert Harkness (1822–1907), John Kneeland (1821–1914), Dio Lewis (1822–1886), Luther Mason (1821–1896), Amory Dwight Mayo (1823–1907), Lewis B. Monroe (1825–1917), Birdsey G. Northrup (1817–1898), Hiram Orcutt (1815–1899), William F. Phelps (1822–1907), John D. Philbrick (1818–1886), Eldridge Smith (1818–1902), Charles V. Spear (1825–1891), Homer B. Sprague (1829–1918), Admiral P. Stone (1820–1902), Thomas Tash (1816–1889), George Taylor (1815–1879), Sanborn Tenney (1827–1877), Thomas W. Valentine (1818–1879), Electa N. L. Walton (1824–1908), George A. Walton (1822–1908), Eben Wentworth (1818–1878), Edward Payson Weston (1819–1879), James P. Wickersham (1825–1891).

A third cohort begins to form about schoolmen born roughly within five years of the date 1845. Here the principal figures would be men like Samuel P. Bates (1847–1902), Thomas Stockwell (1839–1906), Thomas W. Bicknell (1834–1925), G. Stanley Hall (1846–1924), William T. Harris (1835–1908), and Albert Winship (1845–1933). For a theoretical basis for the idea of "generation," see K. Mannheim, "The Problem of Generations," *Essays on the Sociology of Knowl-edge*, p. 306.

2. Hiram Orcutt, *Reminiscences of School Life* (Cambridge, Mass., 1898), pp. ix–x.

3. The only serious effort to explore the connections between the moral rhetoric and the actual behavior of educators in this period is Wilson Smith, *Professors and Public Ethics* (Ithaca, 1956). Smith restricts the study to the moral philosophers who taught in the colleges and usually served as the institution's president. He examines in particular four cases which became political controversies and found in each case that the moral philosophers gravitated to a distinctly conservative position. Particularly interesting in this study is the case of Francis Wayland of Brown University, so often understood as an advocate of university education before that brand of instruction became a model of higher education. His advanced thinking, nevertheless, in many ways paralleled his fellow moral philosophers when fundamental assumptions and values were questioned.

Generally speaking, historians have accepted an easy distinction between thought and action in their studies of the ante-bellum period. The abstract and metaphorical language of the ante-bellum educators has therefore seldom been examined in terms of its actual connections with behavior. Their ambiguities were never seen as having functions themselves. See for example, Merle Curti, *Social Ideas of American Educators* (Totowa, N.J., 1935), p. 59: "It was easier to formulate objectives than to work out concrete methods by which education was to perpetuate republican institutions."

4. An important example of this version of character can be found in the Yale Report of 1828,

cited in Wilson Smith and Richard Hofstadter (eds.), *American Higher Education: A Documentary History*, 1 (Chicago, 1961): 279. At Yale where so many prominent schoolmen studied or aspired to study, this sense of character perdured through the century. See the writings of its later influential president Noah Porter, either *The Human Intellect* (1868) or *American Colleges and the American Public* (1871).

5. Examples of this version of character abound, particularly in the fictional literature of the period. See the writings of men from George Ticknor to the postwar writings of George William Curtis and William Dean Howells. Daniel Aaron, *Men of Good Hope: A Story of American Progressives*, discusses men who shaped, refined and transformed this ideal in the nineteenth century.

6. Though not a peculiar usage of teachers, this version was perhaps most frequently employed by public schoolmen. See, for example, lectures of the American Institute of Instruction like Charles Brooks, "School Reform or Teachers' Seminaries," *Lectures and Proceedings of the American Institute of Instruction*, 8 (Boston, 1837): 161-179. Also, Neil McCluskey, *Public Schools and Moral Education* (New York, 1958), especially pp. 43-44.

7. Ellwood P. Cubberley, *Public Education in the United States* (Cambridge, Mass., 1962), rev. ed. (1st ed. 1934), pp. 18-19. See also: Frank Tracy Carleton, *Economic Influences upon Educational Progress in the United States* (New York, 1965 [1st ed. 1908]), pp. 8-11.

8. Lawrence Cremin, *American Education: The Colonial Experience* (New York, 1971), pp. 181-182.

9. See, for example, John Witherspoon's Account of the College of New Jersey, 1772, in Hofstadter and Smith (eds.), *American Higher Education*, 1: 137; and "Constitution of Phillips Academy (1778)," in Theodore Sizer (ed.), *The Age of the Academies* (New York, 1964), pp. 77-78, 86-89.

10. Michael Katz, *The Irony of Early School Reform: Educational Innovation in Mid-Nineteenth Century Massachusetts* (Cambridge, Mass., 1968), p. 112. While this citation refers to Katz's summary on a single page, his entire book contains an exploration of this fluctuation of hostility. See also David Bruck, "The Schools of Lowell, 1824-1861" (unpublished senior thesis, Harvard University, 1971), and Jay Pawa, "Workingmen and Free Schools in the Nineteenth Century: A Comment on the Labor-Education Thesis," *History of Education Quarterly*, 11 (Fall 1971): 287-302.

11. See Thomas Jefferson's *Notes on the State of Virginia* (Harper Torchbooks, 1964), especially the summary statement of "Query XIV: The administration of Justice and the description of the Laws?" pp. 142-143; Horace Mann, "The Necessity of Education in a Republic Government," *Educational Writings of Horace Mann*, 2 (Boston, 1891): 143-188, for a later example. James McLachlan's *American Boarding Schools: A Historical Study* contains an interesting discussion of how late in the nineteenth century an enriched and largely Republican section of American society turned this older educational tradition to their purposes (New York, 1970)

12. There was important symbolic value in the composition of the first Board ot Education of Massachusetts, the first such directorate in American education. Democrats like Robert Rantoul and Whigs like Edward Everett were among the early members of this group. Shortly thereafter in the early 1840s when the Democratic administration of Governor Marcus Morton waged a strong campaign against Horace Mann and the board itself, the new state agency weathered the storm with bipartisan aid. Though Morton was reelected in 1842 and continued his efforts, his legislature refused to allow his recommendations against the state board. In this support for the state agencies the Massachusetts legislature followed its sister legislature in New York and elsewhere. See Rush Welter, *Popular Education and Democratic Thought in America* (New York, 1962), pp. 64-67.

13. George H. Martin, *The Evolution of the Massachusetts Public School System* (New York, 1894), p. 16. Later historians continued to be impressed with the delicacy of this distinction. Cubberley's *Public Education in the United States* (Boston, 1934) cited it verbatim.

14. Horace Mann describes how the common school muted class differences "to form a happy neighborhood": "Teachers and Teachers' Seminaries," *American Annals of Education*, 7 (February 1837): 55-65.

Also James G. Carter's proposal in Henry Barnard (ed.), *Normal Schools and Other Institutions* (Hartford, Conn., 1851), pp. 76-77.

15. [Mary Mann], *The Life of Horace Mann* (Boston, 1865), pp. 66-67.

16. Mann, *Educational Writings*, 2: 516-517, for a clear endorsement of the schoolman's position on the necessity of an independent will: "If then learning," Mann asserted, "all wills, desires, all costs, labors, efforts, of others, are dependent, at last, upon the will of the learner, the first requirement is the existence in his mind of a desire to learn."

17. The biographies of Horace Mann as one set of examples of his point are examined later in this essay.

18. Stanley Elkins' study, *Slavery: A Problem in American Institutional and Intellectual Life* (New York, 1959), especially pp. 147-156. "Intellectuals without Responsibility," accuses the abolitionist frame of mind of detaching themselves from all responsible behavior because they "abstracted" man. Relying largely on the writings of Transcendentalists (rather than thinkers who were activists like many of the schoolmen), Elkins never assumes that even abstract and nonprogrammatic thought can effect action. Significant ideas reflect organized behavior. Thus, intellectuals who criticized social organization in a fundamental way thereby render themselves useless. By contrast, ideas can be significant, I am assuming, without adhering to institutional allegiances. Even more, they often have significant social functions because of their very inapplicability. This essay then attempts to provide something of a counter-argument to the pragmatic version of intellectual life operating in Elkins and kindred studies such as George Frederickson's *The Inner Civil War* (New York, 1965).

Elkins' effort to use the writings of Emerson as if they were the conclusions of his generation and culture have frequently led to a misunderstanding of both Emerson and other thinkers of the period. Comparisons of Ralph Waldo Emerson and Mann are generally rather superficial, as in Howard Mumford Jones' edition, *Emerson on Education* (New York, 1966), pp. 19-23. For a more informative analysis which concerns the dilemmas associated with nineteenth-century careers, see Henry Nash Smith, "Emerson's Problem of Vocation," in *Emerson: A Collection of Critical Essays*, edited by Milton Konvitz and Stephen Whicher (Englewood Cliffs, N.J., 1962), pp. 60-71.

19. Lawrence Cremin (ed.), *The Republic and the School: Horace Mann on the Education of Free Men* (New York, 1957), p. 87. The quotation is taken from Mann's Twelfth Annual Report to the Board of Education of Massachusetts (1848).

20. *Life of Horace Mann*, p. 142.

21. There is an enormous literature on Horace Mann, the great bulk of it is terribly repetitious. See Clyde S. King, *Horace Mann, 1796-1859: A Bibliography* (Dobbs Ferry, N.Y., 1966). See note 1, p. 193-194, above, for an explanation of the generational split.

22. Amory Dwight Mayo, *Horace Mann and the American Common School* (Washington, D.C., 1898), p. 722. This essay was reprinted as a separate pamphlet. Originally it was Chapter 15 of the *Report of the U.S. Commissioner of Education for 1896-97*. Mayo's viewpoint well represents that of his generation of professional schoolmen.

23. *Ibid.*

24. These notions are true even in the authors who were not native to New England and who could notice some limitations to Mann's work. Even these accounts feel obliged to end their assessments of his work on the positive side. See B. A. Hinsdale, *Horace Mann and the Common School Revival in the United States* (New York, 1898), especially pp. 142-144.

25. Mayo, *Horace Mann*, p. 723. See also *Life of Horace Mann*, p. 10.

26. Albert E. Winship, *Horace Mann, The Educator* (Boston, 1896), p. 5. While Winship (1845-1933) belonged to a third generation of schoolmen and Mayo (1823-1909) to the second, the differences in their accounts are merely idiosyncratic.

27. *Ibid.*

28. In one of his important lectures repeated often to many public audiences, Mann asserted: "Whatever there is of law, of order, of duty, in these works of God, or in the progressive

conditions of the race, all have their spiritual counterparts within him [the man of special preparation]. . . . By tracing the relations between causes and effects, he acquires a kind of prophetic vision and power; for, by conforming to the unchanging laws of Nature, he enlists her in his service, and she works with him in fulfilling his prediction." Horace Mann, "Special Preparation a Prerequisite to Teaching," *Educational Writings*, 11: 113.

29. Jonathan Messerli, "Horace Mann's Childhood: Myth and Reality," *Educational Forum*, 30 (January 1966): 167-168. See also Jonathan Messerli, "Horace Mann: The Early Years; 1796-1837," (unpublished Ph.D. dissertation, Harvard University, 1963), now expanded into his recent book, *Horace Mann* (New York, 1972).

30. Donald M. Scott, "Making It in Ante-Bellum America: Young Men and Their Careers, 1820-1860," paper delivered to the Organization of American Historians, New Orleans, Louisiana, April 17, 1971. See also William E. Bridges, "Family Patterns and Social Values (1825-1875)," *American Quarterly* 17 (Spring 1965): 3-11.

31. Horace Mann to Charlotte Messer, September 15, 1830, Mann Papers, Massachusetts Historical Society, quoted in Messerli, "Mann: The Early Years," p. 145, footnote 2.

32. David F. Allmendinger, Jr., "New England Students and the Revolution in Higher Education," *History of Education Quarterly*, 11 (Winter 1971). Many other features of Mann's career suggest great calculation. E. I. F. Williams' biography provides most of such evidence, but he never draws any inferences which tarnish the older version of Mann's humanitarianism, the opposite of calculated self-interest. See Williams' discussion of why Mann might have selected Litchfield Law School, Mrs. Clarke's boardinghouse or Dedham, Massachusetts as the town suitable for beginning a career in the law. *Horace Mann: Educational Statesman* (New York, 1937), pp. 30, 34, 50.

33. William Mowry, *Recollections of a New England Educator, 1838-1908,* (New York, 1908), p. 3. See also George B. Emerson, *Reminiscences of an Old Teacher* (Boston, 1878), which was serialized in the *New England Journal of Education* previous to its publication in book form; the editors of this serial explicitly urge scrutiny of Emerson's experience to learn how one teacher became successful. *New England Journal of Education* 3 (January 29, 1876): 55. David N. Camp, *Reminiscences of a Long and Active Life* (New Britain, 1917); Edward Eggleston, *Hoosier Schoolmaster* (New York, 1961; 1st ed. 1971); Edward Everett Hale, *New England Boyhood and Other Bits of Autobiography* (Boston, 1900).

34. *Life of Horace Mann,* p. 73.

35. In his contribution to the advice literature, Mann had written: "Free agency necessitates the possibility of perdition; moral compulsion, indeed, may save from ruin; but compulsion abolishes freedom. . . .

"Embued, then with these immortal and energetic capacities to soar or sink; with these heights of glory above him, and this abyss of wretchedness below him; witherward shall a young man set his face, and how shall he order his steps?" *Thoughts for a Young Man,* in *Monthly Literary Miscellany,* 26, "Pamphlets on Education" [University of Wisconsin Collection]: 194.

36. *Ibid.,* p. 80.

37. First Annual Report of the secretary of the Board of Education of Massachusetts (1837) in Mann, *Educational Writings*, 2: 425.

38. *Life of Horace Mann,* p. 80.

39. Cremin, *The Republic and the School* sustains the conception of Horace Mann as a "philosopher" of education by editing out all but the generalized conclusions of his reports. By contrast, the reports themselves must be seen for their argument, since Mann developed them as legal briefs. There was an underlying coherence to Mann's thought but the kind of explicit correlation of fundamental assumptions, essential to philosophy, is missing from his writings.

40. In Horace Mann's very popular address and essay, *Thoughts for a Young Man,* first published in 1850, several of these terms are used. Competency and aptness are among his favorite words when discussing the improvement of teachers in his Annual Reports (1837-1848). The synonym

"balance" is found in the first-mentioned essay and discussed. Career as a "hold" was a prominent idea in the experience of young men aspiring to the ministry. See Donald Scott, "Making It in Ante-Bellum America."

41. Horace Mann, *A Few Thoughts for a Young Man* (Boston, 1850). The copy I used was a popularized version reprinted in the *Monthly Literary Miscellany*. It is bound in the "Pamphlets on Education" in the Memorial Library, University of Wisconsin, Madison. For the several editions, see King, *Horace Mann*, p. 23.

42. *Ibid.*

43. *Life of Horace Mann*, p. 67. Also see the next note.

44. See his own accounts of the shifts into Congress to fill out the remaining term left by the death of John Quincy Adams or else the move to the presidency of Antioch College. In both these cases, and others as well, one finds much deliberation with friends without whose insistence Mann quite likely would not have accepted. Note also his public discussion of his doubts before acceptance as his means of making terms, in the one case with a political party and in the other with a religious sect. Each of these cases resembles his private negotiations with Edmund Dwight, a prominent Boston businessman, in which he states his terms, one of which is a unanimous vote for him as the candidate for the secretaryship. See *Life of Horace Mann*, p. 79. For other evidence of his design of the secretaryship, see the letter of the Reverend John Pierpont to Henry Barnard, Boston, May 7, 1838. Henry Barnard Papers, New York University.

45. Thomas K. Beecher wrote a classic confidential recommendation for a teacher to Henry Barnard: "She has taught a district school one term, and has assisted in an academy for some months. She has nerve and perseverance enough to bear unusual responsibility, while in her estimate of herself she exhibits a self-distrust which in in my estimation is more reliable than showy strength and confidence." Thomas K. Beecher to Henry Barnard, April 4, 1850, Henry Barnard Papers, New York University.

46. This characteristic did not pertain simply to schoolmen. Were one to examine the best of this kind of writing, one might turn to Thoreau's *Walden*, on the one hand, or to *The Education of Henry Adams*, on the other. Both these works as highly individualized accounts tell little about the personal subjects except insofar as their problems coincide with the larger ones of their society and culture.

47. In occasional private references schoolmen specified explicitly how nothing failed to succeed like success. Ariel Parish, principal of Springfield (Massachusetts) High School (1844–1865), expressed this occupational discomfort this way: "Having fully discharged my duty in assisting to give this place [Springfield H.S.] a thoroughly organized system of public schools;—(The school under my immediate charge no longer giving me scope for action, as it has to bring it to its present condition, the inducements to me for remaining here are less than heretofore, except so far as my own *ease* is concerned),—my preference is to spend whatever of *vigor* of age may be continued to me on a broader field if Providence shall see fit to open one for me to occupy." (His italics.) Letter to the Honorable Loren P. Waldo, trustee of Connecticut State Normal School, October 12, 1852 in Henry Barnard Papers, New York University. Barnard and Waldo had made overtures to Parish concerning the Connecticut Normal School principalship.

48. William A. Alcott, "Missionaries of Education," *American Annals of Education and Instruction*, 7 (April 1837): 161-162. N.A., "District School Missionaries," *American Annals of Education and Instruction* 8 (January 1835): 22-23; 8 (February 1838): 71-75.

49. Horace Mann, "Means and Objects of Common School Education," *Educational Writings*, 2: 40.

Chapter IV

1. Some educators, like James G. Carter in Lancaster, Massachusetts, and the Reverend Samuel

Read Hall in Andover, Massachusetts, opened privately supported teacher-training institutions during the 1820s and 1830s. While they prompted much discussion, such schools provided their most lasting contribution by their failures. Private support was insufficient basis for such enterprises. The second major model of teacher training was the department for this purpose annexed to flourishing academies, generally in New York. Like the private institutions devoted solely to teacher training, these departmental appendages seldom survived beyond the 1830s. The introduction of the state-supported normal school represented a qualitatively different level of professional aspiration but not an essentially different kind of institution from its earlier counterparts. The effectiveness of the aspiration in professional circles can be measured by the extent to which problems of teacher training distracted schoolmen from their original concern, the reform of the common school. In a sense, the emergence of professional institutions served to postpone for several decades the transformation of elementary instruction.

See Willard S. Ellsbree, *The American Teacher: Evolution of a Profession in a Democracy* (New York, 1939); Merle Borrowman, *The Liberal and Technical in Teacher Education* (New York, 1956); and Ellwood Patterson Cubberley, *Public Education in the United States* (Cambridge, Mass., 1919; rev. ed. 1962).

2. Vernon Mangun, *The American Normal School* (Baltimore, 1928), p. 135.

3. The origins of the teachers' institute remain disputed. Since the most authoritative work in educational history in this period is still Henry Barnard's *American Journal of Education* (32 vols.), I have merely followed the example of most writers on institutes and have assumed that Barnard's claims to have been the originator are genuine. The most thorough, historical account of the teachers' institute is "Teachers' Institutes: Connecticut; New York; Rhode Island; Ohio; Massachusetts," *American Journal of Education*, 15 (September 1865): 387-414. Also extremely thorough but from the point of view of those who claim the institute originated in New York is: Samuel N. Sweet, *Teachers' Institutes, or Temporary Normal Schools: Their Origin and Progress* (Utica, N.Y., 1848). Whatever the origin, the teachers' institute, like so many other educational institutions in this period, ultimately assumed the characteristics of the New England model. Even if Barnard was not the creator of the institute, he was the commanding figure in its development and influence.

4. Teachers' Institutes: Connecticut," *American Journal of Education*, 15 (September 1865): 388.

5. Henry Barnard (ed.), *Normal Schools, and Other Institutions, Agencies and Means Designed for the Professional Education of Teachers* (Hartford, 1851), p. 76.

6. In addition to previously mentioned works, see M. A. Newell, "Contributions to the History of Normal Schools in the United States," in *Report of the U.S. Commissioner of Education, 1898–1899*, 2 (Washington, D.C., 1900): 2295.

7. Sweet, *Teachers' Institutes*, p. 128.

8. Letter of Emma Willard to S. R. Sweet, November 19, 1847, in *ibid.*, pp. 128-136.

9. "Teachers' Institutes: Connecticut," *American Journal of Education*, 15 (September 1865): 388. Careful selection of institute conductors continued to be a central characteristic of institute work for first-generation schoolmen. See William Russell to Henry Barnard, Merrimac Normal Institute, [Reed's Ferry, N.H.], October 7, 1850, and William Russell to Henry Barnard, Medford, Mass. October 1, 1848, in Henry Barnard Papers, New York University.

10. Horace Mann, *Ninth Annual Report of the Secretary to the Board of Education of Massachusetts, 1845* (Boston, 1846), pp. 43-49.

11. See Wm. H. Wells, principal of Free Academy, Newburyport, Mass. to Henry Barnard, November 1845, Henry Barnard Papers, New York University.

12. Letter of Emma Willard . . . November 19, 1847, in Sweet, *Teachers' Institutes*, p. 130.

13. See, for example, Wilson Smith, *Professors and Public Ethics: Studies of Northern Moral Philosophers before the Civil War* (Ithaca, N.Y., 1956). The particular kind of moral character embodied in the president of the institution played a singular part in Barnard's own evaluation of schools. In a striking passage from his travel journal (actually letters to his brother, Chauncey), sometime between February and March 1833, Barnard described his visit to Georgetown

University, the oldest Catholic institution of higher education in the United States. After an extensive tour of the library (15,000 vols.), which was extremely largé for the period, and all its scientific facilities by the institution's president, the Reverend Thomas F. Mulledy, Barnard could not help expressing approval. Nevertheless, the character of the institution, however scientific and extraordinary, did not derive from the technical facilities of the school. "The discipline of the college," Barnard observed, "is very strict, and were it not for its Catholicism, would be a very eligible situation for a youth from 12 to 17. The situation of the college is delightful; I can't imagine anything finer." This passage is taken from Henry Barnard, "The South Atlantic States in 1833, as Seen by a New Englander," Bernard Steiner (ed.) *Maryland Historical Magazine*, 13 (September 1918): 289.

14. Sweet, *Teachers' Institutes*, p. 129.

15. For a perceptive examination of the relation between poverty and piety in this period, see David F. Allmendinger, Jr., *Paupers and Scholars: The Transformation of Student Life in New England, 1760-1860* (New York, 1975).

16. Sweet, *Teachers' Institutes*, p. 131.

17. Henry Barnard, *Report to the Regents of Normal Schools on the Teachers' Institutes, Held in Wisconsin in 1859*, in Henry Barnard (ed.), *Papers for the Teacher* (New York, 1860), p. 12.

18. For an excellent analysis of revivals in terms of their conceptual and institutional ramifications during this period, see Donald M. Scott, "Watchmen on the Walls of Zion: Evangelicals and American Society, 1800–1860" (unpublished doctoral dissertation, University of Wisconsin, 1968). Also illuminating in this regard is William G. McLoughlin's introduction to his edition of Charles Grandison Finney, *Lectures on Revivals of Religion* (Cambridge, Mass., 1960).

19. Recently some of the most interesting history being written about educational problems tries to account for the lack of controversy in nineteenth-century discussions of common school reform. See Jonathan Messerli, "Controversy and Consensus in Common School Reform," *Teachers College Record* (May 1965), pp. 749-758; Michael Katz, *The Irony of Early School Reform* (Cambridge, Mass., 1968); Albert Fishlow, "The American Common School Revival: Fact or Fancy," in Henry Rozofsky (ed.), *Industrialization in Two Systems: Essays in Honor of Alexander Gerschenkron* (New York, 1966). The basic omission in all these works, however, is the failure to account for the moral dynamic and religious underpinnings which set the context for all discussions of educational and social reform before the Civil War.

20. William Russell, *Suggestions on Teachers' Institutes* (Manchester, N.H., 1852), p. 33.

21. *Ibid.*

22. Sweet, *Teachers' Institutes*, p. 131.

23. The very term "institute" assumed a special meaning and usage in the early nineteenth century. The peculiarity of this meaning suggests much about the concern at this time for effective, educational techniques. Until the nineteenth century, according to the *Oxford English Dictionary*, a "institute" referred to a digest of the elements of a subject, perhaps like John Calvin's *Institutes of the Christian Religion* or, in America, Noah Webster's *Grammatical Institute*. During the early decades of the nineteenth century a "institute" began to refer to the agency for systematizing and disseminating such a digest. In this transition, the word retained several of its former implications, namely, the delineation of a specific body of material or subject, the association with public service, and the intimation of transmitting practical rather than philosophical knowledge. The nineteenth-century version of "institute," especially in reference to mechanics' institutes, manual labor institutes, or scientific institutes, like the Franklin Institute (1842), Marietta Institute (1831), Oneida Institute (1827), and Rensselaer Polytechnic Institute (1824) and most of all, the Smithsonian (1846), took on the added meaning of transmitting not only practical knowledge but also practical skills. Even among those institutes that did not teach practical skills, the designation connoted the immediate and constructive application of certain principles. This characteristic pertains especially to the major educational association of this period, the American Institute of Instruction (1830). At all points, too, an institute retained its

etymological meaning of "founding," "initiating," and "originating"; it inevitably was applied to innovative or experimental efforts.

24. Professor Noah Porter, *Prize Essay on the Necessity and Means of Improving the Common Schools of Connecticut* (Hartford, 1846). This essay was republished by Barnard as soon as he became editor of the *Connecticut Common School Journal* for the second time in 1850. The entire *Connecticut Common School Journal* can be found in the American Periodicals on Microfilm Series, Reels 789, 790, 791. The processor of this series is University Microfilms, Inc., Ann Arbor, Michigan.

Francis Wayland, "Progress of Education for the Last Twenty-Five Years," *Lectures and Proceedings of the American Institute of Instruction*, 25 (Boston, 1855).

Horace Mann, *Ninth Annual Report of the Secretary of the Board of Education of Massachusetts, 1845* (Boston, 1846), pp. 43-49.

Nathan Lord, quoted in "Teachers' Institutes: Ohio," *American Journal of Education*, 15 (September 1865): 403. See also Henry Barnard (ed:), "Progress of Education in Other States: Ohio: Teachers' Institutes," *Journal of the Rhode Island Institute of Instruction*, 1 (April 1, 1846), Extra No. 10, p. 133.

Sweet, *Teachers' Institutes*, pp. 36ff., 78ff.

25. "Teachers' Institutes: Connecticut," *American Journal of Education*, 15 (September 1865), p. 394. Barnas Sears was not specifically mentioned in this article, but since he was in 1848 the highest educational officer of the state, I have assumed the title "superintendent" referred to him. Some confusion about this point has been added by a footnote on the page, asserting that Henry Barnard, though at the time head of the common school system of Rhode Island, actually wrote the reports of the superintendent of Connecticut's school system between 1845 and 1849. During these years Barnas Sears was superintendent of the School Fund of Connecticut. Between the elimination of the office of commissioner of Connecticut common schools in 1842 and the creation of a state superintendency in 1850 (both offices held by Henry Barnard) there was no state superintendent of common schools in the state.

26. Russell, *Suggestions on Teachers' Institutes*, p. 7.

27. Henry Barnard, *Report to the Regents of Normal Schools on the Teachers' Institutes. Held in Wisconsin in 1859*, in Henry Barnard (ed.), *Papers for the Teachers*, p. 12.

28. Teachers' associations had begun to be established in the late 1840s and a decade later nearly all the states that looked to New England as an educational guide had established them. They were distinguished from the institutes by their shorter meetings of one- or two-day duration, by holding their meetings in the cities where they maintained a central office and an official journal, and by the parliamentary rather than pedagogical nature of their proceedings. In addition, they were directed entirely by practicing teachers rather than by a mixture of educators and established, influential citizens of the state who often belonged to professions other than teaching. They were, much less than the institutes, arms of the educational policy of the state, yet received substantial government subsidies for their operation.

29. For a more thorough discussion of this distinction and the significance of these changes, see Stuart G. Noble, "From 'Lectures on School-Keeping' to 'Introduction to Education,'" *School and Society*, 23 (June 26, 1926): 793-802.

30. Among other references, see Cubberley, *Public Education in United States*, and Ellsbree, *The American Teacher*.

31. David Nelson Camp, *Report of the Superintendent of Common Schools to the General Assembly, May Session, 1857-1867* (Hartford and New Haven, 1858-1868). In addition to these state reports the appropriate portions of each issue, usually the section called "Miscellany," in the *Connecticut Common School Journal*, and *The Massachusetts Teacher*, were consulted for the generalizations in this paragraph.

32. Thomas Woody, "David Nelson Camp," *Dictionary of American Biography*, 3 (New York, 1929): 441-443; David Nelson Camp, *Reminiscences of a Long and Active Life* (New Britain, Conn., 1917). See also David Nelson Camp, "Reminiscences of Henry Barnard," in Bernard Steiner, *Life*

of Henry Barnard, United States Bureau of Education Bulletin, No. 8 (Washington, D.C., 1919), Appendix.

33. Merle Curti, "Henry Barnard," *The Social Ideas of American Educators* (Paterson, N.J., 1935; rev. ed. 1961), pp. 139-168.

34. Camp, *Reminiscences*, p. 10.

35. Barnard, *Normal Schools*, pp. 15-16.

36. "Teachers' Institutes," *American Journal of Education*, 15 (September 1865): 387-414; "Charles Northend," *Dictionary of American Biography*, 13: 564-565; "William Bently Fowle," *Dictionary of American Biography*, 6: 561-562; Fowle's enthusiasm for the institutes took the form of a manual for institute organization and operation, *The Teachers' Institute, Or Familiar Hints to Young Teachers* (Boston, 1847), "James B. Thomson: President of the New York State Teachers' Association," *American Journal of Education*, 15 (September 1865): 487; "Asa Dearborn Lord: President of the Ohio State Teachers' Association," *American Journal of Education*, 16 (March 1866): 607-608; for William S. Baker, see John D. Philbrick, "Henry Barnard," *Connecticut Common School Journal and Annals of Education*, N.S. 2 (January 1855): 72, and "The Second Annual Report of the Executive Committee of the Rhode Island Institute of Instruction," *Journal of the Rhode Island Institute of Instruction*, 2 (1847): 155-156.

37. David Nelson Camp, *Report of the Superintendent of Common Schools to the General Assembly, May Session, 1859* (New Haven, 1859), pp. 9-10. (Italics added.)

38. David Nelson Camp, *Report of the Superintendent of Common Schools to the General Assembly, May Session, 1860* (Hartford, 1860).

39. David Nelson Camp, "Report of Lecturers and School Visitations," pp. 113ff., in the *Sixth Annual Report of the Superintendent of Common Schools, May, 1851* (Hartford, 1851), Appendix.

40. *Ibid.*

41. Camp specified his preference for special knowledge and experience over "culture" in a discussion at the American Institute of Instruction. See the proceedings in *Lectures and Proceedings of the American Institute of Instruction*, 62 (Boston, 1862): lxxxv.

42. Camp, "Report of Lecturers and School Visitations," p. 31.

43. David Nelson Camp, "The Relation of the Teacher to Advancing Civilization," *Lectures and Proceedings of the American Institute of Instruction*, 64 (Boston, 1863): 84ff.

44. Camp, "Report of Lecturers and School Visitations," p. 31.

45. *Ibid.*

46. William Mowry, *Martha's Vineyard Summer Institute* (Boston, 1905), p. 23. See also, n.a., "Hints on Teachers' Institutes," *National Journal of Education*, 12 (June 24, 1880); 3-4; n.a., "Speakers and Hearers in Schools Conventions," *National Journal of Education*, 11 (April 15, 1880): 264, in which the author claims: "First let it be understood that a school convention, in distinction from an institute, is *an assembly of teachers and friends of education for general inspiration in educational work and and social communion.*" (Italics his.)

For the mounting controversy over institutes, especially the critical view of superintendents, see, n.a., "A New Art in Education," *New England Journal of Education*, 2 (August 21, 1875): 78. For the summary defense of institutes, check p. 82 in the same volume which reports New Hampshire's abolishment of institutes. On p. 153 of the same volume there is reported the results of a questionnaire in favor of institutes: 103—Yes, 39—No, 20—Undecided. In the same volume see the anti-institute position elaborated on pp. 154 and 178.

47. For example, see Camp on the "self-made man" in his article "The Relation of the Teacher to Advancing Civilization," especially pp. 93-95, and for the shift from Scottish ethics to German science see Camp's colleague, John D. Philbrick, "What Education Should Precede a Strictly Professional One," *Lectures and Proceedings of the American Institute of Instruction*, 68 (Boston, 1869): 101-102.

Chapter V

1. See Alice Felt Tyler, *Freedom's Ferment* (Minneapolis, 1944).

2. The American Institute of Instruction was always given special attention even when its activities repeated those of the state teachers' associations after the Civil War and after it was overshadowed by the National Education Association in the 1880s and 1890s. Nevertheless, scanty attention has been paid by educational historians to the Institute's work. The most recent substantive mention of the Institute occurs in Paul Monroe (ed.), *Cyclopedia of Education*, 1 (New York, 1911): 110. This brief article was written by Will S. Monroe who simply condensed the longer article by Albert E. Winship on the Institute in the *Proceedings of the National Educational Association* (1906), pp. 457-463. (An excerpt of Winship's essay appears in Edgar Knight and Clifton Hall (eds.), *Readings in American Educational History* (New York, 1951), pp. 409-412). In turn, Winship based his entire essay upon a cursory check of the Institute's volumes and George B. Emerson's *The History and Design of the American Institute of Instruction* (Boston, 1849). Other than a few remarks in the standard educational history textbooks, all of which draw from these two basic accounts by Winship and Emerson, historians have simply followed the example of the Institute's later presidents, repeating the same names and same sentiments about the unique contribution of this organization.

3. These generalizations are based upon data drawn primarily from Allen Johnson (ed.), *Dictionary of American Biography*, 22 vols. (New York, 1929), from innumerable references from Henry Barnard's *American Journal of Education*, 31 vols., 1854-1881, from Henry Barnard (ed.), *Memoirs of Teachers*, and many nineteenth-century journals. See also H. K. Oliver, "George Barrell Emerson," *Lectures and Proceedings of The American Institute of Instruction*, 52 (Boston, 1882): 290-296.

4. George S. Hilliard, *Life, Letters and Journals of George Ticknor*, 1 (Boston, 1876), *passim*. See also David B. Tyack, *George Ticknor and the Boston Brahmins* (Cambridge, Mass., 1967).

5. For a thorough description of this crisis and the Boston schools, see Mary Ann Connolly, "The Boston Schools in the New Republic, 1776-1840," unpublished Ph.D. dissertation, Harvard University, 1963; also a fine recent study, Stanley K. Schultz, *The Culture Factory: Boston Public Schools, 1789-1860* (New York, 1973).

6. *Life, Letters and Journals of George Ticknor*, I: 23. In July 1814 Ticknor wrote to a lawyer friend: "The whole tour in Europe I consider a sacrifice of enjoyment to improvement. I value it only in proportion to the great means and inducements it will afford me to study—not men, but books. Wherever I establish myself, it will be only with a view to labor; and wherever I stay,—even if it be but a week,—I shall, I hope, devote myself to some study, many more hours in the day than I do at home." See also in this same connection William R. Taylor, *Cavalier and Yankee: The Old South and the American National Character* (New York, 1961), pp. 31-51.

7. [George Ticknor], "Art. X.—*Letters to William Prescott, L.L.D., on the Free School of New England, with Remarks upon the Principles of Instruction. By James G. Carter. 8 vols., p. 123. Boston. Cummings, Hilliard, and Co., 1824*," *North American Review*, 19 (October 1824): 451. Verification of authorship for this essay may be found in Tyack, *George Ticknor*, p. 206.

8. Connolly, "Boston Schools," pp. 225, 143.

9. William Russell, *Manual of Mutual Instruction: consisting of Mr. Fowle's Direction for Introducing in Common Schools the Improved System Adopted in the Monitorial School, Boston, with an Appendix, containing some considerations in favor of the monitorial method, and a sketch of its progress, embracing a view of its adaptation to instruction in Academies, preparatory seminaries, and colleges* (Boston, 1826), Appendix, p. 75.

10. Quoted in Martin Green, *The Problem of Boston* (New York, 1966), p. 88.

11. George Ticknor, *Remarks on Changes Lately Proposed or Adopted in Harvard University* (Boston, 1825), p. 36. For a further discussion of Ticknor's reforms at Harvard, see R. Freeman Butts, *The College Charts Its Course* (New York, 1939), especially pp. 97-108.

12. Ticknor, *Remarks*, p. 45. One must take care to avoid interpreting Ticknor's insistence upon "thorough" education and systematic instruction as rigid and overbearing. It may well have been so in effect, but in intent Ticknor believed each student became, in proportion as his studies were orderly, more self-possessed and individual. At several points his support of the monitorial system proved an instance of this belief. While many criticized monitorial instruction as mechanized, if not debilitating and militaristic, Ticknor and others such as William Russell insisted the opposite. They felt that only with a particular kind of departmentalization could sufficient attention be given by an instructor to detail when teaching large groups. This same attitude was evident also in Ticknor's explanations of departmentalization in his *Remarks* apropos Harvard University.

13. *Ibid.*

14. Alexis de Tocqueville, "Conversation with Mr. Latrobe, 30th October, 1831," *Non-Alphabetical Notebooks 2 and 3*, in *Journey to America*, trans. by George Lawrence and ed. by J. P. Mayer (New Haven, 1962), p. 78.

15. "The American Institute of Instruction," *American Journal of Education*, ed. by Henry Barnard, 2 (July 1956): 22.

16. [George Ticknor], "Proposals for Forming a Society of Education," *American Journal of Education*, ed. by William Russell, 1 (January 1826): 486-487. Evidence of Ticknor's authorship in this untitled essay is given in "The American Institute of Instruction," *American Journal of Education*, ed. by Henry Barnard, 2 (July 1856): 22.

One member of Ticknor's group, a few years later, articulated the group's implicit suspicion of "political assemblies" and the dubious propriety of enlisting political groups in their work. See William C. Woodbridge, "Courses of Instruction for the Improvement of Teachers, (Hofwyl, February 11, 1836)," *American Annals of Education*, 6 (June 1836): 249.

17. [George Ticknor], "Proposals. . . ."

18. "The American Institute of Instruction," *American Journal of Education*, p. 22.

19. *Ibid.*

20. *Ibid.* Although he does not appear to have been among the actual founders of the American Institute of Instruction, Ticknor nevertheless joined the association in 1832 and in that year delivered before the membership his lecture, "The Best Methods for Teaching the Living Language." His interest in the work of the institute was necessarily cut short after he resigned the Smith Professorship at Harvard and in March 1834 left for Europe and several years' travel abroad. *Life and Letters of George Ticknor*, p. 401.

21. See Table 1, p. 00.

22. "Lectures to Teachers," *American Journal of Education and Monthly Lyceum*, ed. by William C. Woodbridge, N.S. 1 (July 1830): 315.

23. *Ibid.* See also the account in the preface to the first volume of *The Lectures and Proceedings of the American Institute of Instruction*, written by George B. Emerson. Of those attending this meeting only 256 signed the first roster.

24. "The American Institute of Instruction," *American Journal of Education*, pp. 23-25.

25. *Ibid.* These biographical remarks are taken from *The Dictionary of American Biography* ed. by Allen Johnson and from Henry Barnard's *American Journal of Education* as well as the same author's *Memoirs of Teachers*.

26. The details in this and the previous paragraph were drawn from the account of the Institute's proceedings for the first decade of its history. These proceedings are located in published form with the association's annual volumes.

27. For biographical information of these individuals, see *The Dictionary of American Biography*.

28. *Lectures and Proceedings of the American Institute of Instruction*, 1 (Boston, 1831), Preface. This statement of purpose was written by George B. Emerson.

29. [Ticknor], "Proposals," p. 487.

30. "Constitution of the American Institute of Instruction," *Lectures and Proceeding of the American Institute of Instruction*, 1 (Boston, 1831).

31. The monthly salary of district schoolmasters in this period ranged widely. The lowest salaries of about two dollars per month were usually paid to women, although many male instructors did not fare much better. Outside the city and large towns a male instructor rarely received more than twelve to fourteen dollars per month. See, for example, William A. Alcott, *Confessions of a Schoolmaster*.

32. [Ticknor], "Proposals," p. 485.

33. The actual breakdown of the first meeting in 1830 was as follows: 65 from Boston, 116 from non-Boston Massachusetts, 12 from Maine, 10 from New Hampshire, 13 from New York, 1 from Maryland, 4 from Vermont, 3 from Connecticut, 6 from Rhode Island, 9 from Pennsylvania, 2 from Ohio, 1 from New Jersey, 1 from France, 3 from South Carolina, 1 from Tennessee, 1 from Michigan, 1 from Kentucky, and 1 from Virginia. For the next five to seven years the annual increase of the American Institute of Instruction membership, at least with respect to the New England states, retained these proportions. The total membership of the first meeting was 256; however, the Institute would not again admit as many *new* members in a single meeting until 1877 (if one can go by the 1877 list of members). Many members who did attend the first meeting did not register in that year but later. The actual membership lists for that reason are not exactly accurate. Much internal evidence suggests the numbers for many meetings was larger than the official rolls. See "The Members of the American Institute of Instruction from 1830 to 1877," *The Lectures and Proceedings of the American Institute of Instruction*, 47 (Boston, 1878), Appendix, pp. 3-61.

For different statements of attendance numbers see [A.E. Winship], "American Institute of Instruction," *Journal of Education*, 76 (July 18, 1912): 98; and "Bicknell's Meetings," *Journal of Education*, 96 (October 19, 1922): 367.

34. All the meetings between 1830 and 1836 were held in Boston. The number of *new* members for each of these years can be found in Table 2, pp. 99-100. "The Members of the American Institute of Instruction from 1830 to 1877," Appendix, pp. 3-61. Even granting these figures as understatements of real membership and attendance, the drop in registration evidences a problem.

35. The actual number of new members in 1837 was 40.

36. Charles Northend, *The Annals of the American Institute of Instruction 1830:-1883* (New Britain, Conn., 1884), *passim*.

37. See "The Members of the American Institute of Instruction," *Lectures and Proceedings of the American Institute of Instruction*, 47 (1878): Appendix, pp. 3-61.

38. The actual number of new members who joined at this 1849 meeting in Montpelier, Vermont was 73.

39. See Chapter III.

40. Northend, *Annals (passim)*.

41. William Russell, "Suggestions Regarding the Operations of the American Institute of Instruction," *The Lectures and Proceedings of the American Institute of Instruction*, 27 (1857): 140-148.

42. Allen Oscar Hansen, *Early Educational Leadership in the Ohio Valley: A Study of Educational Reconstruction through the Western Literary Institute and College of Professional Teachers, 1829-1841* (Bloomington, Ill., 1923), and Carl Bode, *The American Lyceum*.

43. See the statistical tables in Burritt, *Professional Distribution of College and University Graduates;* see also Allmendinger, *"Paupers and Scholars."*

44. Cubberley, *Public Education in the United States*, pp. 376, 244-257.

45. "The Members of the American Institute of Instruction," Appendix, pp. 3-61.

46. Northend, *Annals (passim)*. For more detail about the events than Northend's handy account gives, see the annual proceedings for the respective years.

47. George B. Emerson, *Reminiscences of an Old Teacher* (Boston, 1878), Papers of George B. Emerson, Massachusetts Historical Society, Boston; Henry K. Oliver, "George B. Emerson,"

Lectures and Proceedings of the American Institute of Instruction, 52 (1882): 290-296; Barnard, *Memoirs of Teachers,* pp. 333-342.

48. *Ibid.*

49. Charles Northend, "Biographical Sketches of the Deceased Members," *Lectures and Proceedings of the American Institute of Instruction,* 52 (1882): 297-299.

50. Barnard, *Memoirs of Teachers,* p. 341.

51. "Presidents of the American Institute of Instruction," *American Journal of Education,* ed. by Henry Barnard, 15 (June 1865): 214.

52. Barnard, *Memoirs of Teachers,* pp. 218-226; "Presidents of the American Institute of Instruction," *American Journal of Education,* p. 214.

53. *Ibid.*

54. Thomas Cushing, *Historical Sketch of Chauncey Hall School with Catalogue, 1828–1894* (Boston, 1895), pp. 83-179.

55. Barnard, *Memoirs of Teachers,* pp. 220-221.

56. Ellwood P. Cubberley, *Readings in Public Education in the United States* (Boston, 1934), p. 230.

57. *Ibid.*

58. Emerson, *Reminiscences,* pp. 66-68.

59. *Ibid.,* pp. 82-85.

60. Cushing, *Chauncey Hall School,* p. 22.

61. Gideon F. Thayer. "On Courtesy and Its Connexion with School Instruction," *Lectures and Proceedings of the American Institute of Instruction,* 10 (1841): 112.

62. Cushing, *Chauncey Hall School,* p. 29.

63. Thayer, "On Courtesy," pp. 83-112.

64. Gideon F. Thayer, *Letters to a Young Teacher,* in Henry Barnard (ed.), *Papers for the Teacher* (New York, 1860), pp. 7-104.

65. Northend, *Annals (passim).*

66. George B. Emerson, *History and Design of the American Institute of Instruction* (Boston, 1849), pp. 3-12.

67. "The Members of the American Institute of Instruction, Appendix, pp. 3-61. It wasn't until 1876, at its forty-seventh annual meeting, that women were elected to the Board of Directors of the A.I.I. That event received favorable mention in the *New England Journal of Education,* 4 (July 15, 1876): 42.

68. These generalizations are based on numerous examples drawn piecemeal from the Miscellany sections of *Connecticut Common School Journal* and the *Massachusetts Teacher.*

69. "The Members of the American Institute of Instruction," Appendix, pp. 3-61.

70. Northend, *Annals,* p. 32. In fact, President Garfield was actually assassinated as he was about to board a train in Union Station, Washington, D.C., for the Institute's annual meeting.

71. Northend, *Annals,* p. 154.

Chapter VI

1. Horace Mann, "First Report of the Secretary of the Board of Education, 1837," *Educational Writings of Horace Mann,* 2 (Boston, 1891): 425. Here he lauds the "voluntary obedience to duty." For alternative ends the teachers might have sought, see Constance Smith and Annie Freedman, *Voluntary Associations: Perspectives on the Literature* (Cambridge, Mass., 1972).

2. William Russell, "Suggestions Regarding the Operations of the American Institute of Instruction," *Lectures and Proceedings of the American Institute of Instruction,* 27 (Boston, 1857): 141.

3. Charles Northend, *The Annals of the American Institute of Instruction: 1830–1883* (New Britain, Conn., 1884), p. 60. Northend's account makes it appear as if there is a perfect harmony between

the institute and the Massachusetts State Teachers Association. Some schoolmen asserted just as explicitly that the organizations represented wholly different attitudes; Russell himself declared the state organizations were compromised agencies. See William Russell, "National Organization of Teachers: An Address to the Convention of Teachers of the United States . . . August 27, 1857, for the purpose of forming a National Organization of Their Profession," *Proceedings of the National Teachers Association, 1857*, 1 (Syracuse, N.Y., 1909): 22.

For accounts of this split historically, see Albert E. Winship, "The American Institute of Instruction," *Proceedings of the National Education Association* (1906), p. 460; George H. Martin, *The Evolution of the Massachusetts Public School System* (New York, 1923 [1st ed., 1894]), pp. 182-183; Raymond Culver, *Horace Mann and Religion in the Massachusetts Public Schools* (New Haven, 1929); [Mary Mann], *Life of Horace Mann*, pp. 244-245.

4. N.a., "American Association for the Advancement of Education," *American Journal of Education*, ed. by Henry Barnard, 5: 857 and 25: 939; Will S. Monroe, "American Association for the Advancement of Education," *Proceedings of the National Education Association* (1906), pp. 471-474; Ellwood P. Cubberley, *Public Education in the United States* (Cambridge, Mass., 1962 rev. ed. [1st ed. 1934]), pp. 706-708.

5. *Proceedings of the National Teachers Association*, 10 vols. (1857-1869). These volumes are usually grouped as the first volumes of the National Education Association. There are only ten during these years because no meetings occurred in 1861 and 1862. Also they remained unpublished until 1909, until they were collected by C. W. Bardeen from the notes and documents of his friend Henry Barnard. See also Will S. Monroe, "The National Teachers Association (1857-1870)," *Proceedings of the National Education Association* (1906), pp. 516-521.

6. Russell, "Suggestions," p. 143.

7. *Ibid.* The year before, Russell made an overture to Henry Barnard to ally his *American Journal of Education* to the work of the Institute. Expectedly he found a harmony of interests in the joint venture. Wm. Russell to Henry Barnard, Lancaster, Massachusetts, January 2, 1855, Henry Barnard Papers, New York University.

8. Henry Barnard (ed.) "William Russell, Editor of the First Series of the American Journal of Education, Boston, 1826 to 1829," *Memoirs of Teachers, Educators, and Promoters and Benefactors of Education, Literature and Science* (New York, 1861), pp. 227-231; *Dictionary of American Biography*, ed. by Allen Johnson *et al.* (New York, 1929), pp. 249-250; Paul Munroe (ed.), *Cyclopedia of Education*, 5 (New York, 1913 [republished by Gale Research Co., Detroit, 1968]): 228.

9. See: William Russell, *The Duties of Teachers: An Address Delivered Before the Associate Alumni of the Merrimack Normal Institute . . . September 4, 1850* (Manchester, N.H., 1850); *Encouragements to Teachers: An Address Before the Associate Alumni of the Merrimack Normal Institute . . . 31st August, 1853* (Manchester, N.H., 1853); *Address at the Dedication and Opening of the New England Normal Institute at Lancaster, Massachusetts . . . May 11, 1853* (Boston, 1853).

10. The manuals abound and are companion pieces to the voluntary associations' work. When the domain of the voluntary association changed and narrowed, the manuals disappeared. Between the publication of Jacob Abbot's *The Teacher* (1834) and Gideon Thayer's *Letters to a Young Teacher*, manuals formed essential equipment for the professional teacher. See Stuart Noble, "From 'Lectures on School-Keeping' to 'Introduction to Education,' " *School and Society*, 23 (June 26, 1926): 793-802. As for their treatments of school architecture, read the recently available reedition of *Henry Barnard's School Architecture* ed. by Robert McClintock as the No. 42 volume of the Teachers College Series (New York, 1970). Earlier than Barnard's seminal volume, the American Institute of Instruction popularized William A. Alcott's *Essay on the Construction of School Houses* (Boston, 1832), a composition which the Institute awarded its earliest educational prize.

11. William Russell, *On Associations for Teachers; An Address delivered at a Meeting Held in Dorcester, on Wednesday, 8th of September, for the Purpose of Forming an Association of Teachers, for Norfolk County* (Boston, 1830), p. 11.

12. Russell, "Suggestions . . . Institute," p. 144.

13. Russell, "On Associations for Teachers," p. 12.

14. *Ibid.*, p. 11.

15. See Chapter III, "The Dynamics of Career Choice."

16. *Ibid.*

17. Russell, "On Associations for Teachers," p. 11.

18. Russell, "National Organization of Teachers," pp. 7-8.

19. William Russell, *Normal Training: The Principles and Methods of Human Culture* (New York, 1863).

20. However sketchy, the only recent discussion of George Jardine can be found in J. J. Chambliss, *The·Origins of American Philosophy of Education: Its Development as a Distinct Discipline, 1808-1913* (The Hague, 1968).

21. Russell, "National Organization of Teachers," p. 19.

22. Russell's most significant work in behalf of Pestalozzi was probably the recruitment of Pestalozzian teachers from Europe. In his New England Normal Institute in the mid-1850s his faculty boasted the Swiss teacher Herman Krusi, Jr., whose father was Pestalozzi's first and long-time associate, and the English art instructor William J. Whittaker. Also on the faculty were some of America's foremost proponents of Pestalozzi, Dana Colburn the author of a series of Pestalozzian arithmetic books [Paul Monroe (ed.), "Dana Colburn (1823-1859)," *Cyclopedia of Education*, 2, p. 48] and Sanborn Tenney, the author of a series of books on natural history [Charles Northend, "Necrology: Sanborn Tenney (1827-1877)," *Lectures and Proceedings of the American Institute of Instruction*, 49 (Boston, 1879), pp. 71-73].

See also Will S. Monroe, *The History of the Pestalozzian Movement in the United States* (Syracuse, N.Y., 1907) and Henry Barnard (ed.), "Memoir of William Russell," *American Journal of Education*, 3: 139-146; Herman Krusi, Jr., "Sketch of the Life and Character of Pestalozzi," *Lectures and Proceedings of the American Institute of Instruction*, 24 (Boston, 1854): 27-52.

George B. Emerson credited Warren Colburn's early textbook on mathematics as the first Pestalozzian textbook in America. Colburn taught in Emerson's English High School in Boston, itself the first school of its kind in the United States. There he and Emerson refined the procedures which found their way into Colburn's mathematics books and into so many American grammar schools. Short biographies of both men can be found in Henry Barnard (ed.), *Memoirs of Teachers*, pp. 195-217 for Colburn, pp. 333-343 for Emerson.

William C. Woodbridge wrote the most scholarly account of Pestalozzian influence before Henry Barnard (ed.), *Pestalozzi and Pestalozzianism* (1863). Shortly after he succeeded Russell [in the early 1830s] as editor of the only English journal on education, he composed a series of articles on Pestalozzi's school at Yverdon and, more intensively, on Pestalozzi's colleague, Phillipe de Fellenberg. Woodbridge's knowledge was firsthand, since he had spent more than three months with both men, most of the time with de Fellenberg at Hofwyl, in Switzerland. "Memoir of William C. Woodbridge," *Memoirs of Teachers*, ed. by Henry Barnard, pp. 268-280. In 1842 a London publisher put out Woodbridge's articles as a book, *Letters from Hofwyl, by a parent, on the educational institutions of de Fellenberg.* See "William C. Woodbridge," *Dictionary of American Biography*, 20: 484-485.

23. Monroe, *Pestalozzian Movement.*

24. For a superb analysis which accounts for the Calvinist influence upon Swiss and Scottish education, see Lawrence Stone, "Literacy and Education in England, 1640-1900," *Past and Present*, No. 42, pp. 126ff. For an excellent analysis of Scottish education and Glasgow University during Russell's formative years there, see W. M. Mathews, "The Origins and Occupations of Glasgow Students, 1740-1839," *Past and Present*, No. 33 (April 1966), and John Clive and Bernard Bailyn, "England's Cultural Provinces: Scotland and America," *William and Mary Quarterly*, 3rd Ser. 11 (1959): 203-207. Also Douglas Sloan, *The Scottish Enlightenment and the American College Ideal* (New York, 1971), pp. 24-66.

25. The literature on Oswego is not large: Mary Sheldon Barnes (ed.), *The Autobiography of*

Edward A. Sheldon (New York, 1911); Dorothy Rogers, *Oswego: Fountainhead of Teacher Education* (New York, 1961), pp. 44-45. Herman Krusi, Jr., went to Sheldon's school at Oswego, New York in 1862 from William Russell's New England Normal Institute, at Lancaster, Massachusetts.

The other experiment in using Pestalozzian educational methods to initiate an extensive social reform (though not an urban one) developed through the work of William MacClure at the Owenite community, New Harmony in Indiana. See J. F. C. Harrison, *Quest for a New Moral World: Robert Owen and the Owenites in Britain and America* (New York, 1968); also, Clarence Karier, *Man, Society and Education* (Glenview, Ill., 1967), pp. 220-226; and Merle Borrowman and Charles Burgess, *What Doctrines to Embrace: Studies in the History of American Education* (Glenview, Ill., 1969), pp. 36-50.

26. The great majority of textbook writers, like Russell, were university graduates. Among those men the followers of Pestalozzi more often seem to have employed his ideas in their educational manuals than in practical instruction. A large number of those who receive biographical sketches in the *Cyclopedia of Education* (1913) bear out this pattern. (Textbook writers seem to have received special consideration in that five-volume work, since their American educational historian, Will S. Monroe, was then compiling material for his study of American textbooks. He had just published his study of Pestalozzian movement in America.) One hundred and thirty-three American schoolmen listed here by Monroe, over 90 percent of the American educators included, belonged to the American Institute of Instruction.

See also Ruth M. Elson, *Guardians of Tradition* (Lincoln, Neb., 1964) and Clifton Johnson, *Old-Time Schools and Schoolbooks* (New York, 1904).

27. Russell, "National Organization of Teachers," p. 10.

28. See n. 32, below. Even in his essay to the National Organization of Teachers, Russell attempts to use the "service-to-community" argument, though only in his introductory remarks. The weight of his argument rested on other factors, which forced him to discuss relationships among institutions rather than those between an institution and its community.

29. Russell, "National Organization of Teachers," p. 16.

30. One of the few major figures who did voice alarm over the increase of educational institutions was Philip Lindsley, long-time faculty member at Princeton and later president of the University of Nashville. Actually his objections registered fears for the waste of resources and the unchristian intolerance of Protestant sectarianism. As in Russell's case, the problem of diversity, though suffusing his essays and addresses, never became the formal subject of any of his writings. See selections under the heading, "Philip Lindsley on the Problems of the College in a Sectarian age, 1829," in Hofstadter and Smith, *American Higher Education,* 1: 233-237.

31. As Lindsley's own critical remarks bear witness, diversity in educational institutions was rampant. See Daniel Boorstin, "Culture with Many Capitals: The Booster College," *The Americans: The National Experience* (New York, 1965), pp. 152-161.

32. Russell, "National Organization of Teachers," p. 15.

33. *Ibid.*

34. *Proceedings of the National Teachers Association,* 1: 14.

35. Russell, "National Organization of Teachers," p. 17.

36. *Ibid.*

37. *Ibid.*, p. 16.

38. *Ibid.*, p. 20.

39. *Ibid.*, p. 18.

40. *Ibid.*

41. Louis Agassiz (1807–1873), a noted Swiss scientist before coming to America in 1846, served from 1847 to his death in 1873 in Harvard's Lawrence Scientific School. He developed an international reputation as a teacher, wrote a famous textbook on methods for teaching natural history and founded a summer school for teachers in 1873 on the island of Penikese. *Cyclopedia of Education,* I: 55.

Arnold Guyot (1807–1884), like Agassiz born in Switzerland and graduated from the College of Neufchâtel, had also developed a distinguished reputation as a geographer before coming to America in 1848. Between his arrival and 1854 when he began his thirty-year tenure at Princeton, he lectured to normal schools at the request of the Massachusetts Board of Education. Also like Agassiz, Guyot wrote popular textbooks on his special interest, geography in this case. *Cyclopedia of Education,* III: 195.

Russell's special mention of these two Swiss scientists suggests how closely he saw his work for rendering his own special subject, elocution, parallel to theirs. In all three cases the thrust of their writings and teaching was to establish for their respective subjects a claim for scientific standing.

42. Russell, "National Organization of Teachers," p. 19.

43. *Ibid.,* p. 20.

44. *Ibid.,* p. 21.

45. For a shorthand view of the proceedings, see Charles Northend, *The Annals of the American Institute of Instruction.* For the remaining twenty-five years (1883–1908), consult the *Lectures and Proceedings of the American Institute of Instruction.* Edgar Wesley's *NEA: The First Hundred Years: The Building of the Teaching Profession* discusses few genuine educational controversies in that organization during the nineteenth century. When educators become critics in that time, generally they are speaking to other critics outside the NEA's membership.

46. Before Herbert Spencer's *Education: Intellectual, Moral and Physical* (1860), Russell's theory of education was the only body of thought sufficiently coherent and systematic to merit the term "philosophy." In many respects his thought resembled and laid a foundation for Spencer's writing, which enjoyed an extensive vogue in America, particularly among American teachers. For an excellent analysis of Spencer, see Henry D. Aiken, "The Apostle of Evolution, Herbert Spencer (1820–1903)," *The Age of Ideology* (New York, 1956), pp. 163-182; Richard Hofstadter, "The Vogue of Spencer," *Social Darwinism in American Thought* (Boston, 1944), pp. 31-50; Andreas Kazamias (ed.), *Herbert Spencer on Education* (New York, 1966). Not least among the reasons for schoolmen's attraction to Spencer was William James' later explanation of the Englishman's popularity. "Spencer," James wrote, "is the philosopher whom those who have no other philosopher can appreciate." In *Memories, Studies,* p. 126, cited in Hofstadter, p. 219.

47. *Proceedings of the National Teachers Association,* 1: 14; See also Wesley, *NEA,* pp. 20-24.

Chapter VII

1. Arthur Clarke Boyden, *Albert Gardner Boyden and the Bridgewater State Normal School: A Memorial Volume* (Bridgewater, Mass., 1919), p. 25.

2. *Ibid.*

3. See Table 13, p. 174, concerning college men who belonged to the American Institute of Instruction. Over the 86 years of its existence the scale for this grouping drops slightly. In the context of the increases over the same period in the association and more dramatically in the teaching profession as a whole, the college men compose a progressively narrower minority among teachers over the nineteenth century.

4. See Table 8, p. 163.

5. Albert G. Boyden, *History and Alumni Record of the State Normal School at Bridgewater, Mass., to July, 1876* (Boston, 1876), p. 167.

6. Rev. Samuel J. May, "Cyrus Peirce," in Henry Barnard (ed.), *Memoirs of Teachers, Educators, and Promoters and Benefactors of Education, Literature, and Science* (New York, 1861), pp. 405-436; also Paul Monroe (ed.), "Cyrus Peirce," *Cyclopedia of Education,* 4 (New York, 1913): 623.

7. "Samuel Phillips Newman," *Dictionary of American Biography,* ed. by Allen Johnson *et al.* (New York, 1929), 13: 466-467. As his middle name indicated, Newman belonged to the Phillips family which founded both Exeter and Andover academies.

In an official description of Newman's views on normal training the Massachusetts Board of Education acknowledged different social roles for the college and normal school. Newman believed, the board proclaimed, "that he regards the office of the principal of a normal school as neither less dignified in its character nor less elevated in its objects than that to which his life has been hitherto devoted [the notice also explained that Newman had served as acting college president of Bowdoin just before coming to the normal school at Barre, Massachusetts]; believing that any station which aims at the welfare and improvement of large numbers of mankind cannot be less honorable or devoted than an office which, though it may give its possessor the power of conferring higher priveleges, limits those priveleges to a few." *Semi-Centennial and Other Exercises of the State Normal School at Westfield, June 25, 1889* (Boston, 1889), Appendix, p. 61.

8. "Emerson Davis," *Lamb's Biographical Dictionary of the United States,* ed. by John Howard Brown (Boston, 1900); also Paul Monroe (ed.), "Emerson Davis," *Cyclopedia of Education,* 2: 256.

9. John W. Dickinson, "Historical Address to the Westfield Normal Association on the Fiftieth Anniversary of the Normal School," *Semi-Centennial and Other Exercises,* pp. 32-33, 35, 62.

10. Albert G. Boyden, *History and Alumni Record,* pp. 42-57.

11. "Memoir of Rev. Samuel May," *American Journal of Education,* ed. by Henry Barnard, 16: 141.

12. Dickinson, "Historical Address," pp. 32-33. Dickinson was speaking of David S. Rowe.

13. Charles Northend *et al.* (eds.), "John D. Philbrick," *Connecticut Common School Journal and Annals of Education,* 5 N.S. (January 1858): 1-8; also Larkin Dunton (ed.), *A Memorial of the Life and Services of John D. Philbrick* (Boston, 1887).

14. For David Camp see Chapter IV of this study.

15. For John W. Dickinson, see George Walton, "In Memoriam: John W. Dickinson," *Lectures and Proceedings of the American Institute of Instruction,* 71 (Boston, 1901): 19-23.

16. For George N. Bigelow, see Albert E. Winship (ed.), "Diverse Points," *Journal of Education,* 26 (September 1, 1887): 125.

17. For Dana P. Colburn, see Albert G. Boyden, *History and Alumni Record,* p. 58.

18. *Ibid.;* also Arthur Clarke Boyden, *The History of the Bridgewater Normal School* (Bridgewater, Mass., 1933), p. 21; and Paul Monroe (ed.), "Richards Edwards," *Cyclopedia of Education,* 2: 411.

19. "William Franklin Phelps," *Dictionary of American Biography,* ed. by A. Johnson, 14: 532-533; also, Rachel M. Jarrold and Glenn E. Fromm, *Time the Great Teacher: One Hundred Years of the New Jersey State Teachers College at Trenton, 1855-1955* (Princeton, 1955), p. 11.

20. Arthur C. Boyden, *History of the Bridgewater Normal School,* especially pp. 37ff.

21. For classic statements of this principle, see Albert E. Winship (ed.), "Politics and Pedagogy," *Journal of Education,* 24 (September 2, 1886): 148-149; and "The Schoolmaster and Politics," *Journal of Education,* 26 (September 1, 1887): p. 120.

22. Arthur O. Norton (ed.), *The First State Normal School in America: The Journals of Cyrus Peirce and Mary Swift* (Cambridge, Mass., 1926), p. 63.

23. *Ibid.,* p. 60.

24. *Ibid.,* p. 67.

25. *Ibid.,* p. 46.

26. *Ibid.,* p. 42.

27. *Ibid.,* p. 50.

28. It was such illnesses and involuntary forces which compelled so many teachers from their professional positions. See the commentary on this facet of the teacher's work in Chapter III, "The Dynamics of Career Choice."

29. From numerous passages one senses how the formal restrictions upon Peirce's official powers did not inhibit his informal and "suggestive" powers. One passage, from October 23, 1840, offers an example: ". . . one [of] my Pupils, after school, desired leave of absence to go to Framingham. I do not like this interruption in school matters; and mean to grant less and less favors of this sort. If young ladies enter the school and mean to *make* teachers, *efficient* Teachers,

they must give their minds, hearts, and time to the Business—They must make school the great object of their attention and of their affection. It must be uppermost in their souls. If they are not willing to do this, they have not yet countered the cost. I did not approve the scheme,—though I did not refuse,—she *left* in TEARS." Italics and capitals are Peirce's. *Ibid.,* p. 59.

30. *Ibid.,* p. 51.

31. *Ibid.,* p. 65.

32. *Ibid.,* p. 33.

33. Cyrus Peirce to Henry Barnard, 1851, in Norton, *The First State Normal School,* p. 283.

34. Rev. A. D. Mayo, "The Oswego Normal School," *Journal of Education,* 24 (December 16, 1886): 391.

35. See the four articles devoted to the "Liberal Arts College in the Age of the University," *History of Education Quarterly,* 11 (Winter 1971).

36. Dickinson, "Historical Address," pp. 28-29.

37. Albert G. Boyden, *History and Alumni Record,* pp. 112-136.

38. An analysis of the fathers' occupations of Bridgewater students indicated that the clothing industry of Fall River and the shoe manufactures of Worcester dominated the work of skilled laborers, especially after the Civil War. See Table 8, p. 163, for the complete breakdown. See also Joseph Kett, "Growing Up in Rural New England, 1800-1840," in *Anonymous Americans: Explorations in 19th Century Social History,* ed. by Tamara Hareven (Englewood Cliffs, N.J., 1971), pp. 1-16.

39. Paul Monroe (ed.), "Military Education in the United States," in *Cyclopedia of Education,* 4 (New York, 1913): 238-242. Even in 1913 West Point insisted that it was not a "war college" and that the quality of its education rested on the character of the men rather than the course of study, suggesting how slowly social and economic realities penetrated the ideology of character.

40. Albert G. Boyden, *History and Alumni Record,* pp. 80-95.

41. The collegiate norms, though never flaunted, were most effectively applied to the schoolmen's work in the first two decades of the nineteenth century. As other norms crept into professional agencies like the American Institute of Instruction as well as the normal school, Henry Barnard attempted an energetic private effort to establish chairs of education, at least at Yale, Trinity, Brown and Michigan. Concerning a Yale professorship, Noah Porter to Henry Barnard, July 24, 1848; Noah Porter to Henry Barnard, August 21, 1848; Noah Porter to Henry Barnard, November 20, 1848; concerning Trinity, the Reverend Thomas H. Vail to Henry Barnard, June 28, 1828; concerning Brown, John Kingsbury to Henry Barnard, May 3, 1848; concerning Michigan, Dr. Z. Pitcher to Henry Barnard, May 12, 1848. Henry Barnard Papers, Fales Collection, New York University.

Actually the only chair to materialize before the Civil War was at Brown. The Chair of Didactics there was for teachers, was occupied by Samuel S. Greene, and was quickly transformed and reorganized into the Rhode Island State Normal School (1854). Willard S. Elsbree, *The American Teacher,* p. 151.

For the rationale of college presidents against such chairs *in colleges,* see Thomas Hill, "Remarks on The Study of Didactics in Colleges," *American Journal of Education,* 15 (1865): 177-179.

42. *Report of the Board of Visitors,* May 28, 1857.

43. Arthur C. Boyden, *Bridgewater Normal School,* p. 32.

44. *Book of the Records,* v. 1 (1840-1854). Bridgewater Archives, Massachusetts State College at Bridgewater, Bridgewater, Mass. See also Jordan Fiore, *Bridgewater and the Sciences: The Record of the First Century* (Bridgewater, 1964), pp. 4-8.

45. See p. 137 for the Tables 5 and 6 on Bridgewater Normal School, 1840-1912. The generalization is based on the general assertion that Massachusetts taught more males in their normal schools than any other state. According to one history (Richard Boone, *Education in the United States* [New York, 1889], p. 379), "after twenty years' experience in Massachusetts with four normal schools [in 1886] eighty-seven percent of the students were found to be women." In that year Bridgewater, its percentage of women students increasing erratically, enrolled 80 percent

females. See also Amy Bramwell and H. M. Hughes, *The Training of Teachers in the United States* (London, 1894), p. 147.

46. Richard Edwards, "Memoir of Nicholas Tillinghast," in *History and Alumni Record,* pp. 47-48. Equally practical-minded, Marshall Conant, the second principal at Bridgewater, used a similar set of norms to describe his work. Marshall Conant to William F. Phelps, December 26, 1856. Bridgewater Archives, Massachusetts State College at Bridgewater, Bridgewater, Massachusetts.

47. Edwards, "Tillinghast," p. 50. The classic statement on "unconscious teaching" was offered in 1856, the year that Edwards penned this memoir of his teacher. See F. D. Huntington, "Unconscious Tuition," *Lectures and Proceedings of the American Institute of Instruction,* 26 (Boston, 1856): 101-139. Boyden's endorsement of this notion can be found in Albert G. Boyden, "The Distinctive Principles of Normal School Work," *Journal of Education,* (June 11, 1885): 371-372.

48. A. G. Boyden, *History and Alumni Record,* p. 39.

49. A. C. Boyden, *History of Bridgewater,* p. 17. According to an 1853 salary scale a male teacher in Massachusetts, which paid male teachers more than double any other state at that time, could make about $250 teaching 7½ months a year. The assistants on a normal school salary like Bridgewater were paid higher than average teachers in public schools. Their salaries were "reduced" in terms of the other professions and other occupations with greater recompense. For the appropriate salary table see, Elsbree, *American Teacher,* p. 275.

Apparently too the "experimental status" of the normal school justified a lower salary scale than those in institutions like the public high school where assistants were paid half the principal's salary. In Boston, 1861-1862, a high school principal was paid an annual salary of $2,400, neither high nor low by comparison with other cities, and the assistants (male) received $1,200. (Female assistants received $500.) Elsbree, *American Teacher,* p. 278.

50. *Register of Graduates* (1912), pp. 179-180.

51. A. C. Boyden, *History of Bridgewater,* pp. 20-23, 35.

52. *Ibid.,* p. 14. Tillinghast's fellow normal schoolmen developed such objections into a significant professional problem. See *American Normal Schools: Their Theory, their Working, and their Results as Embodied in the Proceedings of the First Annual Convention of the American Normal School Association held at Trenton, New Jersey, August 19 and 20, 1859* (New York, 1860), afterward cited as *Proceedings of American Normal School Association.*

53. *Catalogues and Circulars of the State Normal School at Bridgewater 1859-1870* (Boston, 1859-1870). Members of this group were: E. Ripley Blanchard (music), the Reverend Birdsey G. Northrup (mental philosophy), the Reverend John L. Russell (botany), Professor James C. Sharp (chemistry), O. B. Brown (music), Dio Lewis (gymnastics), Sanborn Tenney (natural history), William Russell (elocution), Hosea E. Holt (music), Professor William P. Atkinson (English literature), Joseph White (civil polity), Lewis G. Lowe (anatomy), Professor E. Thore (French).

54. A. C. Boyden, *History of Bridgewater,* p. 46.

55. *Ibid.,* pp. 36-45.

56. Dorothy Rogers, *Oswego: Fountainhead of Teacher Education* (New York, 1961), especially pp. 58-59, 117; for the emergence of a new type of teacher-training institution, Nicholas Murray Butler, "Founding Teachers College," *Across the Busy Years: Recollections and Reflections,* 1 (New York, 1939): 176-187; see also Bramwell, *Training of Teachers,* pp. 86ff.

Compare Bridgewater and Oswego in 1880: "Massachusetts," *National Journal of Education,* 11 (January 29, 1880): 77, and Mary R. Alling, "The Oswego State Normal and Training School, N.Y.," *National Journal of Education,* 11 (January 15, 1880): 36.

57. M'Ledge Moffett, *The Social Background and Activities of Teachers College Students* (New York, 1929), pp. 16-17. This study contains excellent tables which illuminate these patterns.

58. Charles DeGarmo, "The Character of Academic Work in Normal Schools," *Journal of Education,* 24 (October 7, 1886): 223-224.

59. It is important to remember that until the 1890s nearly half of the normal schools in the United States were private institutions. Little is known of them, so little in fact that their exact number remains obscure. One account ("This and That," *Journal of Education*, 24 [July 8, 1886]: p. 53) insisted that one-half of the normal schools were private and compared the 370 universities and colleges in America with their 65,522 students to the 255 normal schools, public and private, with their 1,937 instructors and 60,063 students. For the same year another study (Boone, *Education in the United States*, p. 135) computed the total number of normal schools at 168. His breakdown gave 87 state normal schools with 19,382; 49 private normal schools with 8,065 students; and 32 city normal schools with 4,987. Together the three types accounted for 32,384 students.

While many state normal schools claimed to be *the* model of normal school training, U.S. Commissioner of Education William T. Harris acknowledged Massachusetts' claim, in J. P. Gordy, *The Rise and Growth of the Normal School Idea in the United States* (Washington, D.C., 1891), p. 43. In actual fact, most such claims served the celebrationist graduation or anniversary exercises where they were delivered rather than the interests of historical accuracy. More important, the frequent claim itself reveals much about the fragmentation of professional values engendered by the normal school's regionalized and localized orientations after the Civil War.

60. George A. Walton, *Training of Teachers* (n.p., 1888), pp. 6-7.

61. A. G. Boyden, *History and Alumni Record*, p. 167.

62. See Table 8, p. 163. Note the relatively substantial increase in fathers who were unskilled laborers, from .8 percent in the Civil War period to 11 percent of the total by the end of the century.

63. Albert G. Boyden, "The General Work of the Normal School," *National Education Association: Report of the Committee on Normal Schools, July, 1899* (Chicago, 1899), p. 55.

64. *Catalogue and Circular of the State Normal School at Bridgewater, Mass., 1869* (Boston, 1869), p. 9.

65. Frederick Rudolph, *The American College and University: A History* (New York, 1962), p. 232. "The Lawrence Scientific School & Normal Students," *Journal of Education*, 85 (March 24, 1892): 182.

66. A. C. Boyden, *History of Bridgewater*, pp. 57-58. Curiously, the first mention of these scholarships in the official catalogue came in 1896, sixteen years after the relationship between Bridgewater and Harvard's Lawrence School was actually arranged. *Catalogue and Circular of the State Normal School at Bridgewater, Massachusetts, 1896* (Boston, 1896), p. 36. See also "New England Department: Massachusetts," *National Journal of Education*, 11 (April 22, 1880): 269.

For a highly informative statement in an influential teacher journal, examine the awareness of different levels of instruction and their matching social status (especially the comparative place of the college and normal school) in "How a Poor Boy May Obtain an Education," *New England Journal of Education*, 2 (August 28, 1875): 96.

67. *Catalogue and Circular of the State Normal School at Bridgewater, Massachusetts, 1907–1908* (Boston, 1908), p. 54; *Catalogue and Circular of the State Normal School at Bridgewater, Massachusetts, 1909–1910* (Boston, 1910). From the view of the normal schoolmen "many" graduates took advantage of this arrangement, although until the 1880s the figures argue otherwise. Apparently so few did apply for the scholarships that in 1904 they were reduced from eight to four. *Catalogue and Circular of the State Normal School at Bridgewater, Massachusetts* (Boston, 1904), p. 56.

In some educational quarters the lack of enthusiasm for the program was considered "humiliating" or at least "surprising." Between 1880 and 1886 "but three have applied for these scholarships, and one of these held his but one year." This same article attributed the circumstance to the great demand for teachers. To overcome that attraction the author advanced an argument to take the scholarship in order to gain a good education at Harvard without incuring the time and expense, presumably wasted for the teacher's purposes, on the classical studies of a collegiate course. "Aid at Harvard for Normal Graduates," *Journal of Education*, 24 (November 18, 1886): 325. See also A. C. Boyden, *Albert Gardner Boyden*, p. 75.

68. *State Normal School, Bridgewater, Mass., Semi Centennial Exercises, August 28, 1890: Dedication of the New Normal School Building, September 3, 1891* (Boston, 1892), p. 23.

69. Boyden would likely have been as pleased as was the editor of the *Journal of Education* to report an account of a visit to Bridgewater where a professor of the classics from a western college admired Bridgewater's instruction as equal to a "university course." "In other words," the editor interpreted, "our friend was disposed to say that the students at Bridgewater were receiving a liberal education. Indeed we were not inclined to dispute the statement." One reason the editor, Albert E. Winship, would not dispute the statement was because Bridgewater was not only his alma mater but the school where he had served Boyden as an assistant teacher for three and a half years. "The Bridgewater Normal School," *Journal of Education*, 21 (April 23, 1885): 264.

70. *Ibid.*

71. "Teachers in Council: New England Normal School Teachers Association," *Journal of Education*, 21 (February 21, 1885): 107.

72. Albert G. Boyden, "Is Massachusetts Making a Mistake?" *Journal of Education*, 23 (March 25, 1886): 179. The sentiment was repeated in the memorial volume to Boyden. A. C. Boyden, *Albert Gardner Boyden*, p. 56.

73. Journal of Cyrus Peirce, in Norton, *The First State Normal School in America*, p. 58.

74. "Principles of the School," *Catalogue and Circular of the Bridgewater Normal School, at Bridgewater, Mass.* (Boston, 1904), p. 50.

75. For schoolmen both literary culture and vocational training served as extreme ends of the educational spectrum. Each excluded the other. Manual training continued to be the banner for a combination of both as a professional ideal. Albert G. Boyden, "Manual Training in Public Education," *Journal of Education*, 23 (May 26, 1886): 307-308.

76. A. C. Boyden, *History of Bridgewater*, p. 56.

77. The textbook notion that academies were channels to colleges seems to be a highly questionable generalization. One extremely interesting list ("Statistics of New England Academies," *New England Journal of Education*, 7 [March 28, 1878]: 205) of forty-five academies (the list is not complete) with 5,111 students, only one student in eighteen graduated from the academy and only one in twenty-nine pursued "college-preparatory" studies. Our understanding of such institutions has been aided by the recent study of James McLachlan, *American Boarding Schools: A Historical Study* (New York, 1971), but much more needs to be done beyond this restricted group of the academy genre.

78. Initially special accommodations were made on an individual basis, usually for college graduates who desired some study at a normal school. *Catalogue and Circular of the State Normal School at Bridgewater, 41st year* (Boston, 1881), p. 5. Ten years later these individualized accommodations became regular features in the course offerings, and were designated as "Special Courses." *Catalogue and Circular of the State Normal School at Bridgewater, 51st year* (Boston, 1891), p. 19.

79. *Catalogue and Circular of the State Normal School at Bridgewater, Mass., 1861* (North Bridgewater, 1861), p. 6.

80. See Table #7, pp. 154-155, on students' ages.

81. *Catalogue and Circular of the State Normal School at Bridgewater, Mass. . . . 1873-74* (Boston, 1874), p. 11. Later statements specifically give the teacher the responsibilities of the parent: A. G. Boyden, "Is Massachusetts Making a Mistake," *Journal of Education*, 23 (March 23, 1886): 176.

82. *Catalogue and Circular of the State Normal School at Bridgewater, Mass. . . . 1869* (Boston, 1869).

83. *College Yearbooks* ("The Normal Offering"), *1858-1912*. Bridgewater Archives, Massachusetts State College at Bridgewater, Bridgewater, Massachusetts. See also A. C. Boyden, *Albert Gardner Boyden*, pp. 116-118.

84. *Semi-Centennial Exercises . . . 1890*, p. 31.

85. Jordan D. Fiore, *Leadership in Perspective* (Bridgewater, Mass., 1967), pp. 12-15.

86. See *The Autobiography of Edward Sheldon*, ed. by Mary Sheldon Barnes (New York, 1911), and Rogers, *Oswego*, pp. 75-116; "In Memoriam: John W. Dickinson," *Lectures and Proceedings of the American Institute of Instruction*, 71 (Boston, 1901): 19-23.

87. Arthur C. Boyden, *History of Bridgewater*, pp. 21, 23.

88. At the Boston Normal School, Larkin Dunton served as principal for twenty-seven years and passed the office on to Wallace Boyden, a son of Albert G. Boyden and a Bridgewater graduate who served there for more than twenty-five years. Wallace Boyden, "A Historical Address . . . On the 70th Anniversary of the Boston Normal School, May 26, 1923," in *School Document No. 20: Boston Public Schools: Annual Report of the Superintendent* (Boston, 1923), pp. 150-169.

89. *Register of Graduates* [Bridgewater Normal School], (1912), pp. 180-82.

90. In this period the Massachusetts Board of Education time and again made formal systematization explicitly secondary as an educational and professional goal. Speaking of the success of Ellen Hyde, principal of the Framingham Normal School, the board affirmed: "While the Board provides for a uniform system, it also desires to secure the greatest possible freedom within the system, and it values the personal element above every other. . . ." Quoted in Mangun, *The American Normal School*, p. 351.

91. A. G. Boyden, "General View of the Work of the Normal School," *NEA Report 1899*, pp. 52-53.

92. Mangun, *The American Normal School*, p. 269.

93. See Table 8, p. 163, for distribution of the fathers of Bridgewater students. The twentieth-century patterns did not change for the better, and in some areas the divisions became starker; see Moffett, *Social Background*, pp. 16-17.

94. *Semi-Centennial Exercises . . . 1890*, p. 31.

95. Daniel B. Hagar, "Prof. Alpheus Crosby," *New England Journal of Education*, 1 (January 16, 1875): 25-26.

96. *Proceedings of the American Normal School Association*, p. 20. Social regimentation and Europe were synonymous ideas for schoolmen by the time Crosby spoke. For examples of earlier sentiments in the educational literature, see "Educational Convention in Vermont," *American Annals of Education*, 9 (December 1839): 572.

97. Statements supporting Crosby's view are easily found; see, for example, "Normal Schools," *Journal of Education*, 33 (May 28, 1891): 344. However, from the beginning responsible spokesmen predicted that normal schools would serve the poorer classes more than any other. Vernon Mangun, *American Normal Schools*, p. 173.

98. *Ibid.*, p. 21.

99. *Ibid.*, p. 22.

100. In addition to the references earlier in this chapter, see the more general remarks in Henry Barnard to Daniel Coit Gilman, June 23, 1856, and Daniel Coit Gilman to Henry Barnard (no date but clearly a reply to the June 23rd letter of HB), 1856. Most explicitly, see William Russell to Henry Barnard, February 4, 1856, where Russell stated: "I can easily imagine how irritating you found your connection with Dr. Peters [co-editor with Barnard in the first two volumes of the *American Journal of Education*], he, as you express it, hide-bound in his notions of higher education, in the idea of an American College and all improvement to be an expansion of that, when your plan embraced comprehensive views of the entire field. I am glad that you now stand free for a wider scope of action and usefulness." Henry Barnard Papers, Fales Collection, New York University.

Barnard explicitly stated that he himself agreed to accept the chancellorship of the University of Wisconsin only when he was permitted to adapt the university to the functions of teacher training. Henry Barnard to Professor Salisbury of Whitewater, Wisconsin, May 9, 1876, Hart-ford, Connecticut. Henry Barnard Papers, New York University.

Similarly Horace Mann turned Antioch College, Yellow Springs, Ohio, of which he was the first president, to a pattern resembling an early normal school. Mary Mann, *Life of Horace Mann*, p. 425.

101. The sources for these statistics are: *Book of the Records*, vols. 1-2; *Record of Scholars, 1854-1863*, Vol. 3; *Roll of Membership, 1864-1909*, vols. 4-8. Bridgewater Archives, Massachusetts State College at Bridgewater, Bridgewater, Massachusetts. My special thanks to Cora Vining and Jordan Fiore of the Massachusetts State College at Bridgewater for making these archives available to me.

The categories of *farmer* and *teacher* are uncomplicated. The *professional category* included doctors, lawyers and ministers. *Unskilled laborer* designated those who registered their occupa-tions as laborer, painter, expressman, hack driver, teamster, whaleman, nailer, steward, hostler, livery stable keeper, sailor, gardner, peddler, drummer, gate-tender, watchman and the like. *Mechanic* and *craftsman* designated wheelwright, shop-foreman, carpenter, shoemaker, confec-tioner, actor, policeman, deputy sheriff, postmaster, dentist, mason, jeweler, weaver, canner, navigator, carriage maker, architect, land surveyor, sea captain, railroad engineer and the like. *Merchant* represented bookkeeper, auditor, paymaster, grocer, hotelkeeper, broker, many vari-eties of "dealer"—ice, leather, furniture, grain, etc.—flourist, druggist, auctioneer, bank cashier, insurance salesman, clerk, freight agent, real estate broker, furrier and the like. *Manufacturer* indicated paper-mill superintendent, mill owner, shoe manufacturer, superintendent of gas works, and anyone in general charge of producing goods or services.

The groupings span eight-year sequences in order to accommodate the first period for which there are figures. Actually each year represents two terms in the 1854-1862 sequence. The manuscript records contain information on fifteen rather than sixteen terms. I have averaged the fifteen terms to give me figures for the sixteenth and to give me a full eight-year sequence for comparison with the other groupings.

Corroborating figures for the Salem Normal School can be found in *Proceedings at the Quarter-Centennial Celebration of the State Normal School at Salem, Mass.* (Salem, 1880), pp. 26-27; Also for Rhode Island Normal School in 1875, see "State Departments: R.I.," *New England Journal of Education*, 3 (February 5, 1876): 71; Section III, *Sixty-Fourth Annual Report of the Massachusetts Board of Education . . . , 1899-1900* (Boston, 1901), pp. 34-75.

102. A. C. Boyden, *History of Bridgewater*, p. 116.

103. *Ibid.*, p. 79.

104. *Ibid.*, p. 119.

105. Arthur C. Boyden to David Snedden, October 3, 1913. Bridgewater Archives, Massa-chusetts State College at Bridgewater, Bridgewater, Massachusetts. See also Walter H. Drost, *David Snedden and Education for Social Efficiency* (Madison, Wis., 1967), especially pp. 101-143.

This effort to maintain normal schools on a level with colleges had an eye to the future. Eventually the college degree would serve a traditional, professional function, the prerequisite for normal training. Boyden was not alone in this hope. See, for example, C. F. Carroll's comments, "The City Normal School of the Future," *Proceedings of the National Education Associa-tion* (1903), p. 547.

106. Asbury Pitman (ed.), *Essentials of Education: Essays of George Henry Martin* (Boston, 1932). The editor introduced these essays with a lengthy biographical account.

107. Drost, *Snedden*, pp. 96-100.

108. Pitman, *Essentials*, p. 16.

Chapter VIII

1. See Table 2, pp. 99-100.

2. [Albert E. Winship], "Teachers at Bethlehem," *Journal of Education,* 34 (July 16, 1891): 78.

3. *Ibid.*

4. One of the Institute's presidents, Samuel S. Greene, experienced a career in all these offices, ending with a professorship at Brown University (1855-1875). His experience was not typical but reflected combinations of positions which his fellow schoolmen also shared. See "Samuel Stillman Greene," *Dictionary of American Biography,* 8: 574-575, and "Obituary," *Journal of Education,* 17 (February 3, 1883): 89.

5. See Table 11, p. 172. In Table 1, p. xix, the superintendents there bear out the previous assertion.

6. See Table 1, p. xix.

7. "Who—Where—What," *Journal of Education,* 55 (February 20, 1902): 127.

8. Edward Krug, *The Shaping of the American High School, 1880-1920* (Madison, Wis., 1964), p. 2.

9. [Albert E. Winship], "The Institute's Future," *Journal of Education,* 34 (July 16, 1891): 72.

10. Bailey B. Burritt, *Professional Distribution of College and University Graduates, U.S. Bureau of Education Bulletin No. 19* (Washington, D.C., 1912), pp. 74-75, 77.

11. "The Institute's Future," p. 72; and *Lectures and Proceedings of the American Institute of Instruction* (Boston, 1891).

12. For Paul Hanus, see especially Arthur Powell's essay on Harvard's School of Education in Paul Buck (ed.), *Social Sciences at Harvard* (Cambridge, Mass., 1965), and his essay, "Speculation on the Early Impact of Schools of Education on Educational Psychology," *History of Education Quarterly,* 11 (Winter 1971): 406-412; and "Who—Where—What," *Journal of Education,* 55 (February 20, 1902): 124.

For Royce, "Who—Where—What," *Journal of Education,* 55 (February 27, 1902): 137. For James, "College Notes," *Journal of Education,* 55 (February 6, 1902): 94. For Hyde, "Personal," *Journal of Education,* 22 (August 20, 1885): 133. For Gates, "Amherst College," *Cyclopedia of Education,* 1: 113.

13. See Table 13, p. 174.

14. *Ibid.* For an illuminating essay on colleges like Dartmouth and the others of this period, see David F. Allmendinger, Jr., "New England Students and the Revolution in Higher Education, 1800-1900," *History of Education Quarterly,* 11 (Winter 1971): 381-389.

15. "The Institute's Future," p. 72.

16. See Table 1, p. xix, and Table 11, p. 172.

17. See Table 1, p. xix.

18. Ray Greene Huling analyzes the membership of the Institute in *Lectures and Proceedings of the American Institute of Instruction,* 62 (Boston, 1891): xxxvi-xxxvii.

19. *Ibid.* Huling gave a geographical breakdown on the basis of the membership's current addresses. Further research should illuminate that the "Massachusetts" category here distorts the number of Massachusetts-born teachers in the Institute or in the profession.

20. The following ten are the only ones which appear to me to be public grammar schoolmasters of Boston: Thomas H. Barnes, Alfred Bunker, Quincy Dickerman, Charles W. Hill, Daniel W. Jones, Charles F. King, James A. Page, John J. Sheehan, Augustus D. Small, James Webster Walker.

21. See Table 1, p. xix.

22. See Table 15, p. 177. Later lists include extensive comparative information on the normal schools. See "Statistics for Normal Schools for 1877," *American Journal of Education,* ed. by Henry Barnard, 29: 356-365.

23. See Tables 16 and 17, p. 177.

24. See Table 1, p. xix.

25. See Table 1, p. xix.

26. See Table 2, pp. 99-100.

27. See Edgar Wesley, *NEA: The First Hundred Years* (New York, 1957), Appendix B.

28. The most acerbic and effective critics were probably Richard Grant White, "The Public School Failure," *North American Review*, 131 (1880), and Gail Hamilton whose criticisms were collected in *Our Common School System* (Boston, 1880). From a different point of view, see the informative discussion of Michael Katz in "The Emergence of Bureaucracy in Urban Education: The Boston Case, 1850-1884," *History of Education Quarterly*, 8 (Summer 1968): 155-188, and 8 (Fall 1968): 319-357.

For a convenient thumbnail sampling of the spokesmen's positions, see Daniel Calhoun's "The Climax of 19th Century Reform: Fresh Criticism," in *The Educating of Americans: A Documentary History* (New York, 1969), pp. 295-325.

29. *Boston Evening Transcript*, February 5, 1880, quoted in Michael B. Katz, "The Emergence of Bureaucracy" (Fall 1968), p. 327.

30. Michael Katz, "The Emergence of Bureaucracy" (Summer 1968), p. 177.

31. See Table 2, pp. 99-100. See also, Wesley, *NEA*, Appendix B.

32. In addition to the Katz articles and the documents in Calhoun, *Educating*, Adams' essay can be found in his three-part pamphlet, *The New Departure in the Common Schools of Quincy and Other Papers* (Boston, 1879).

33. See Table 18, p. 181.

34. Charles Francis Adams, "The Development of the Superintendency," *NEA Addresses and Proceedings* (1880) pp. 61-76.

35. Marion Foster Washburne, "Col. Parker, The Man, and Educational Reformer," in *Memorial Edition: Francis W. Parker, Talks on Teaching* (New York, 1893), especially pp. 12-14.

36. Arthur C. Boyden, *The History of the Bridgewater Normal School*, pp. 26-27; and "Examinations of Norfolk County (Mass.) Schools," *National Journal of Education*, 11 (March 18, 1880): 185.

37. Adams, "Superintendency," pp. 63-64.

38. See Chapter III, "The Dynamics of Career Choice."

39. Adams, "Superintendency," p. 69.

40. *Ibid.*, p. 75. Another Bridgewater graduate supported Walton's view in the American Institute of Instruction discussions. See the remarks of Edwin P. Seaver, at the time superintendent of Boston Schools, in response to an address, "The State Normal College—The Next Step in Normal Work," *Lectures and Proceedings of the American Institute of Instruction*, 61 (Boston, 1890): 107.

41. See Adams' essay *A College Fetish: Address . . . Harvard Phi Beta Kappa* (Boston, 1884, 3rd ed.). For an orthodox collegiate view taking exception to Adams' address, see Hon. D. H. Chamberlain, "Not a College Fetish," *Lectures and Proceedings of the American Institute of Instruction*, 55 (Boston, 1884): 139-182.

42. An excellent essay on the political uses of the "scientific" argument in the redesign of the superintendent, see Elinor M. Gersman, "Progressive Reform of the St. Louis School Board, 1897," *History of Education Quarterly*, 10 (Spring 1970): 3-21.

43. *Register of Graduates* [*Bridgewater Normal School*] (1912), p. 2. The fifth graduate of the Bridgewater Normal School who served the American Institute of Instruction as president was John Kneeland (1821-1914), Class 3 (March 10, 1841). At the time of his American Institute of Instruction tenure (1868-1869) he was a school supervisor in Boston. "John Kneeland," *American Journal of Education*, ed. by Henry Barnard (September 1865), p. 526.

44. George A. Walton, participating in a discussion of physical culture in *Lectures and Proceedings of the American Institute of Instruction* 62 (Boston, 1891): xxi.

45. *Ibid.*, p. xxii. The academy men were Edward P. Jackson, principal of Boston Latin School from 1877 to 1905; George A. Williams, principal of the Saxton's River Academy in Vermont; Moses Grant Daniell, principal of the Roxbury Latin School for seventeen years and then principal of the Chauncey Hall School in Boston for twelve years; William A. Mowry, principal of the classical school for boys in Providence known as Mowry and Goff's, for over twenty years;

and James S. Barrell, long-time master of the Harvard School in Cambridge, Massachusetts. All were active in the Institute during the middle period and well represented the second-generation schoolmen.

46. See: Nicholas Murray Butler, *Across the Busy Years.* v. 1 (New York, 1902); Elsie Hug, *Seventy-Five Years in Education, New York University, 1890–1965* (New York, 1965); also Amy Bramwell and H. Millicent Hughes, *The Training of Teachers in the United States* (New York, 1894), pp. 97-98.

47. Wallace C. Boyden, "Report of the Committee on Affiliation of New England Educational Associations," *Lectures and Proceedings of the American Institute of Instruction,* 78 (Shelton, Conn., 1908): 330-334.

48. The eight meetings after 1908 did not produce annual volumes as had the previous seventy-eight conventions. The last meetings were held consecutively in Castine, Maine (1909), Providence, Rhode Island (1910), North Conway, New Hampshire (1912), Harvard University, Cambridge, Massachusetts (1914 and 1915), Cambridge, Massachusetts, Massachusetts Institute of Technology (1917), and Boston, Massachusetts (1918). I have not been able to establish where the 1916 meeting was held.

The final Boston meeting had been arranged as a joint venture by the American Institute of Instruction, the New England Association of School Superintendents, the Massachusetts Superintendents Association and the Massachusetts Teachers Association. (See "Educational News: Massachusetts," *Journal of Education* [November 29, 1917], pp. 554-55.) The meeting actually attracted other groups like the New England Teacher-Training Association and the Massachusetts Teachers Federation. Their collective force attracted the attention of politicians like Massachusetts Governor Calvin Coolidge who offered them welcome to his state. Ironically the teachers who had so consistently avoided politicization in the nineteenth century, held their last meeting in 1918 in the exact place as their first convention in 1830, Boston's State House. "The Annual Convention of the New England Educators," *Journal of Education,* 92 (December 9, 1920): 569-71.

Bibliographical Notes

There has been surprisingly little study of the history of the American teacher. Apart from the material in such secondary works on education as Ellwood Cubberley's *Public Education in the United States* or Lawrence Cremin's *The Transformation of the School,* there are only a few works that give the teacher primary attention. Merle Borrowman, in *The Liberal and the Technical in Teacher Education,* fashions his picture of the teacher from a study of the debates and problems concerning curriculum development. In Merle Curti's *Social Ideas of American Educators* the practicing teacher is studied only indirectly, since the author's purpose is to show the interrelations of educational and social issues, especially the deference educators pay to the business community. The encyclopedic work by Willard Ellsbree, *The American Teacher: Evolution of a Profession in a Democracy,* catalogues impressively the many facets of the teacher's work. His study is, however, less about the professional development of the teacher than an orderly presentation of the external aspects of the occupation of teaching. The dynamics of the development are omitted.

The present study presumes to examine the teacher in terms of the teacher's own experience, to use his own preferences and conceptions and to locate the changes of the profession at those points in his individual development when one aspect of his work gains or loses significance for him. The importance of autobiography and biography in such an effort is self-evident. While the *Dictionary of American Biography* contains material on an extraordinary number of appropriate men in this period (approximately one hundred), additional historical scholarship seemingly has not been able to

221

collect much information on teachers. There are little manuscript data or papers, and where those are available, as in the case of George Emerson's papers in the Massachusetts Historical Society, the papers are of a highly personal nature, pertaining little to educational work. The vast collections of Henry Barnard's papers at New York University and Horace Mann's papers in the Massachusetts Historical Society and Antioch College have been only partially examined. This limitation might be very serious had much of their personal and public writings not already been published or had there been only a small secondary literature on them. Much biographical information was collected from a systematic study of the appropriate journals of the period, particularly in the Miscellany section. Apart from works like William Alcott's *Confessions of a Schoolmaster* and David Camp's *Reminiscences of a Long and Active Life*, there is little autobiographical writing by teachers. Nor is there any fictional literature to speak of which might have served the purpose of examining the teacher's view of himself. The tale *Locke Amsden: or The Schoolmaster* by Daniel P. Thompson and the "Young People's Story" *Breaking Away: or The Fortunes of a Student* (1870), by Oliver Optic [pseudonym for William T. Adams] fall into this category, however, together with numerous reminiscences printed in educational and other journals. The limited nature of this type of material has been a serious restriction of the present study.

From beginning to end the institutional context for this work has been defined by the history and work of the American Institution of Instruction, the first major association for teachers in the United States. The seventy-eight volumes of the Institute's lectures and proceedings are perhaps the most unused yet authoritative collection of educational writing available to historical research. After checking all the obvious libraries and societies, such as the Essex Institute, the American Antiquarian Society, the Boston Atheneum, the Boston Public Library and the Massachusetts Historical Society, I have concluded that the archives of the Institute are not still extant. Still, the published proceedings afford more than adequate documentation of the problems and strategies of this early and long-lived association. Its significance to this study may be indicated by the fact that all the persons treated in detail here belonged to the organization. A systematic study of institute membership has provided the basis for practically all my generalizations about the profession of teachers. All previous historical discussion of the Institute has been highly repetitious and, if it is not based on George Emerson's short *History of the American Institute of Instruction*, has been drawn from a very cursory examination of their published proceedings. The most recent essay on this organization was written in 1906!

For the study of shifts in rhetoric and conception of teaching by the professional teacher, the educational journals of the period are indispensable. Fortunately the Memorial Library of the University of Wisconsin and the Wisconsin Historical Society contain much of this material, and what they lack was supplied by the highly useful *American Periodicals on Microfilm*, Ann Arbor, Michigan.

A large portion of the published material which can be used as primary sources for educational history remains uncatalogued or without indexes. There are, however, a few exceptions which proved very useful. *The History of American Education* (1973), by Jurgen Herbst, is the most thorough presentation of sources both primary and secondary. The only comprehensive index for a major educational journal for the period under study was that compiled under the direction of William Torrey Harris while he was U.S. commissioner of education. This work, *The Analytical Index to Barnard's American Journal of Education: 1855–1881* (1892), is far superior to the catalogue compiled by Barnard himself and included at the end of v. 16 of the *American Journal of Education* as well as in v. 1 of the *Report of the U.S. Commissioner of Education, 1867–1869*, pp. 17-40. In addition, there is much primary material about educational problems in this period which Clyde S. King has gathered in his book, *Horace Mann; 1796–1859: A Bibliography* (1966), although, of course, the focus upon Mann restricts this index. Most of the state educational journals contain indexes at the end of each volume but have published no comprehensive index. A recent and highly serviceable index to scholarship in educational history is Murray Shereshewshy's *Ten Year Index: History of Education Quarterly, vols. 1-10, 1961–1970* (1973).

For a comprehensive bibliography for this study, including many works not actually footnoted, consult pp. 441-472 in an earlier version of the study, *The Origins of Professional Schoolmen, 1820–1900*, U.S. Office of Education Project No. 1-0530B (1972).

Index

Graduates of, in professional association, 177;
Graduates as presidents of the American Institute of Instruction, 172;
See Tables 5-9, 12, 16-17;
Photos of, 116.
Brooklyn (Conn.) Convention, 2, 14, 16.
Brooks, Reverend Charles, 20, 68.
Brown University, 30, 39, 91, 98, 105, 108, 172, 173, 174, 175, 212;
Graduates who become professional schoolmen, 172, 174.
Bruce, Orasmus B., 170.
Bulkley, John W., 133.
Bunyan, John, 75.
Bureaucracy, xvii, 149, 188.
Bureaucratization, xvi;
By means of voluntary associations, xvii, 119, 128, 183-184.
Bushnell, Reverend Horace, 68.
Butler, Nicholas Murray, 149.

Calhoun, William, 96, 103.
Calkins, Norman, 73.
Camp, David Nelson, xvi, 74-83, 97, 110, 138;
Photo of, 114.
Career, choice, 44-60, 132-133, 174.
Career, status, 106,
Career, professional and training, 46, 136, 154.
Career success,
Ambiguity of, 48-49, 52;
As a balance of individual and social benefits, 57-58;
Less important than career choice, 136.
Careers,
In historical analysis, xiv;
Statistical alignments within the teaching profession, xix;

And career planning, 44-60, 137;
And normal school patterns, 138-139, 144-145, 161, 198.
Carter, James C., 84, 86, 96, 103, 198, 199.
Carleton, Isaac N., 103.
Channing, Walter, 105.
Channing, Reverend William Ellery, 19, 58, 107.
Chapin, Reverend W., 29.
Chapman (Boston, Mass.) School, 147.
Character,
definition of, xii;
As apolitical, xiii, 46-47, 53-54;
As ideological force, xiv, xv;
Its indirect strategies, xx;
Its effect upon career choice, 44-60;
And the teaching profession, 118, 122, 123, 126-133, 135, 142, 146, 149, 152, 159, 160, 167, 179, 180, 184, 194, 195, 199-200.
Chauncey Hall (Boston, Mass.) School, 109, 110, 219.
Church, George E., 170, 175.
Circuit, lecture, as a voluntary structure, xv, 36, 43.
Circuit rider, 42, 67, 193.
Class, social, xiii, xvi, 90, 124, 131, 135, 139, 141, 143, 149, 150, 152, 153, 155, 160, 161-168, 216;
Taken for granted by schoolmen, xvi;
And its effect on first and second generation schoolmen, 53;
Downplayed by teachers, 57.
Classical study, 46, 86, 108, 109, 138, 145, 146, 153, 185.
Classless profession, xi, xvii, 161-168.
Cogswell, Dr. Mason, 25, 26.
Colburn, Dana, 138, 208;
See Group Photo, Frontispiece.

An instrument of public instruction, 16-17;
A bridge from rural to urban teaching positions, 19;
Relationship between permanent school and lyceum, 33-39;
And the work of Josiah Holbrook, 35-39;
Proliferation of, 43;
The Boston, 90.
Lyceum Seminary, 37, 38.
Lyon, Merrick, 103, 111.

Mann, Horace, xii, xv, 19, 20, 44, 47, 49, 63, 65, 71, 75, 84, 97, 109, 119, 120, 137, 168, 175, 183, 195, 197, 198, 217;
Professional significance of, 50-60;
Photo of, 113.
Manuals, teachers, 49, 189, 207;
In the form of biographies, 51-60.
Manual training, 37;
Different from vocational training, 153, 215.
Marietta (Ohio) Collegiate Institute, 33, 200.
Martha's Vineyard Summer Institute, 82.
Martin, George H., 158, 159, 167, 170, 185.
Mason, Wallace E., 170
Massachusetts Teacher, The, 108.
Massachusetts State Teachers' Association, 108, 175.
May, Reverend Samuel J., xiv, 2-5, 7, 14, 16-20, 38, 146.
Merrimack Normal Institute, 121.
Michigan, University of, 174.
Middlebury College, 174, 175;
Graduates who became professional schoolmen, 174.
Middle States Schoolmasters Associations, 155.

Missionary work and the professional schoolman, 29, 38, 59-60.
Monitor, 10, 70.
Moral ambiguity as a social force, 58-60; *See* Character.
Morrison, Henry C., 170.
Mowry, William, 101, 103, 219.

National Education Association, 120, 150, 155, 173, 179, 180, 203, 207.
National Teachers Association, 120, 122, 125, 126, 129, 130, 132, 133.
New Britain (Conn.) Normal School, 74, 82, 98. *See* Connecticut State Normal School.
New Britain (Conn.) Seminary, 74.
New England Normal Institute, 121.
New England Normal Teachers Association, 155.
New England Association of Colleges and Preparatory Schools, 155, 173.
Newman, Samuel Phillips, 138, 146, 210-211.
New York University, 174, 185.
Normal Lyceum, 157.
Normal School, 62, 64, 65, 68, 71, 73, 77, 78, 81, 82, 84, 98, 118, 121, 133, 134-168, 171, 182, 184;
As a generic institution, xvi;
In Massachusetts and Connecticut, 8;
First in America, 29;
Its principal as a professional type, 134-139;
As a revival agency, 139-143;
Compared with college, 143-153, 155n;
As a regional school, 149;
Its second generation purpose, 143-168;
In the United States, 177;
Public and private compared, 214;